"KING LEHR"
AND
THE GILDED AGE

"KING LEHR"
AND THE GILDED AGE

BY
ELIZABETH DREXEL LEHR

WITH EXTRACTS FROM
THE LOCKED DIARY OF
HARRY LEHR

Published in cooperation with
THE PRESERVATION SOCIETY
OF NEWPORT COUNTY

APPLEWOOD BOOKS
Bedford, Massachusetts

King Lehr was first published in 1935
by J. B. Lippincott Company

Thank you for purchasing an Applewood
book. Applewood reprints America's lively
classics—books from the past that are still
of interest to modern readers. For a free
copy of our current catalog, write to:

Applewood Books
P.O. Box 365
Bedford, MA 01730

ISBN 1-55709-963-4

TO MY MOTHER
LUCY WHARTON DREXEL
FOR WHOSE SAKE
I ENDURED
MANY THINGS

CONTENTS

"KING LEHR"
AND
THE GILDED AGE

CHAPTER I

HARRY LEHR AND I

❧

HARRY LEHR DIED IN BALTIMORE ON JANUARY 3RD, 1929, and the news of his death flashed over two continents. I was in Paris, whither I had rushed back from a visit to Colonel and Mrs. Jacques Balsan at their Riviera villa. My maid greeted me with a sheaf of newspapers. One glance at her face told me the truth.

I sat down slowly on my bed . . . no need to hurry now . . . and began to read them. The headlines flared up at me . . . "Harry Lehr, America's Former Social Leader, Dies" . . . "The Beau Brummell of Twenty Years Ago" . . . "Once the Four Hundred's Playboy" . . . "Death Takes Society's Jester. . . ." Long columns were filled with the exploits of the man whose claim to fame had been that he had found out the way to make a jaded world laugh; his freak parties were recounted at length, his "bons mots" quoted, his social triumphs commented upon, his many eccentricities remembered.

Reading them I looked back into the past, visualizing those twenty-eight years of our life together, years that had brought him success and laughter and approbation, years when he had been acclaimed as the "King Lehr" whose wit had enlivened the drawing-rooms of New York

13

and Newport. For me those same years had held sorrow and disillusion. I had known loneliness in the midst of crowds, had learnt to endure agonies of humiliation in secret.

And now it was all over. The tragic farce of our marriage had ended.

For days I shut myself up in my home in the Rue des Saints Pères, while reporters clamoured at my door in vain.

My lawyer called to see me. He hesitated in explaining his business. Harry Lehr had left a will, bequeathing $200,000, all the money he possessed in the world, to his brothers and sisters. It was just what I had anticipated. I had never thought to inherit money from him, or wanted to. But there was a strange codicil attached:

"I bequeath to my wife, Elizabeth Drexel Lehr, my houses, lands, silver plate, tapestries, pictures, carriages, yachts, motor cars, in all parts of the world, excepting in the United States of America and in France, absolutely and for ever."

I took the document and stared at it incredulously. Houses, lands, yachts? Harry had never owned any at any time during our married life! How could he leave me what did not exist? Surely such a codicil must have been made during his illness when he was not responsible for his actions? No. It was dated some years before. Then my lawyer enlightened me.

"I am afraid you will have trouble, unless you take instant precautions, Mrs. Lehr. Your husband has made you residuary legatee, which means that you would be liable for all taxes, all claims which may be made on his estate, and for the payment of any debts incurred by him. You will have to renounce this bequest legally even though it only exists on paper."

So I had to make a solemn, formal declaration that I refused to accept my imposing fictitious inheritance, that I would never lay claim to it.

The few friends of Harry Lehr who heard of the wording of the codicil laughed at what they called his final and best joke. So like him to get the last ounce of fun out of life, to waste the time of pompous lawyers drawing up codicils to bequeath imaginary possessions. But their laughter was tinged with affectionate regret for the man who had been able to jest while death knocked at the door. Not one of them guessed the real meaning of the codicil. That remained for me. It had always been thus in my life with Harry Lehr; always the jest for the world and the bitterness for me.

So now after many years let me write the truth of our story, in order that those who knew us both may perhaps understand for the first time. Many wounds have been healed for me, and at last I can look back on the past seeing it in its true perspective. I want to be fair to Harry Lehr, to write of him as he really was; not only as "The Funmaker" as he liked to call himself, America's Court Jester; nor yet as the man who embittered the best years of my life. As Stevenson wrote: "There is so much bad in the best of us, and so much good in the worst of us . . ."

CHAPTER II
MYSELF

❧

Most fitting to begin our story with the simple statement that I was born Elizabeth Drexel, for it is almost superfluous to add that had I not been thus born I should never have been married to Harry Lehr. My grandfather Francis Martin Drexel founded the Drexel family in America. From the little Tyrolese town of Dornbirn on the shores of Lake Constance he arrived in Philadelphia in 1817, a young artist with a stock of paints and brushes as his principal capital, and remained to become first one of the most fashionable portrait painters in America, and secondly the founder of a banking house.

My father, named Joseph William, was his youngest son. I was scarcely out of my childhood when he died. A big, bearded man with fine dark eyes, sensitive, beautifully shaped hands, and a low musical voice rather at variance with his habitual sternness and the iron discipline that ruled our household. He was perpetually tired. Every hour of his day was given over to work, even at home he was constantly harassed by messages from his secretaries. When he came back from the office at night he was more exhausted than a field labourer; I have often known him to fall suddenly asleep even at the dinner

16

table in the middle of a conversation that was obviously interesting him, although when he made an effort he could be a delightful companion and talk well on nearly every subject.

My mother was younger than my father, small and golden-haired, with a little heart-shaped face that was nearly always smiling and big china-blue eyes that reminded me of those of my beloved Paris doll. Before her marriage she had been Miss Lucy Wharton and she was immensely proud of her descent from the Duke of Wharton.

The winters we spent in New York in a big house at 103 Madison Avenue, only a few blocks from J. Pierpont Morgan's house, and since they were so closely allied in business the two families saw a great deal of one another.

"Jackie," as everyone called him, ruled his entire household like the autocrat he was, and I do not think that anyone in the family would have dreamt of disobeying him, unless indeed it was his youngest daughter, little Anne Morgan. A thin, lanky child with an elfin face and penetrating eyes, she had a personality and a will as strong as his own and a disconcerting habit of putting her elders in the wrong. On one occasion when Mrs. Morgan was giving a dinner party, Anne was brought into the dining-room after dessert, and with her usual self-possession started to amuse those sitting near her. After she had announced her intention of never marrying and of making a career of her own instead, her father asked her what she intended to be when she grew up. "Something better than a rich fool, anyway," she replied with infinite contempt, and the scornful child's voice rang through the room, making more than one millionaire look uncomfortable.

．　　．　　．　　．　　．　　．　　．

The New York of my childhood was a city of changes. Fifth Avenue which bounded my small world was the first to reflect them all. While I grew up I watched it pass from the era of modest, discreet-looking brick and brownstone houses, each with its high stoop striving to look as much like its neighbour as possible, to the splendours of the great, gaudy palaces which proudly reared their Italian, Gothic or Oriental structures to house the new millionaires. In my school-days when Twenty-third Street was the fashionable shopping centre, when a cock horse waited patiently at the corner of Thirty-fourth Street to help the bus horses up Murray Hill, and the colossal right hand of the Statue of Liberty, installed in Madison Square pending the arrival of the statue itself from France, was considered one of the sights of the city, you could have counted the great homes of New York on your fingers. A. T. Stewart's white marble house at the corner of Fifth Avenue and Thirty-fourth Street was one of the pioneers—visitors from the provinces used to stand before it in open-mouthed admiration. They were as interested in the Astor houses at the corners of Thirty-third and Thirty-fourth Streets, twin structures of red brick joined by a garden, though here their curiosity was defeated by the high red wall which safeguarded the pri-

vacy of the most exclusive family in New York. Jay
Gould had a fine house at the corner of Forty-sixth Street
and Fifth Avenue, and Pierpont Morgan another on
Madison Avenue, but they still conformed to the solid
brownstone tradition and indulged in no flights of fancy.

Then almost imperceptibly there came a change. The
new architecture adapted itself, like everything, to meet
new standards, the standards of a society in the melting
pot, an ever-shifting kaleidoscope of dazzling wealth,
restless endeavour, ambition and rivalry. The "Gilded
Age" had dawned. It merited its name. There was gold
everywhere. It adorned the houses of men who had become millionaires overnight, and who were trying to forget with all possible speed the days when they had been
poor and unknown. It glittered on their dining-tables
when they sat down to unfamiliar awe-inspiring ban-
quets of rare dishes whose high-sounding names conveyed
nothing to them; it enriched the doors of their carriages
in which their wives and daughters drove round Central
Park behind the high-stepping thoroughbreds imported
from England. Gold was the most desirable thing to have
because it cost money, and money was the outward and
visible sign of success. They cultivated the Midas touch
to such good purpose that truth to tell they were often
bewildered by their own magnificence.

They sent their experts to Europe to seek out the art
treasures of France and Italy, gave them carte blanche
to buy regardless of cost. Mediæval châteaux of the
Touraine yielded up their tapestries and carvings, whole

wainscotings, panel by panel; ancient Florentine palaces bade farewell to their frescoes. Suits of armour that had gathered the dust of centuries in grim old Scottish castles were ruthlessly packed and shipped across the Atlantic to lend realism to the newly-built feudal home of some baron of trade.

Plain, sensible houses were out of favour now, everyone wanted to outshine the rest in architectural originality, and they all looked to the past for inspiration. The Astors transferred themselves to other and more splendid twin houses, built in the François I style, connected this time by a magnificent ballroom instead of a garden. Harry O. Havemeyer acquired an imposing feudal castle of granite bristling with culverin towers. Cornelius Vanderbilt built a sumptuous palace of red brick and white marble at the corner of Fifty-seventh Street, which was only eclipsed in splendour by the supposedly Venetian Palace designed to the order of his sister-in-law, Mrs. W. K. Vanderbilt. Opposite the Park a bewildering row of mansions sprung up like toadstools.

On Saturday afternoons we went to the Opera. My father, who was passionately fond of music and was President of the Philharmonic Society, was one of the directors of the Metropolitan Opera House, and all through the season we had a box. My mother, who was not musical, had little interest in the performance, especially if the opera happened to be one of Wagner's, whose music she detested. She regarded the Opera purely as a social function and never failed to occupy her box on Monday evenings, like everyone else with any claim to being fashionable. On these nights the house would be crowded, every box in the "Diamond Horseshoe" would present the spectacle of two women superbly gowned and bejewelled sitting in the front row, while four men grouped themselves behind. In the *entr'actes* the velvet curtains at the back of the box were drawn aside and they would all retire to the salons behind, which were decorated according to the individual taste of their owners, draped in costly brocades or massed with flowers. Lily Hamersley, who afterwards became Duchess of Marlborough, used to have the entire walls and ceiling of hers concealed by festoons of orchids.

In those days it was considered fashionable to be unable to understand Wagner and to despise him accordingly. He was described as "vulgar and immoral." I remember my uncle, Anthony Drexel, once holding forth on the subject at a dinner party at his house. . . . His loud voice boomed through the room. . . . "There's going to be a concert next week and I want no child of mine to go to it. Some fool whose name is Dam . . . Dam . . . some kind of bug or other . . . Roach, that's what it is, Walter Damroach, and he's going to play the music of that miserable Wagner! None of you go to it, you understand."

·　　·　　·　　·　　·　　·　　·

Every summer we, in company with the whole fashionable world of New York, used to flock to Saratoga Springs, to fill the two ornate hotels, "The United States" and "The Grand Union" (the latter owned by A. T. Stewart, already famed as the pioneer of the department store). There were of course other hotels, but socially speaking they did not exist. They might even expose their guests to the dreadful indignity of meeting the chosen race of Israel, a catastrophe against which both "The United States" and "The Grand Union" took care to insure themselves by placing conspicuous placards at all entrances bearing the stern warning . . . "No Jews or Dogs Admitted Here."

How well I remember the mornings on the sun-bathed piazza of The United States Hotel watching the fashion parade. The women in their latest dresses imported from Paris, skin-tight bodices, skirts of yards and yards of shining silk looped over enormous bustles that swayed as they walked slowly up and down, their waists squeezed into twenty-inch stays, their feet encased in boots at least a size too small for them, their hands buttoned into hot kid gloves. Their lace parasols, opened to shelter their complexions from the sun, were like a forest of gaily coloured trees.

.   .   .   .

In contrast to the artificial atmosphere of Saratoga Springs was our daily life, which was very simple. Over our home loomed the shadow of Queen Victoria of England, who was my mother's ideal of wifehood. Every English newspaper and magazine which informed its readers of life at Windsor or Balmoral was sure to be found in

our drawing-room. We did our best to model ourselves
upon it.

The Queen of England did not countenance divorce;
neither would Mother. In the midst of a fast-changing
New York social world, where already the old standards
enjoined by a Puritan ancestry were slipping farther and
farther into the past, she remained unshaken. She refused
to receive divorced persons in her house.

.   .   .   .

Many friends came to my father's house; among them
was Ward McAllister, of whom years afterwards Harry
Lehr said to me. . . . "I begin where Ward McAllister
left off. He was the voice crying in the wilderness who
prepared the way for me. . . ." I used to smile, thinking
that McAllister would scarcely have liked this definition
of himself, for his conceit was equal to Harry's own.

I rather liked this Shepherd of the "Four Hundred"
and the most complete dandy in America, his pleasant
lazy drawl, his hearty laugh, but Mother used to raise her
eyebrows at many of the things he said. . . . "I cannot
admire a man who spends all his time pushing some people into society and pushing others out of it," she would
say.

He took his responsibilities very seriously. Knowing
that his decision was regarded as the verdict of the Supreme Court of Appeal where matters of etiquette were
under discussion, he devoted his whole life to compiling
his famous set of rules for the guidance of social New
York. He read books on heraldry and precedence, studied

the customs of every Court in Europe. He revelled in forms and ceremonies, his cult of snobbishness was so ardent, so sincere, that it acquired dignity; it became almost a religion. No devout parish priest ever visited his flock with more loyal devotion to duty than did Ward McAllister make his round of the opera-boxes on Monday evenings. He would listen to plans for forthcoming parties with the utmost gravity, offer his advice as to whom should be invited, restrict the number of guests. He would spend ten minutes discussing the wording of an invitation, the colour of a sheet of note-paper. And all the while his watchful eyes would be observing the neighbouring boxes, noting the new-comers, whom they were talking to, "who was taking them up. . . ." "You can never be absolutely certain whether people are in society or not until you see them at four or five of the best houses. Then you can make advances to them without the danger of making a mistake," was his favourite dictum. He took precautions to make no mistakes.

Almost as much in demand as Ward McAllister was old Mr. E. N. Tailer, who rarely missed a social occasion of any importance on account of his diary. All his friends knew of the existence of this all-important document; not a few were afraid of what it might contain. It was known that he never went to bed without devoting at least an hour to writing up the events of the day. Even the most trivial incidents were recorded with a wealth of detail, conversations were reported verbatim, every party was described, the names of guests noted. As the years

passed by the diary was augmented, volume was added
to volume. People who wanted to be certain of the precise date of any happening had only to refer to him, and
he would delve into the past for them. He would produce
pages of conclusive evidence in his neat, clear handwriting, adding the last word to any argument. The hostesses
who entertained him at their country houses knew that
one of his trunks was sure to contain the famous diary
and that they would figure in its pages; so he never lacked
invitations, despite the fact that he was noted for a rather
caustic wit. His diary was useful on more than one occasion. When produced in court it settled discussions
over wills.

.   .   .   .

I used to look forward for weeks to the Coaching
Club's Annual Parade which was held on the first Saturday in May. My sisters and I were always allowed to drive
to Central Park with our governess to see the start, and
my childish imagination could conceive of no greater
bliss. How vividly the scene comes back to me today!
The shrill blasts of the horns, the clatter of hooves as
coach after coach swung past to take its place in the long
line awaiting the starting signal from Colonel Jay,
the President of the Club. The sunlight gleaming on
brightly-polished harness and sleek coats of chestnut, bay
or black; the grooms in their smart liveries backing the
teams slowly into position, springing to the heads of the
leaders as they reared and fretted, impatient to be off.
How I envied my mother as she climbed into her seat

on Colonel Jay's coach, a breath-taking adventure in those days of voluminous trailing skirts when the least slip might have exposed her to the everlasting shame of affording the spectators the view of a pair of feminine legs. All around her other women would be mounting the steps to the accompaniment of timorous giggles and a great display of lace petticoats, while their escorts gallantly stood beneath in readiness to catch them should they fall. Soon the tops of the coaches looked like so many flower-gardens, for every woman had put on her most be-trimmed hat and loveliest dress in honour of the most important event of the season. Silk capes and lace ruffles fluttered in the breeze, painted parasols were unfurled to shield delicate complexions from the sun, jewelled buckles sparkled on Paris-made shoes. Even the men conceded to the gaiety of the day by wearing enormous bouquet buttonholes of red and white to brighten their regulation Coaching Club livery of black coats, check suits, tan aprons and buckskin gloves.

I used to think Oliver Belmont one of the handsomest men at the Coaching Parade, with his dark eyes, clear-cut profile and slender, faun-like grace. Mrs. W. K. Vanderbilt often sat at his side on the box behind the four famous bays, Sandringham, Rochingham, Buckingham and Hurlingham. The women glanced at her as she sat wide-eyed and innocent-looking, and whispered to one another.

Marion Langdon was easily the most beautiful woman there, as she was at any gathering. All the men's eyes fol-

lowed her as she swept past with Roy Phelps Carroll in
devoted attendance and mounted the coach of whoever
happened to be the most favoured admirer of the moment. Her little head with its crown of dark curls was
held high, her silken skirts rustled as she walked. Her
tightly-boned waist revealed "the most perfect figure in
New York."

Lily Hamersley was perhaps her only dangerous rival
to the claim of being the loveliest woman in the "Four
Hundred," Lily, who had been born Lily Price of Troy,
with no money or social position, but a face as fair as the
legendary Helen's. So Gordon Hamersley, adored son of
a millionaire father, fell in love with her the first time
he saw her, married her and brought her to New York
to reign as an acknowledged queen. She was nearly always
dressed in white, an affectation that annoyed other
women, but it suited her opulent rose and gold beauty
better than any other colour. She used to create a sensation when she appeared at the Coaching Parade in
white from the ostrich plumes trimming her big hat to
the French shoes on her tiny feet.

As the coaches lined up Colonel Jay would drive slowly
up and down exchanging greetings with everyone, his
hearty laugh ringing out above the babel of sounds. He
had many friends, for there was about him an infectious
gaiety that endeared him to everybody. One sensed that
here was a man well pleased with life. A proud man,
proud of the traditions of his family, of his descent from
John Jay. Proud of his handsome wife, of his fine place

on the Hudson River, of the fortune he had built up.
Not one of the hundreds who knew and liked him could
have believed it possible that he would die tragically!

   .   .   .   .

In the winter sleighing took the place of coaching and
there was keen rivalry for the ownership of the smartest
equipage. Everybody wanted to devise something new.
Tassels grew longer and more elaborate every season,
harnesses were so gaily decorated that they began to look
like the trappings of mediæval chivalry, real aigrettes of
every imaginable shade waved from the horses' heads.
On midwinter afternoons the air was full of the tinkle
of sleigh bells; the snow churned up by the beat of the
hooves fell in a glittering spray as the sleighs passed and
repassed each other in Central Park. The keen frost
whipped colour into the women's cheeks, brightened
their eyes as they sat back wrapped in their luxurious
fur rugs watching the occupants of the other sleighs. Mrs.
Cornelius Vanderbilt would flash by in a blaze of red
. . . dark red liveries, red carriage work . . . crimson
plumes, red and gilt tassels . . . carved gold bells on the
horses. The Townsend Burden's turn-out was in tones of
blue, graded from a dull peacock to turquoise. Everybody
said it was the smartest of all until Hooker Hamersley
imported a real troika from Russia complete with coachman and footman.

   .   .   .   .

My father died during the great blizzard of '88, worn
out and prematurely aged. My mother was adamant in

her conception of decorous widowhood and its obligations. Her ideal of all wifely virtues, Queen Victoria, had gone into perpetual mourning for Prince Albert. She ordered us all to wear black for four years—crêpe veils for two. No parties, no theatres. The days passed in an atmosphere of silence and hushed voices.

Then into the grey monotony of it all came John Dahlgren, so young and ardent and vital that he seemed like a being from another world. From the first moment I met him at a friend's house we were always together. Without knowing why, I began to be happy once more. We walked together, rode together, drove together, came back hand in hand to the silent house, silent no longer. His merry laugh would ring out in the sombre rooms dispelling the shadows.

Within a week he proposed to me. "I've only known you such a short time. What on earth will Mother say?"

"I like him and he is the son of Admiral Dahlgren. Your dear father always admired and respected the Admiral," said my mother.

So I was married in St. Patrick's Cathedral. My white satin wedding dress with its point lace trimmings and long train was the first grownup dress I had ever worn. I felt very superior in it and rather inclined to patronise my youngest sister to whom I had just passed on my collection of dolls.

Our happiness was short-lived. When the autumn came John caught a cold that developed into an incessant cough. The doctor examined him, told me the truth very gravely. John's lungs were seriously affected. One could only take him to the most favourable climate. . . . "The one certain thing you can do for him is never to let him know how ill he is. As long as he goes on fighting there is always a chance. . . ." How eagerly I caught at the thread of comfort, forced myself to be gay, to laugh and chatter as we left the doctor's.

We stayed in Washington a few weeks longer to wait for the arrival of our little son, whom we called John after his father. Then we started for Colorado Springs, the doctor's choice of a suitable climate for my husband.

How I hated the little town at the foot of the Rockies that was to be my home for so many months! We found a big villa on Colorado Avenue and moved in there.

We soon got acquainted with the rest of the little colony who had come down like ourselves in search of health. One of our neighbours was a prominent New York business man who, with his wife, had taken a villa there. He was terribly ill, and Mrs. Blank (who later became the wife of a titled Englishman) made no secret of the fact that she expected shortly to be a widow. She had even brought down all her mourning with her from New York to be in readiness for her husband's death. She insisted on taking me up to her room to see it.

"You can't hope to get anything fashionable in this god-forsaken place," she explained, "so I just put through the whole mourning order at my dressmaker's. The only disadvantage is that my husband has lived so much longer than the doctors thought possible that it will be out of fashion before I begin wearing it."

I felt wretchedly uncomfortable as I waited while she tried on the dress she intended to wear at the funeral, for I could not help picturing the possibility of the poor man, who happened to be out of bed that day, opening the bedroom door to see his wife pirouetting in front of the mirror while she arranged her widow's bonnet and crêpe veil at a becoming angle!

The days slipped by peacefully, uneventfully, lengthened into weeks, months. The wet season came with its torrents of rain that poured down without a break for hours on end, then gave place once more to the dry, burning heat of the sun-scorched plain. And at the end of a golden summer day, a happy day in which we had driven through the gorge in our new pony carriage, laughed at Baby's attempts to walk, and talked of the things we meant to do when he was well, John took my hand in his and fell asleep, at least I thought he slept, until the doctor came and told me the truth.

With him died my youth.

CHAPTER III

HARRY

~♥~

Our moments of destiny steal upon us so quietly, generally so unperceived, that we are hardly aware of them until they have passed by. Only in after years can we look back on them and see them from their true perspective, know that they made or marred our whole lives.

Such a moment came to me when I met Harry Lehr.

I had not expected anything more than a pleasant, mildly entertaining evening when I accepted Mrs. George Gould's invitation to her opera party. I had been to many such parties, I had heard "Lohengrin" more times than I could remember.

I looked at myself critically in the long mirror before I left my room that night. I had discarded for the first time the black I had worn ever since John's death, and I thought that I was looking my best in my dress of diaphanous while tulle. It emphasised the magnolia-like pallor of my face and the darkness of my hair and eyes.

The dinner was a long one and we arrived at the Opera late during the second act and took our places in silence. I noticed a man sitting back in the shadows of the box, but beyond the fact that he was tall and powerfully built

I could see nothing of him. Suddenly the lights went up
and Edith Gould turned to me . . .

"My dear, I want you to meet the most amusing man
in New York. . . ."

I looked up into eyes of vivid blue that seemed to hold
the very spirit of gaiety. There was something challenging in the laughing mockery in their depths, the eyes of
one who had few illusions, who took life lightly, gave
back jest for jest. For the rest I saw that their owner was
big and blond, with white teeth that parted in a slow
attractive smile, and a pleasant lazy voice, curiously high-
pitched.

He sat down at my side and we began to talk. In five
minutes I had decided that Edith Gould was right; he
was certainly the most amusing man that I had ever met.
It was not so much the things he said as the way he had
of saying them. Conversation rippled around him. Impossible for anyone to be bored in his company. There
was something so magnetic in his gaiety that other people
instinctively responded to it. He had a flair for drawing
out unsuspected conversational talents, for holding up
even the dullest gathering through the sheer force of his
personality. All women were happy in his society. He
liked them and understood them. He had an almost feminine intuition, an unfailing instinct for saying the right
thing, and a great desire to please. In his presence every
woman unconsciously felt at her most attractive.

"Who is Harry Lehr?" I asked Edith Gould after he

had left the box. . . . "Tell me something about him."
She laughed . . .

"There, I thought you would fall under his spell. We all do. I don't really know very much about him except that it's impossible to have a party without him. He has hardly any money but he goes everywhere. The men don't like him very much. They call him one of 'the little brothers of the rich,' but that's because they are jealous of his popularity."

The next day Harry Lehr came to call on me, and after that he came many times. I was falling under the spell of his charm. I had only known him a fortnight when I wrote in my diary:

"What does he think of me and how does he look upon me? His opinion means much to me and there are so few good and attractive men in the world, and none so lovely as Harry Lehr. . . ."

He filled my sombre house in West Fifty-sixth Street with gaiety and laughter. He was always bringing people to see me, arranging parties on the spur of the moment, inviting me out to dine at the house of one or other of his friends. . . . "You are far too young and pretty to remain a disconsolate widow . . ." he would say. . . . "I am going to wake you up and teach you how to enjoy life again. . . ." There was something infectious in his radiant vitality; gradually it communicated itself to me. The ice that had lain round my heart since the day John died was melting in the sunshine of this new friendship. I felt that my loneliness had gone for ever.

When he went away on a round of visits I realised how much I had come to rely on his friendship. I wrote in my diary:

"Mr. Lehr came late at the Opera and we sat in the little room behind my box and talked about the most interesting things, about his going away tomorrow and how much I would miss him. Oh, I really admire him from the depth of my heart and can understand any woman falling in love with him, he is so honourable and so handsome! He said he would write to me, when . . . ?"

While he was away there were letters for me every few days. On March 22nd I wrote:

"I got a letter from Harry this morning; it was written at Mr. Wanamaker's house in Philadelphia. He said he was en route to the Goulds' at Lakewood and expected to stay with them over Sunday and would come to New York on Monday—shall I see him then . . . ?"

Entries in my diary every day now:

"I got a letter from Harry this morning, it was written at Georgian Court. He is coming to New York today and will telephone to me at five o'clock and find out when he can see me tomorrow. The letter is lovely. I have read it twice and could do so many more times with pleasure, there is so much in it and it is so very interesting. I really think I have given my whole heart away! A thing I told myself that I would never do. It is useless to struggle against a higher power, and I am content. Mr. Lehr telephoned to me just now (about five o'clock). He says he will take lunch here tomorrow. . . ."

I was counting the days until his return to New York. He came to see me at once. . . .

"Harry came to lunch—I could not eat anything at all, I was so excited. I enjoyed having him here—it was the first time he had ever had lunch in my house. He has invited me to lunch with him at Sherry's tomorrow. . . ."

Next day he came to call for me. . . . "I have invited four of my best friends to meet you," he said as we drove there. "You cannot imagine how important this luncheon party is going to be to me."

Rather to my surprise I found that he had asked no men; his only guests besides myself were Mrs. Astor, Mrs. Stuyvesant Fish, Mrs. Hermann Oelrichs and Mrs. Oliver Belmont. They were all charming to me, but I could not quite rid myself of the impression that they were taking stock of me. Evidently the result was satisfactory, for as we rose to leave the restaurant I heard Mrs. Oelrichs say, "I think she is delightful, Harry. We four are going to take her up. We will make her the fashion. You need have no fear. . . ."

On the way home Harry asked me to marry him. "You must have guessed I have been in love with you ever since that first evening. I know that you don't love me, but you are lonely, you need someone to take care of you. I believe I can make you happy. . . ." He left me at my house, begging me to think it over at least until the next day. I was leaving next day to stay with my mother at Pen Rhyn. I promised to give him his answer there.

That evening I dined alone and sat by the fire trying

to make up my mind. I was not sure that I loved him, but it was true that I was desperately lonely. How much more so would I be without him! How could I send him out of my life, this dear companion who had filled so many empty days for me? I reflected that sincere friendship and affection was perhaps a more solid basis for marriage than romantic love.

He came to Pen Rhyn and I wrote:

"I went to Mass in the church and received Holy Communion. I prayed that I might be guided right and if I ever married again that I might be happy and make my husband happy. God is all-powerful and all-good; I place my trust in him. Harry came about two o'clock. I cannot write more. I was too happy for words—we walked on the shore and drove and had—at least I had—a lovely time. Harry kissed me! I honour him and I love him. . . ."

He stayed the week-end with us at Pen Rhyn. His presence dispelled any lingering doubts I had.

"He told me many things," I confided to my diary, "which all went to strengthen my admiration for his character and virtues. He said he was not 'animal' or 'emotional' (neither am I, but I thought all men were). He is the one glorious exception, the one pure and Godly man. I love him more than ever before but feel sure I would never have been drawn to him had he been other than he is, though till today he never told me. If I am to marry him I really think I shall be happy. That he is honourable and high-minded I know—I am also sure that

I truly admire him. I do not believe in what novelists are pleased to call 'romantic love': it is low and bestial and not worthy of men and women, who are made in God's image. True love which lasts to the end and which strengthens with years is founded on respect, not on passion. . . ."

For the first time in many years I began to dream of the future, to make plans for our life together. The days passed in a happy dream. On April 25th I wrote:

"My birthday. Harry sent me a beautiful rosary of coral and gold in a sweet heart-shaped box. I am deeply touched by his kindness—he also wired me, 'Every good wish to you today from my heart.' How can I ever show how much I value his thoughtfulness and his gift? I shall always say at least one decade of the rosary (*The* rosary) for him every night. I must say it *now* for the first time. I have written to Harry to thank him. . . ."

I was rather hurt and disappointed to find that Harry was infinitely more interested in the precise details of the fortune my father had left me than in anything else. Before our engagement had been announced more than a week he was talking of incomes and settlements. "My dear, you won't have to worry over money," I told him; "you know I will give you everything, as much as ever you want. I understand perfectly that you have to provide for your mother, and we will arrange all that. . . ."

He laughed with his characteristic charm . . . "I don't suppose you have any idea of the way I live," he said. "Well, I shall have to enlighten you. I live not on

my wits, but on my wit. I make a career of being popular."

I remember the light half-bantering tones of his drawling voice, that his eyes were full of their faintly cynical
laughter as he told me "how one could live for nothing"
—as he put it.

Wetzel made all his clothes free. . . . "He has an idea,
which I naturally encourage, that it is a privilege to dress
the man who according to newspapers 'sets the fashion
for American manhood,' " Harry explained. "He never
even suggests anything so vulgar as payment for his
suits. . . ." Kaskel and Kaskel supplied him with the
latest designs in shirt and pyjamas on the same understanding, only asking him as a favour to let it be dis-
creetly known where his underwear came from. Black,
Starr and Frost lent him jewels, an unending supply, for
they were always renewing them. How had I supposed
he had been able to afford them? I was beginning to
understand now, to remember how often I had heard
choruses of admiration over his thin gold watches, the
signet rings that were always in such perfect taste, the
cigarette-cases that no one else seemed to have. His casual
comment, "Black, Starr and Frost of course. Just got
them in from Paris."

"I never pay for one single thing I wear, not even a
tie or a handkerchief," he concluded. . . . "Now you
are probably thinking that clothes are only a small part
of a man's yearly expenditure, and that other things must
cost far more. They don't. I get everything else in the

same way. . . . It is quite easy to do it once you become the fashion."

His beautiful rooms over Sherry's cost him nothing, for they were part of Tom Wanamaker's permanent apartment there, and Tom was only too pleased to loan them to anyone as amusing as Harry. His meals were supplied free whenever he chose to take them there, and in the restaurant downstairs he could entertain as many guests as he chose, for the management was perfectly aware that no better advertisement could exist than Harry Lehr's patronage. Wherever he led, the whole of the smart crowd would be certain to follow. The Waldorf and Delmonico's competed for his favours, suave maîtres d'hôtel smiled their delight when he ordered meals that must have cost the management hundreds of dollars. They knew that his guests would be of such social eminence that their presence could only be regarded as an honour to be received in all humility.

The same system was applied to everything, to even the most trivial details. Postage stamps might have involved some expense, so he preferred to send telegrams and cables. . . . "Harry must send more cables than any man in America, so original . . . Much better than bothering to write letters," said his friends. They did not know that every one of his affectionate messages flashing across the wires night and day was franked. Mrs. Clarence Mackay and the wives of other cable magnates were only too pleased to arrange such a small favour with their husbands . . . "Oh, do let Harry Lehr send his cables

free. He is always hard up . . . so generous . . . what
that boy must spend . . . and then he's so amusing!"

No railroad expenses! He boasted that he could
travel free on any line in America. Mrs. Fish got him
passes for the Illinois Central, Mrs. Gould and Mrs. Vanderbilt obtained similar concessions from their husbands.
Such a thing as distance should never be allowed to worry
him, to prevent him perhaps from coming to their house-
parties.

George Kessler, the wine merchant, astute, far-seeing,
a fine business man for all his dignity and his pride in his
resemblance to King Edward VII of England, saw the
possibilities in co-operation with the most popular man
in New York society. He called on him. . . .

"Mr. Lehr, you and I can be useful to one another. I
will give you six thousand dollars a year to sell my champagne. . . ." So Mrs. Oelrichs and Mrs. William Astor
and many another great hostess stocked her cellars with
champagne she did not particularly want merely for the
pleasure of having Harry Lehr at her parties. No need to
worry over ready money!

"Now you see how it is all done," Harry explained.
. . . "But it has this one disadvantage. It can only last
while I am a bachelor. People see me from quite a different angle now that they know I am going to marry a
rich girl. The day after our engagement was announced
everyone started bothering me. The shops won't give me
things free any more. They say that now I can afford to
pay for them myself. Even Kessler says he does not sup-

pose I shall want to go on selling wine after I marry. So you see, darling, I am afraid there is only one solution. You will have to realise that I am giving up a perfectly good livelihood because I love you far more than my career . . . and you will have to supply me with all that I am losing. . . ."

I appreciated his frankness and there was something so irresistibly funny in his point of view that I could only laugh and agree. I promised that I would make a marriage settlement on him. A few days later our lawyers drew up an imposing agreement by which I undertook to pay him twenty-five thousand dollars a year as pocket money, and to provide all the expenses of our life together. It was witnessed by Tom Wanamaker and Samuel Newhouse and afterwards we all lunched at Sherry's.

In describing that lunch I wrote:

"I like to meet Harry's friends and I don't want to meet any others. I trust his judgment in all things and am sure I shall be as happy as it is possible for anyone to be on earth. Harry returned and we worked with Miss de Baril at the wedding invitations. I cannot realise yet that I am to be married so very soon. I consider myself fortunate. I love Harry and deeply respect him. No one can read the future but there seems to be every chance of our combined happiness and peace. Harry has a most lovable disposition. . . ."

On the eve of our wedding I dined with him and wrote:

"We had a lovely dinner, Harry was awfully clever and

witty and lovely and handsome and oh! I was so proud
of him! There is no other like him in the whole
world. . . ."

I was married in the Cathedral where years before I
had stood in my simple white dress by the side of John
Dahlgren. This time the nave was crowded; the whole
of fashionable New York had come to see its most popular bachelor married. My dress had been designed by
Callot; the church blazed with light. But I missed something of the sweet content I had once known. I felt desperately alone among all those people. I looked at Harry
for comfort. Was it my fancy that the gaiety seemed to
have gone out of the vivid blue eyes, leaving only the
spirit of mockery that had once so fascinated me? A vague
sense of foreboding swept over me; it was as though a
cold hand had been laid on me.

As we left the church together I looked up and saw
that the sky that had been so bright was overcast.

.   .   .   .

We arrived at the Stafford Hotel, Mount Vernon
Place, Baltimore. It was our wedding evening and I lingered over my dressing for this our first dinner alone,
pinned a diamond brooch into my rose brocade gown,
hoped that Harry would think me beautiful. In the adjoining dining-room of our suite the table was being laid
—the sheaves of crimson roses I had ordered filled the
room with their fragrance. Caviar, quails in aspic, his
favourite brand of champagne, the cabinet of cigars I had
bought for him; I had forgotten nothing. By the side of

his plate lay the gold and enamel watch I had chosen so carefully. I wanted us both to remember this evening all our lives.

My maid came in. Her face was flushed, her eyes downcast. . . . "Madame, I thought I had better tell you," she hesitated. . . . "There must be some mistake. The maître d'hôtel tells me that Mr. Lehr has just given him orders to serve him dinner in his own room. He says that you will dine alone."

I forced myself to speak lightly as I made some casual excuse, said that probably Mr. Lehr was not feeling well, that he was tired after the ceremony.

A few minutes later my husband came into the room. His face was very pale, the laughter had left his eyes. Something in their expression made my heart stand still. He sat down facing me. . . .

"There are some things I must say to you, and it is better that I should say them now at the very beginning so that there can be no misunderstandings between us. You have just heard my orders to the servants, I presume?"

I nodded. My lips were too dry to speak. . . .

"Well, I intend that they shall be carried out for the rest of our life together. In public I will be to you everything that a most devoted husband should be to his wife. You shall never have to complain of my conduct in this respect. I will give you courtesy, respect and apparently devotion. But you must expect nothing more from me. When we are alone I do not intend to keep up the miser-

able pretence, the farce of love and sentiment. Our mar-
riag will never be a marriage in anything but in name.
I do not love you, I can never love you. I can school
myself to be polite to you, but that is all. The less we
see of one another except in the presence of others the
better."

"But why did you marry me?" The words were scarcely
above a whisper. He laughed and there was such bitterness in the sound that I shrank back involuntarily. . . .

"Dear lady, do you really know so little of the world
that you have never heard of people being married for
their money, or did you imagine that your charms placed
you above such a fate? Since you force me to do so I must
tell you the unflattering truth that your money is your
only asset in my eyes. I married you because the only
person on earth I love is my mother. I wanted above
everything to keep her in comfort. Your father's fortune
will enable me to do so. But there is a limit to sacrifice.
I cannot condemn myself to the misery of playing the
rôle of adoring lover for the rest of my life."

I sank into a chair, unable to speak. Perhaps something
in my stricken face aroused his pity, for he continued in
a more human tone:

"After all have you so much to complain of? At least
I am being honest with you. How many men in New
York, how many among our own friends, if it comes to
that, have entered their wives' rooms on their wedding
night with exactly my state of mind? But they prefer hy-
pocrisy to the truth. If I am never your lover when we

are alone, at least I will not neglect and humiliate you in public. What is more, I believe you will actually gain by marrying me. You will have a wonderful position in society. As my wife all doors will be open to you. Perhaps you will remember that luncheon to which I invited you to meet my four best friends? That was because I wanted to be sure that they would approve of my choice. Much as I wanted to marry you, nothing would induce me to forfeit my position in society to do so. But when I heard their decision to take you up I knew that you were going to be invited to all the most important houses in New York, and therefore there could be nothing to fear. . . ."

I did not speak, and for a moment he paced up and down the room in silence. Then he turned to me once more . . .

"I suppose I am what the novelists would call an adventurer. I am not ashamed of it. I would do more than I have done for the sake of my mother. If you will try and accustom yourself to the position, and realise from the start that there is no romance, and never can be any between us, I believe that we shall get along quite well together. But for God's sake leave me alone. Do not come near me except when we are in public, or you will force me to repeat to you the brutal truth that you are actually repulsive to me. . . ."

A second later and he was gone. I was left alone sitting by the fire, staring into the ruins of my life. Then I undressed and crept into the great bed that was to have been our marriage bed, and lay sobbing in the dark till the pillow was drenched with my tears.

On the next day I wrote in my diary:

"My happiness is gone. Mamma must never know. . . ."

. . . .

Pride came to my rescue. My marriage had broken up, my illusions had been swept away, but the world should never know, never even guess my hurt. I would not ask for sympathy from the friends who flocked to our house to congratulate us on our "happiness." Still less would I let Harry know how deeply he had wounded me. A thousand times better wear the mask of casual indifference, let him think I cared as little as he! I knew now that this marriage had been no escape from the loneliness I had hated, that I was to be more solitary than ever; alone among the crowds that surrounded me every hour of the day. Well, I would accept my destiny with what grace I could. I would be an observer, learn to look on at the happiness of others, pretend that I shared it.

I found myself swept into the gay set to which Harry Lehr belonged, or rather of which he was the pivot. We were invited everywhere, parties were given in our honour, we entertained in our own house, faced one another at the dining-table. He would pay me little compliments, fetch my wrap . . . "Don't get cold, darling. The garden is very chilly. You see I have to take care of her. She's so precious. . . ." Kind motherly Mrs. Astor would smile her approval . . . "So nice to see young people so much in love. . . . I am so glad to see dear Harry with such a charming wife . . ." and she would go to spread the story of how that confirmed bachelor Harry Lehr was madly in love with his wife. The other women would envy me. They had not learnt to read the mockery in the blue eyes!

He continued to avoid me when we were alone. Sometimes he would say grudgingly, "You make a better hostess than I should have guessed. That dinner tonight was really delightful. Everyone enjoyed it. You see I did not make a mistake. You are becoming the fashion."

Slight praise, but the highest he could bestow! It warmed my heart a little. Hoping against hope I determined to make some sort of a success out of my marriage. I flung myself into the gay social whirl that was to be my *raison d'être*. Vain substitute for the love I had longed for!

CHAPTER IV

"*TOUT COMPRENDRE, C'EST TOUT PARDONNER*"

"I NEVER CONFIDE IN ANYONE," HARRY LEHR WAS FOND OF saying . . . "explaining oneself is the refuge of the weak; it always puts you at a disadvantage."

He puts his maxim into practice. Looking back on the long years we spent together I realise how rarely he talked about himself. On the few occasions when he did so it was usually to boast of some fresh triumph, some social fortress that had fallen to his siege, for he had the vanity of a child. It was months before I gained a glimpse of the real personality of this strange man I had married, years before I grew to understand him. Only in unguarded moments did he ever lift the veil, generally when he was smarting from some wound to his self-esteem, for he was morbidly sensitive to snubs, and then as though he feared having said too much he would scarcely speak to me for days. Since his childhood he had so cultivated the habit of reticence that it was almost impossible for him to break it. This is his story, as he told it to me in snatches of conversation.

Henry Symes Lehr was born in Baltimore on March 28th, 1869. His father, Robert Oliver Lehr, was a pros-

perous tobacco and snuff importer; his mother, Mary
Moore, had been a beauty. Harry, the third son in a
family of six, grew up in the conservative background of
a city which prided itself on its exclusive society composed of people whose ancestors had been pillars of Baltimorean respectability for generations. Such a community was inclined to despise New Yorkers as vulgar, and
affected disdain of the new aristocracy of wealth.

In spite of his connection with trade, Robert Lehr had
a fashionable position in Baltimore, a fine town house
with a ballroom and a country place in Green Spring
Valley. He was Consul of Portugal and Belgium and
Governor of the Maryland Club, which widened his circle of friends and, as Harry once told me, "was the means
of wafting up the family to social summits which they
would not otherwise have scaled." Mrs. Lehr travelling
in Europe met the Duchesse de Bassano (née Symes of
Montreal) and the two women laid the foundations of
a lasting friendship which resulted in Harry having the
Duchesse for a godmother and Symes for one of his
names. . . . "So you see I started off well," he said, with
that light laugh of his.

I think that his childhood was happy enough until the
crash came when he was just seventeen and his father
died leaving the family practically penniless. The eldest
daughter, Alice, was already married to a Frenchman,
John Morton of the famous wine firm of Bordeaux; Mrs.
Lehr decided to take her children over to Europe. They
settled in Cologne, where one son, Louis, studied medi-

cine and Harry got a post as clerk in a bank. He only spoke to me once of those days, "It was like Hell . . . the wretched poverty, the greyness and squalor of it all. One day passing just like the next behind the counter of the bank, getting spoken to like a dog, always counting out sums of money for other people to spend, money that would have lifted us out of all our worries, and then drawing one's own miserable pittance of a salary."

They had furnished rooms in the poorer part of the city. . . "We were all herded together. Such frightful furniture, cheap oleographs on the walls. What I felt coming home to it at night, that one shabby sitting-room with its smell of stale food, finding my sister Fanny doing all the housework, seeing Mother sitting by the window, crying quietly because she had no clothes to go out in, not even enough to eat. Oh, how I loathed it!"

I could guess what he must have suffered, for he had an almost fanatical love of luxury and beautiful surroundings. After his death I read his diary and came upon this passage, "I must have beauty, light, music around me. I am like Ludwig of Bavaria, I cannot bear the cold greyness of everyday life. It withers my soul. Other clod-like people can stand it if they choose—I cannot!"

Those days in Cologne gave him a horror of poverty that he never lost even in the days when he had the great fortune my father had left me to draw upon. . . . "I have been spending the whole morning paying bills and writing cheques," he wrote in his diary years afterwards.

. . . "Such enormous sums of money they almost frighten me. I get a nightmare horror, supposing there should not be enough, although it is really absurd, for I can never be poor again, no matter what else I may be."

After two years the unexpected happened. Robert, the eldest son, was offered the chance of a post in the business that had been once his father's, and they all returned to Baltimore. In one way the move was infinitely better; it meant more comfort, comparative security, but to Harry it was almost more painful than those days in Cologne. . . . He could not accustom himself to the new circumstances since his father's death, the changed attitude of their former friends. . . . "People treated us so differently. In our days of success there had been so many invitations; now we got more snubs than anything else. We could not afford to entertain, so people did not want to bother with us. . . ." He grew bitter and sarcastic, shut himself up at home, avoided going anywhere where he would meet acquaintances of the old days.

"But I was too sensible to let that mood last long," he told me once. "I realised that no one ever got anything out of life by retiring into a shell, and that the only wise thing to do was to adapt oneself to one's circumstances. I found out that it was no good dwelling on the past and expecting people to sympathise with me because of it; it did not take long to show me that if I wanted to get back into the social set I had been in in my father's lifetime, I should have to offer something in place of the money and position we had before."

So he offered them laughter. . . . "I saw that most human beings are fools, and that the best way to live harmoniously with them and make them like you is to pander to their stupidity. They want to be entertained, to be made to laugh. They will overlook most anything so long as you amuse them. I did not mind cutting capers for them if I could gain what I wanted through it."

So that had been the secret of the faintly ironical gleam which was never completely hidden in those laughing blue eyes! "How could anyone take me seriously, dear lady? I'm only your fun-maker, your jester. . . ." How often I had heard him say it to Mrs. Astor or Mrs. Belmont, and they had laughed and beamed upon their protégé. And yet how seriously he had taken himself. How he had planned his campaign, voiced the bons mots which had made him famous throughout America, devised new eccentricities, new entertainments to amuse society while he had remained aloof and unamused behind that blandly smiling mask, cynical, calculating. And he had done it all because he had been afraid, afraid of having to face the poverty, the ugliness he loathed.

"Other men have to sweat in offices. I made up my mind I never would. I had only to be amusing to get a living, much better than working for one. . . ."

His first chance came with the success he had in "The Paint and Powder Club" theatricals. The whole of Baltimore society rang with praises of his performance of feminine parts in the different operettas which the Club presented. I only realised after his death, when I was looking through his papers, how much those early triumphs of over forty years ago must have meant to him, for he had cut out every single press notice and kept them carefully. I read:

"Mr. Harry Lehr was simply a picture. Nature having been very kind in figure and grace of movement was further enhanced by two stunning gowns. Add to this a faultless pair of shoulders and a throat which might be the envy of many women, and a natural aptitude for dancing and posing, and an idea will be formed of his success. He was one of the hits of the evening. . . ."

Another critic wrote:

"Mr. Harry Lehr presented a picture of female loveliness as Princess Genevieve in the comic opera 'Joan of Arc' produced by 'The Paint and Powder Club' at Ford's Grand Opera House yesterday. He wore white silk with low square corsage, puffed sleeves and white gloves, and bodice ornamented with open green iridescent work. The skirt which reached only to the knees was also of white silk with panels pendant from the waist of green iridescents and his shoes and stockings were of white. The fashionable audience showered applause on Mr. Lehr. . . ."

I could imagine how he had enjoyed choosing those gowns! He delighted in women's clothes and was never so happy as when he was helping some woman or other of his acquaintance to choose dresses. Although it was part of his pose to be a dandy, buying men's suits bored him. In his diary he wrote: "I went to Wetzels and had my clothes fitted on. I did the very best I could to hide

how it bored me. Oh, if only I could wear ladies' clothes;
all silks and dainty petticoats and laces, how I should
love to choose them. I love shopping even for my
wife. . . ."

He always longed for the picturesque clothes of the
Middle Ages—for the lace ruffles and jewels of the French
courtiers. Over his bed always hung the picture of the
Duc de Joyeuse, the famous "mignon" of Henri III of
France.

Those who admired him on the stage found that he
was just as amusing off it. No need now to look for invitations, they came to him by every post; every hostess
wanted to have such an entertaining young man to her
parties. As one newspaper put it:

"Harry Lehr is of all the young men in this city the one
who does the most entertaining, not at his own home but at
other people's. He is one of the few men of leisure in Baltimore, and has the one object of making himself agreeable.
He is in frequent demand, and is constantly invited to houses
where amusing people are desired. He is most versatile and
has many accomplishments. Playing the piano, dancing the
ballet, telling funny stories, pouring afternoon tea, designing
his hostess's smartest costume, or speaking French with the
foreign fellow-guests are all matters of equal ease. In winter
he flits about and in house party season is always present. . . ."

He wanted to widen his horizon. His opportunity came
when Mrs. Evelyn Townsend Burden (née Evelyn Moale
of Baltimore) invited him to stop at her Newport house,

"Fairlawn," where she dispensed hospitality on a lavish scale. Another great Newport hostess, Mrs. Elisha Dyer, also insisted that he should join her house parties. It was the beginning of that dazzling social career which flashed like a meteor across the sky and animated every season. From that first visit to Newport came all his success. The reigning queens of New York society, arrived for the season in search of new diversion, were delighted with so modest and entertaining a young man. He was so tactful, so obviously anxious to please, so resourceful. Every luncheon he attended was enlivened by his wit; he could always be relied on to come to the rescue when the spirit of a house party was beginning to flag, and suggest some new scheme for amusing the guests. His laugh made him famous. During his first visit to Newport "The Morning Telegraph" wrote:

"This seaside Valhalla of swaggerdom is dull—dull as a Presidential message or a 'Punch' joke. It is also as hot—hot as a conning tower in a sea fight, and even dinner dances, barn dances and all other species of hops, including the kind that comes in mottoed steins at the Dutch pavilions, are boresome even to the death.

But what cares Newport? It can console itself with its new bona fide sensation—Harry Lehr's laugh. Haven't you heard 'Harry' Lehr's laugh? That shows that you have not been within a hundred miles of Newport this season. Everybody within rifle range of Newport has 'Harry's' laugh down by heart. Not that it is stentorian, clangorous or of the ten-ton gun variety. Not at all. But its vibrations, once started, have an initial velocity of a mile a second, and by the end of the third peal, the very earth is undulating in unison, the church steeples begin to wag in perfect time, and the jaded souls of Newport's 'h'inner suckles' seem acted upon by some new and potent stimulant.

Well may 'Harry' Lehr echo the poetess: 'Laugh and the world laughs with you.' In 'Harry's' case the world simply cannot do anything else.

Mr. Lehr is a Baltimorean. He has money—a little, as Newport riches go; good looks—more, as Newport beauty goes; but it was the laugh that made him king. As Newport's court jester 'Harry' is a wonder. He simply laughed himself into the bosom of the ultra exclusives. He has held up the town with his irresistible chuckle, and robbed it of invitations to dinners, musicales, yacht cruises, barn dances, and heaven knows what not, at his piratical pleasure."

He was an expert on human nature. He had studied it to good purpose in those lean years in Cologne. He knew just what to say, what to leave unsaid, for he had reduced tact to a fine art, knew when to flatter, when to show restraint. He whetted the jaded appetities of Newport. He realised that people who had gone to the same place year after year, met the same familiar faces, exhausted one another's resources, needed novelty more than anything else. And he supplied it. They welcomed him, his inexhaustible vitality appealed to them, his incessant supply of conversation amused them. The Newport millionaires were for the most part dull companions at a dinner table. They might give evidence of brilliance of mind in Wall Street; in their homes they gave none. They might hold up the market but they could not prevent conversation slumping heavily at their own tables. They either talked of business or sat silent and apathetic through course after course, too nerve-racked by the strain of building a fortune to be able to relax. They were prepared to spend their last cent in gratifying the whims of their womenfolk, but they were incapable of amusing them themselves. This was where Harry Lehr found his opportunity. No business worries ever intruded into his flow of light chatter, no office in the city ever sapped his vitality, no tape machine ever put lines round his mouth or silenced his merry laugh. He was never obliged to rush back to New York, he was practically the only man in Newport who could be relied upon for parties in midweek. Like the lilies of the field he toiled not neither did he spin. The men were pleased enough to have him always in the company of their wives. They knew that he would give them no cause for jealousy; they did not even fear him; his friendships with women were so completely sexless.

"That is the secret of my success," he said to me once, commenting on this fact. . . . "Love affairs are fatal to ambition. I have seen the shore strewn with the wrecks of people who have given way to their passions, and I don't intend that mine shall be among them. If you have an affair with a single girl you have to marry her whether it is a suitable marriage or not. If you are fool enough to go after a married woman it always ends in disaster. Either she tires of you or you tire of her, and then what happens? At the best it means a rift in a friendship and someone's house closed to you; at worst you have a horrible scandal. I'm running no such risks. My position is not stable enough for that."

So he rejoiced in the fact that the men saw in him a sort of watchdog who would keep their wives amused and therefore out of mischief. One door after another opened to him, he became persona grata in the most exclusive circles. He chose his friends with a nicety of discrimination, avoiding the failures, picking out with unerring instinct those whose stars were in the ascendency. He saw Elisha Dyer leading cotillions at the great houses of Newport and modestly suggested that he should help him. Each made a perfect foil for the other—Elisha, immaculate dandy, tall, slim, elegant, black-haired at one end of the room; Harry, plump, heavily-built, blond and smiling, at the other. Soon he had proved himself so invaluable that Elisha could scarcely lead a cotillion without him. They were always bickering, and jealous of one another's popularity, yet no matter how acrimonious the dispute it was always certain to be settled before the next ball, and they would be on the best of terms once more. It was extremely difficult to quarrel seriously with Harry, for he had acquired a perfect self-mastery. He never permitted himself to show offence.

"There are three ways of taking an insult," he would say. . . . "You can resent it and walk out of the room, in which case you have committed yourself to a quarrel you may later regret; you can pretend not to hear, or you can laugh and turn it into a joke. I always choose the last, for I find it the most disarming. No one can quarrel with a man who laughs like an idiot." In those first seasons in Newport he extricated himself from many an awkward situation with an easy debonair grace that was one of his most potent charms. He became a legend. The newspapers loved to see his name down at any gathering. . . . "King Lehr" . . . "New York's Beau Brummell" . . . and catalogued even his most trivial sayings. Columns were devoted to his parties, to the clothes he was wearing. Every escapade of his—and there were many—was exaggerated to give small town readers their full share of wonderment that the sober twentieth century could produce so dazzling a figure. . . . He was held up as an object of admiration in some of the papers, of ridicule in others. . . . One journalist wrote:

"Harry Lehr of Baltimore is at last beginning to be appreciated at Newport, where there was formerly a disposition to make merry at the expense of his charms. To see Harry at his best one should visit Bailey's Beach any morning at the bathing hour. He has always been famous for the elegance of his legs.

But let nobody discount Harry's mental abilities while lost in admiration of his person. He is not only a wise young man in his day but knows where the good things of life grow, and how best to attain them. . . ."

Another notice ran:

"Mr. Lehr has been cutting a wide swathe recently in the select social field of New York. . . . He has been entertained and fed like a prince and is generally considered a lucky dog in consequence. Had Mr. Lehr lived a hundred years ago he would have made a veritable Beau Brummell or a Beau Nash. Clever in a way, he has all the requisite qualities to push himself to the front and render himself conspicuous. Without possessing wealth himself he has obtained a place among the most wealthy and the most refined in the land . . . and all this comes of being a good fellow, observing the conventionalities and wearing an individuality which is sui generis on all occasions."

Some of the writers made merry at his expense:

"Harry Lehr, I hear, will spend most of the summer visiting friends at Newport, R. I. As bathing has become fashionable again among the swagger set there, Harry has provided himself with a particularly cute bathing suit of his own designing with which to ravish the eyes of the 400. The vest will be cut décolleté in order to expose the whiteness of his snowy neck, and the trunks abbreviated so as not to deprive his admirers of a full view of his shapely limbs, which will be modestly incased with silken hose. A chic sun-bonnet will protect his peach-blow complexion from the ardent rays of the fiery sun. . . ."

"Mr. Lehr holds rather a unique position in society, and he has an individuality not to be compared with that of anyone else. His family is not wealthy, he has no profession or business, and I am often asked the question 'How does Harry Lehr live?' No one ever thinks of designating the gentleman by the name of Henry, and every Tom, Dick and Harry takes the liberty of speaking of Harry Lehr as though he were a bosom friend. Mr. Lehr has acquired a reputation for wading in fountains and taking headers from Bar Harbor yachts that has immortalized his name, but his fame does not rest upon exploits of this nature solely. He is an expert with the needle and would be an invaluable addition to a swell millinery establishment did he consider work compatible with his station in life. . . ."

wrote another columnist with withering sarcasm.

Scarcely a week passed without his being in the news. Long descriptions of his latest cravats, of how his Louis XV costume had taken the gentlemen's prize at the Bradley Martins' ball.

Then he was said to be engaged to May Van Alen; for days the papers were full of them both, the affair was discussed from every angle:

"There is much gossip anent the rumoured engagement of Mr. Harry Lehr to Miss May Van Alen, and it has now been announced in the dailies for about the sixteenth time. Mr. Lehr spent Christmas at the residence of Mrs. Astor, Sr. This, coupled with the fact that Mr. Van Alen has gone abroad with his younger daughter, leaving his elder daughter on this side of the water, would imply that Miss Van Alen's Astor relatives favour her engagement with Mr. Lehr, that her father does not approve of it and that it will not be an actuality until the young lady is twenty-one—an event not very far off—and becomes her own mistress. . . ."

"Reported denials of the engagement of Miss May Van Alen, of New York and Newport, to Mr. Harry Lehr of this city, by the friends of the lady, should be accepted as a satisfactory disposition of the rumoured alliance, yet notwithstanding the affirmation is made every week or so much to the annoyance, it is said, of both Miss Van Alen and Mr. Lehr. Mr. Van Alen, who is at present in Europe, has time and again emphatically denied that anything more than a friendly social relation existed between Mr. Lehr and his daughter. Mr. Lehr himself has intimated that the report connecting his name with that of Miss Van Alen is not founded upon fact, and the whole story resolves itself into a fiction fabricated by imaginative minds. . . ."

"The talk is that the engagement of Miss Mary Van Alen and Harry Lehr, of Baltimore is likely to be formally announced at any moment, says the New York 'Journal.' Mr. Lehr paid Miss Van Alen marked attention at the Assembly. Strangers thought he was a detective guard looking out for her jewels. Attached to the diamond necklace she wore a pendant with a solitaire in it very generally compared to a robin's egg in size. She was quite loaded down with magnificent jewels. Now that she is of age, Miss Van Alen feels privileged to adorn herself with diamonds. One-half of the collection of her mother, who was the eldest daughter of Mrs. William Astor, is now hers. . . ."

The Fountain episode caused another sensation, for the entire press came out with the story of how Harry Lehr and lovely Louise Gebhard, returning at midnight from a Baltimore party, were attracted by the cool plash of the fountain in Mount Vernon Place and dared one another to wade into the pool beneath it. The night watchman passing on his rounds was regaled with the spectacle of Louise with the skirt of her evening dress rolled up far above her shapely knees, and Harry, his trousers bedraggled, his evening pumps sodden with water, dancing about in the basin of the fountain, splashing one another to the accompaniment of shrieks of laughter from Mildred Morris, Moncure Robinson and Adele Horwitz who were looking on.

Of course the watchman had to tell his story, and to make the most of it in the telling, and the incident was distorted into a sort of Bacchanalian orgy with the result that Harry Lehr was denounced from half a dozen pulpits for his "scandalous conduct."

CHAPTER V
AFTER MY MARRIAGE

AFTER THE FIRST HEARTBREAKING REALISATION THAT MY marriage had been a cruel farce, a marriage in name only, I began to accustom myself to the situation. My pride at least was left to me; no one should suspect the agony of disillusion and humiliation through which I had passed, the bitter irony of my pose as a happy young wife. It was almost a relief that Harry played his part of a devoted husband so perfectly when we were with other people, for at least it saved me the necessity of painful explanations. We were rarely alone together. The locked door that divided our rooms was symbolical of the perpetual barrier between us. At first I tried to break it down. I knew so little of this man I had married; I could not believe that we were not both the victims of some tragic misunderstanding that had turned the love he had once seemed to have for me to hate. Perhaps he guessed what was in my mind, for he did not spare my illusions. . . . "Do you imagine that I am the type of man who would let himself be influenced by any woman's attractions, least of all yours? Let me tell you once and for all that love of women is a sealed book to me. I have not wanted it, or sought it, and I never shall. . . ."

He was incessant in his demands for money, and still more money. I gave it to him with open hands, never even discussed his extravagance. I found a fierce satisfaction in the giving; it salved my pride a little. He had married me for my money, and for that alone. . . . Well, he should have it.

And so the years slipped by and the world accounted us happy. I went to balls and receptions, entertained at Newport, in New York, travelled in Europe. One day succeeded another in the continual round of entertaining and being entertained against the background of that brilliant, glamorous social life which New York will never see again. It was easy to cheat oneself, to imagine that one was as happy as the majority of one's friends.

We spent most of the year in New York at the house which I had bought in West Fifty-sixth Street. We entertained a great deal, for by mutual consent we avoided whenever possible being left in each other's company.

There were always luncheons and dinner parties either at home or at someone else's house; on the rare occasions when we had an evening free I would dine in my room and Harry would go to Tom Wanamaker, his best friend. "I went to supper at Sherry's alone with Tom Wanamaker," he writes again and again in his diary. . . . "As always his company was like a draught of wine to me. How different from the chatter of women . . ." he comments in describing an evening spent with him.

We lived in the midst of a perpetual whirl. In those first golden years of the twentieth century, when every season could be called "brilliant," each week brought its quota of parties. Stately musicales at the beautiful house in East Sixty-fourth Street where Orme Wilson, handsome, grey-haired, distinguished with his air of a Louis XVI courtier, and his wife, gentle, lovely Carrie Astor, dispensed dignified hospitality. Informal dinners given by Mrs. Stuyvesant Fish, leader of the gayest set, often frowned upon by older, staider society matrons for her unconventionality, when the whole table would be convulsed with laughter at the sallies of Harry Lehr and his hostess. Dinners of lavish Southern hospitality at the Pembroke Jones' house, newcomers from North Carolina who had burst triumphantly into society, perhaps because they had profited by Harry Lehr's tip given in their first season, "Feed New York well enough and it will eat out of your hand. . . ." And so their table groaned under the weight of rare Southern delicacies, rice birds and Indian corn brought up from their own estates, chicken and corn fritters, Sally Lunns and muffins cooked to perfection by their negro cook who had his special little kitchen while their famous Russian chef, lured from the Czar's own household by a fabulous salary, prepared his elaborate menus in his own domain. The combined efforts of these two culinary artists were so successful that those who were inclined to raise disdainful eyebrows at Pembroke Jones' full-flavoured jokes and noisy laugh dined with him and thereafter became his staunch champions.

Splendid costume ball . . . Louis XVI . . . Roi

Soleil . . . Elizabethan . . . Venetian . . . Stuart. Strange complex that made us who belonged to a society so new seek always inspiration for our amusements in the past! No one would have dreamt of anything so plebeian as modern fancy dress; we had all to be kings and queens and courtiers. Princes of trade could represent none lower than princes of the blood; it was like children playing some fascinating game of make-believe. Cotillions with a dozen lovely intricate figures, original features introduced by Harry Lehr . . . an enormous papier-mâché watermelon dragged in at the Pembroke Jones' ball out of which sprang a tiny negro picaninny to distribute gold cigarette-cases and enamel watches to the guests . . . a huge pasteboard box delivered with ceremony in the Rollins Morse ballroom and opened to reveal Mrs. Lawrence Townsend picturesquely attired in the costume of a Chinese doll.

Harry Lehr was the acknowledged cotillion leader now. He had outstripped Elisha Dyer in popularity. There were occasional bitter words over it. . . . They took themselves very seriously. . . .

"I dined at the Dyers' and Elisha and I had a fight about the Jones' dance," writes Harry in his diary. . . . "He was very nasty and I was calm and quiet. He will not realise that it is useless for him to challenge my supremacy. . . ."

But there had to be a truce next day for they were both to lead the cotillion at the Oliver Harrimans' ball. . . . "I led with Elisha as my second. . . ." "I was dignity it-

self and did not speak to him more than was strictly necessary, but afterwards we had an awful fight, he and I
and Mrs. Fish. We went at it hot and heavy. Mrs.
Fish took my side, which was just what he did not expect. . . ."

Those were the days of magnificence, when money
was poured out like water. Nothing but the best was good
enough and so the best had to be procured regardless of
cost. The new kings of trade might work at their offices
twelve, fourteen hours a day, but their wives would have
something to show for it. Festoons of priceless jewels
draped ample bosoms, yards of historic lace trimmed un-
derpetticoats, the greatest dress designers of Europe vied
with one another to create costumes that would grace
some splendid ball for one night and then be thrown
away.

Gold plate gleaming on dinner tables laid for a hundred and fifty guests . . . fleets of lorries coming up
from the South in depth of winter laden with orchids to
decorate the ballroom of some great hostess. No one
thought of the cost. Cotillions with jewel favours, diamond bracelets for the women, sapphire cravat-pins for
the men . . . ball suppers of terrapin and quail, vin-
tage wines, nothing but the choicest champagne. . . .
No one would have dreamt of giving anything else! The
entire entertaining floor at Sherry's redecorated and up-
holstered in rose brocade just for one night . . . the entire staff of musicians, footmen and attendants equipped
with Louis XVI liveries—a hundred thousand dollars as

the price of an evening's amusement! James Hazen Hyde's ball cost twice that sum—but it also cost him his position in New York society.

When Henry Baldwin Hyde died, leaving his only son just graduated from Harvard complete control of the powerful Equitable Life Insurance Company, every hostess held out welcoming arms to one of the most eligible young bachelors in New York. All doors were open to him; he was fêted everywhere. Only his father's old business friends looked grim and prophesied disaster. It was enough to turn any young man's head, they said.

Everyone began to talk of his extraordinary clothes, his affectations. He imported his horses from the greatest studs in Europe, stabled them at his town house.

James Hazen Hyde began telling us about his costume ball which was to eclipse in splendour any entertainment that had ever been given in New York. All the dresses were to be of the period of eighteenth century France. Stanford White was hard at work with an army of painters and sculptors transforming Sherry's into a replica of the court of Louis XVI. He had engaged Réjane to come over specially from France to recite "Racine." In all it would cost him a cool $200,000. "Don't let that get into the newspapers," said Harry Lehr. . . .

Even New York, accustomed to scenes of splendour, was startled at the magnificence of that ball. Stanford White had surpassed himself. The whole floor of the supper-room was strewn with rose petals, thousands of orchids were massed in clusters on the walls, priceless statuary brought over from France stood in niches garlanded with flowers. All the waiters wore the authentic dress of Louis XVI lackeys. Caviar and diamond-back terrapin on the supper menu, the most expensive wines that France could produce. Harry Lehr dismayed the waiters by asking for hard-boiled eggs and a glass of cold milk. . . . "I always love to do it at a party of this sort . . ." he explained maliciously. . . . "Champagne may flow like water, but you will see the whole staff won't be able to produce a glass of milk. . . ." He got it in the end, but he had to wait half an hour for it.

.   .   .   .

Evenings given over to balls, to dinner parties. Evenings at the Opera, where every woman wore full regalia, to outshine her neighbours. Diamond tiaras, ropes of pearls, enormous sapphires and emeralds, such a profusion that the problem was to find a novel way of wearing them. Mrs. John Drexel, "Cousin Alice" as Harry Lehr insisted on calling her, wore her priceless pearls set in a wide band which crossed over her imposing bosom and down her back like a Sam Browne belt. Mrs. Frederick Vanderbilt having heard that the Venetian beauties liked to toy with a single jewel on the end of a chain decided that it would be even more original to have hers hanging before her feet. So she always progressed to her loge at the Opera kicking a great uncut sapphire or ruby attached to her waist by a rope of pearls.

Evenings at the theatre where I wept over the pathos of "Camille," where Harry Lehr left in the middle of

"Everyman" ("which surpassed anything I ever knew in the line of boredom," he described it in his diary), where we both laughed at the drolleries of Raymond Hitchcock in "The Yankee Consul" and enthused over Fritzie Scheff in Victor Herbert's operetta "Babette," and Elsie de Wolfe in "The Other Girl."

Harry and I and Mrs. Fish went sometimes to Barnum's Circus in Madison Square Garden.

It recalled vivid memories of my childhood when I had crossed the Atlantic with my parents in the old-fashioned paddle-steamer "The Scotia" and a particularly bad voyage had been enlivened by the endless good-humour and high spirits of the famous showman Barnum who was a fellow passenger.

We loved the story of how he had once been held up at a wayside station when he was in a desperate hurry to get to Philadelphia. To his intense dismay he was told that there was no train available until late that evening, which meant a wait of many hours. "But the express passes right through your station in an hour and a half," he exclaimed; "you will have to hold it up for me." The station clerk shook his head. His orders were that under no circumstances was the express to be stopped except for a large party of travellers. . . . And there won't be a large party today, or I should have heard about it."

Barnum walked off dejectedly in the direction of the village.

A few minutes later a small boy arrived hot and breathless at the station. . . .

"Here, Mister, you've got to stop the express. There's a large party from Barnum's Circus travelling to Philadelphia, and they've got to catch it." The astonished station clerk wasted no time on further enquiries. He had heard of the great Barnum, everyone in the States had. When an hour later the Philadelphia express drew up alongside the platform with much grinding of brakes and ringing of bells, only one passenger answered its shrill summons. He was stepping into the coach with leisurely dignity when the irate clerk accosted him:

"Here, you, what's the meaning of this? I was asked to stop the train for a large party from Barnum's Circus!"

"Well, so you did. I am P. T. Barnum and," tapping his huge chest, "ain't I a large party?"

. . . .

Shopping in the mornings, with Harry Lehr to choose my dresses. He had an unerring instinct about clothes and consequently his advice was always sought by all our friends. He would spend whole mornings happily at the dressmaker's with Mrs. Fish and Mrs. Hermann Oelrichs, comparing models, choosing colours, telling them what they ought or ought not to wear.

As one journalist wrote:

"Mrs. Harry Lehr will sport some remarkable toilets at Newport this summer. Everyone may be included in the catalogue that spells 'dreams,' for everyone has been carefully thought out by her liege lord. I ran across him at Worth's recently, where he had the whole establishment in commotion that was heard even out on the Rue de la Paix, while the presiding genius of the temple of clothes was literally tearing his hair out in handfuls in his atelier. The particular creation that was troubling Mr. Lehr's brain, the morning I saw him, was a combination of five colours which he insisted could be made into a unit. When Mrs. Lehr trips across the lawn of the Newport Casino in this characteristic get-up she will look like an animated rainbow. . . ."

In the afternoon we would drive in the Park. Those were the days when you had to love, or pretend you loved, horseflesh or be socially damned. Every house with any claim to fashion had its stables of horses from the finest strains in Europe and Kentucky, its smart turn-outs for every occasion. The John Drexels boasted of twenty-six different carriages, Mrs. Fish and the Pembroke Jones' must have had nearly the same number. Even the most moderate stables included light phaetons for morning, with silk-fringed white canopy tops in summer, small one-horse victorias driven by a coachman in corded livery for shopping; a more elaborate version of the victoria with two men on the box for afternoon drives, and the resplendent "grand daumont de visite" with its liveried footmen perched up behind for state occasions. In the fashionable afternoon hours there would be a long procession of carriages round the Park, Oliver Belmont driving his spider phaeton, the Orme Wilsons' victoria, Mrs. Astor's chestnuts and green-liveried men, Mrs. Fish's strawberry roans, Mrs. Hermann Oelrichs' magnificent daumont.

Harry and I would often drive on James Henry Smith's

coach. "How I admire that man," wrote Harry Lehr in
his diary. . . . "It takes a lot of personality to bring a
newcomer to society to the front like that. . . ."

Actually I think it was wealth rather than personality
which made his social career, for no one seemed to have
discovered much charm in the plain, stocky, undistin-
guished little man who went by the name of "Silent
Smith" until his eccentric old uncle died and left him a
fortune of forty million dollars. Thereafter he was presented to the world anew, so richly gilt and covered with
diamonds, with such an aura of wealth around him, that
no one ever thought what he was like himself. He immediately bought the William C. Whitney house with its
famous gates imported from the Palazzo Doria, and there
he lived alone, the quarry of all the match-making
mothers in New York. He was dazed at the sudden change
in his fortunes, uncertain where to look for interests. He
wanted to get into society, he did not know how to do it.
Edith Gould and Mrs. Stuyvesant Fish came to the rescue. . . . "We are going to launch you in the right set.
You must give a ball. We will organise it for you."

He gave them carte blanche to order what they would,
choose the decorations, buy the gold cotillion favours.
His ball at the Waldorf was the greatest success of the
season, and from that moment he became "the fashion."

Not so fortunate was another newcomer who wanted
to get into society, Harry Blank, eccentric young millionaire. Harry Lehr had a contempt for him. . . . "The
man's a snob and an opportunist," he wrote in his diary

. . . "and he is not even clever enough to disguise it," and his comment was dated at the time of the Bobby Hargous party.

There was no doubting the fact that the Hargous family was "IN" (as Ward McAllister said of those fortunates who were acceptable in the inner circles of the social pasture), so when Bobby, a rich and agreeable young bachelor, issued invitations for a ball at the Waldorf-Astoria there were few refusals. Then just about a week before the date of the ball the host was taken very ill. His sister Mrs. de Forest was sent for, and he was ordered into a nursing home immediately for an operation. "Of course the ball will have to be postponed . . ." said everyone. . . . But they had not counted upon Harry Blank, who at that time had not many friends, and presumably wanted to acquire more. While Bobby Hargous lay at death's door his sister was completely mystified to receive a telegram which read:

"If brother lives will take on party. If dies will call party off. Send list of guests.

HARRY."

Upon investigation she discovered that the sender of the wire was anxious to replace her brother as host at a party which was expected to be one of the season's smartest affairs. Not wishing to be worried with the question at such a time she wired back that as far as she was concerned he might do anything he liked with the party and sent the list of guests. The result was that all the guests were solemnly notified that the fate of the evening's entertainment rested on the knees of the gods. They must be prepared to write letters of acceptance to a new host or letters of condolence to the Hargous family.

Fortunately for all Bobby Hargous took a turn for the better, and the ball was a great success.

. . . .

Every Sunday Harry Lehr and I went to High Mass at Saint Patrick's Cathedral together, and he would stand beside me devoutly telling his exquisite carved jade rosary, his eyes half closed, his lips moving in prayer, only pausing to hiss at me, "What a perfect fright you are looking! Why on earth did you put on those shoes?"

Going to church was a social function. Everyone was religious. The more successful in business you were during the week, the more devoutly you attended church on Sunday. Pierpont Morgan took up the collection at Saint Bartholomew's, the Vanderbilt men roared out the hymns untunefully at Saint Thomas's. Everyone lionised the popular preachers; they were invited to the smartest houses in New York.

Bishop Henry C. Potter was one of them. He was stately and magnificent, a man of the world, a lover of rich food and rich houses. He had actually two forms of saying grace before meals. The first which he used at the table of Mrs. Fish and other wealthy hostesses was delivered in a rich and fruity voice, "Bountiful Lord"—rolling the words round his tongue—"we thank Thee for all these Thy blessings. . . ." In the homes of lowlier parishioners where the fare was of uncertain quality he would begin meekly, in a minor key, "Dear Lord, we give thanks for even the least of these Thy mercies. . . ."

In striking contrast to Bishop Potter was the æsthetic Dr. ——, rector of a fashionable New York church, who adopted a pose of humility and conversed in a low musical voice. He was greatly in demand at Newport as a fashionable addition to dinner parties where the women described him as "magnetic." Handsome and faultlessly dressed, he loved to carry about with him a string of amber beads which he fingered incessantly to display the lily-whiteness of his long slender hands.

Archbishop Corrigan, kindly, sincere, tactful, as popular in the houses of his flock for his charm of manner as he was unpopular in the pulpit for the length of his sermons, would come to call on us. He was overjoyed at the smacking price for which he had sold the two entire blocks on Fifth and Madison Avenues occupied by the Roman Catholic Orphan Asylum, which had acquired them years before, when they were far outside the city, for the merely nominal sum of two dollars a lot. Knowing their tremendous value the Archbishop was determined to sell them. He waited until an Irish Catholic, Hugh J. Grant, was elected Mayor of New York, then went to call on him. . . .

"Isn't it a pity now that the city is getting no taxes from those grand blocks we have for the children there on Fifth Avenue? I've been thinking you might like us to sell them. . . ."

The Mayor declined shortly. Then the Archbishop played his strongest card:

"Have you thought that an epidemic might break out at any moment among these hundreds of children?" he suggested quietly. . . . "And if it did, what would save the city?" Mayor Grant was strong on the question of health and sanitation. His schemes for improving the city had been an important part of his campaign.

"If you are wanting to give up the sites and take the children to the country where it will be healthier for them I'll not be hindering you," he conceded. "The City will buy back your lots but at the price you paid for them, and maybe a bit over. But it is no good expecting to sell to us at a fancy price."

"I want a new orphanage in the Bronx for my boys and girls, and I mean to have it. Unless you will help me to get it we will keep our property. But I tell you what I will do: I will write letters to all the newspapers and point out the peril to the health of New York, and I will let the public judge. . . ."

"Ah, don't do that now. . . ." The Mayor was alarmed for his popularity. . . . "Let's talk it over first. . . ."

In the end the Archbishop got his way. He was allowed to sell the land at his own price.

CHAPTER VI
A QUEEN AND HER JESTER

HARRY LEHR ALWAYS SAID THAT HE OWED A DEBT OF gratitude to Mrs. Astor, for without her help he could never have scaled the social peak. Queen of the Four Hundred as she was, in New York society she reigned supreme and her decisions as to things social were final, from which there was no appeal. She could make or mar the ambitious climber.

She made Harry Lehr. She liked him from the moment she met him at the Elisha Dyers' house in Newport, invited him to lead the cotillion at her next ball, and ever afterwards her loyalty was unswerving. She was naturally sincere and gracious and her friendship once given was not lightly withdrawn. There were many attempts to dislodge Harry from her favour, but none succeeded. She had taken him under her wing. She was one of those women to whom one instinctively applies the adjective "motherly" in no matter what walk of life they may be placed. . . . "A real woman in a real woman's atmosphere," wrote Harry Lehr in his diary. . . . "She has been kindness itself to me. . . ."

Only the other day I came upon one of the letters she wrote him in his bachelor days, a letter full of tact and sympathy, very characteristic of her. He had evidently consulted her as to whether he should marry, for this letter was her answer, written from her beautiful Paris apartment, 146 Avenue des Champs Elysées.

"I have received two charming letters from you, and they have given me much pleasure, one page interested me more than all the others. Of course I have no right to advise but it seems to me your present life is an ideal one, so many good friends, such a hearty welcome everywhere, a life so free from serious anxieties, it seems to me better to let well alone, at least for some years, you have all life before you. Of course this is all in confidence and I could only repeat the same thing if I were talking to you. To a woman a home is a necessity, not so for a man, whose life is so free and independent. I am speaking in a general way as I do not know the lady you refer to, but you are happy now and there is a risk in changing a certainty. . . .

And now I must tell you of Paris. . . . We are all busy doing nothing. . . . I am sure of your ready sympathy when I tell you that two of my hats are unbecoming, the others are quite lovely. . . . The Opera seemed tame after ours at home. . . . The Porters have a very handsome house here and entertain continually. . . . The trees and flowers are all in bloom here and when the sun does shine it is lovely, but I am tired of these weeping skies. . . . I am so sorry to hear of your mother's illness. . . . Please remember me very kindly to her and your sister. . . ."

She showed him many little kindnesses. Every night of the week during the Opera season a seat was reserved for him in her box whether he chose to use it or not. He it was who induced her to go to the Bradley Martins' ball, the first time she had ever been known to honour an hotel with her presence. There was a little stir of excitement as she swept regally into the room on Harry's arm. Her black satin costume, copied by Worth from a Van Dyck picture, with its lovely lace collar and cuffs, was the personification of elegance and richness; the diamonds she wore were incomparable. To please him she even lifted her self-imposed ban and dined in a public restaurant, a procedure so entirely without parallel that the papers were full of it next day.

"Harry Lehr and his legs and his piano playing and his singing and his witticisms and all the rest of it have completely fascinated Mrs. Astor. To see that august lady—for whom I have the greatest respect and whom I think one of the few veritable *grandes dames* in New York society—in a coquettish raiment of white satin, with the tiniest hair dress, at Sherry's on Sunday last, *dos-à-dos* almost with Lillian Russell, I could hardly believe my eyes. And she seemed to enjoy it, and nodded her head to the rag-time tunes, and took the most gracious interest in everything. She wore her famous pearls, and was indeed a stunning sight.

I did not think that the company was particularly lively, and how everyone did stare at them! Perry Belmont was a bit triste, and even Mrs. Cornelius Vanderbilt, Jr., who has always plenty to say for herself, seemed suddenly struck dumb. And every one of the old table d'hôte stagers was there —Bourke Cockran nodding to friends, W. E. D. Stokes grasping people by the hand, and Fenelon Collier, as usual, tripping about; the Baron Rosenkrantz and Frank Munsey and the Westervelts and all the first-nighters. And I am sure it was the Lehr-Astor party whom they came to see, and I wonder if the great star cast enjoyed it. I think they had stage fright. . . ."

"But what are we coming to?
Mrs. Astor at Sherry's table d'hôte!
Even in the palmiest days of the Waldorf-Astoria one never saw the very ultra people dining and breathing the same air as that of the 'middle classes.' Now and then people who were on the tip-top, and who had good sense enough to enjoy themselves and go wherever they pleased, would drop into the Waldorf-Astoria. . . .
But I never dreamed that it would be given to me to gaze on the face of an Astor in a public dining-room.
But Harry Lehr, dear child, is irresistible. He will be Mrs. Astor's favourite grandson-in-law. The dinner is to take place this evening.
The fact of Harry Lehr giving anything is so extraordinary that all Baltimore, his native town, is up in arms. He was never known to give anything there but infinite amusement, which perhaps, after all, is better than nothing, and certainly very grateful in these days, when one is bored to death.
Every table in the place is taken in view of the event.
What, a great dinner party on Sunday night in a restaurant, with all the women in evening clothes and the famous stomacher and tiara in evidence! Surely it cannot be! I am sure that there is some mistake!"

I was only a very young girl when I first met Mrs. Astor, and her dignity, her air of reserve rather over-awed me. It was only years afterwards when I began to know her better that I was able to appreciate her. She was a *grande dame* in everything she said or did, but, despotic and strong-willed as she was, she could on occasion be sentimental. When her sixteen-year-old daughter, Caroline, fell in love with Orme Wilson, who was only two years older, she was bitterly opposed to the marriage. They were both far too young to know their own minds, she said, and she had other plans for her daughter. For a long time the Astors refused their consent—neither Carrie's tears nor the representations of the Wilsons had the least avail.

Then one day Mrs. Astor saw the young couple coming out of church hand in hand. They had been to the service together, and they looked so serenely contented, so completely absorbed in one another that her heart was touched.

"I felt that I could not stand in the way of their happiness a day longer," she told my mother—and thereupon withdrew her opposition. Carrie was allowed to marry the man of her choice.

Mrs. Astor was always dignified, always reserved, a little aloof. She gave friendship but never intimacy. She never confided. No one ever knew what thoughts passed behind the calm repose of her face. She had so cultivated the art of never looking at the things she did not want to see, never listening to words she did not wish to hear, that it had become second nature with her. New York would ring with gossip concerning the latest doings of William Astor; stories would be circulated of wild parties on board his yacht. . . . The rumours grew more and more exaggerated as they flew from mouth to mouth. Everyone wondered what Mrs. Astor, giving her stately dinners and "musicales" at her Fifth Avenue house, thought of it all, but their curiosity was never satisfied. When someone would ask tentatively after her husband she would reply placidly: "Oh, he is having a delightful cruise. The sea air is so good for him. It is a great pity I am such a bad sailor, for I should so much enjoy accompanying him. As it is I have never even set foot on the yacht; dreadful confession for a wife, is it not?" And her smile would hold nothing but pleasant amusement over her inability to share her husband's interests.

Whatever the world might think of William Astor his wife would never give vent to the faintest criticism of anything he did. She always spoke of him in terms of the greatest affection and admiration: "Dear William is so good to me. . . . I have been so fortunate in my marriage. . . ." There was something disarming in her quiet loyalty.

It was the same when her daughter, Mrs. Coleman Drayton, figured in a divorce case. Everyone wondered what Mrs. Astor would do. Would she, who had hitherto turned her back on anyone who had come before the divorce courts, apply her rigid code to her own daughter? The first reception at the Astor house after the case was crowded to the very doors. Every friend of the family was there to support, or condole, as the necessity might be. But whatever it was the Queen could do no wrong. They would follow her faithfully. Their eyes turned anxiously towards her as they entered the salon . . . then they sighed with relief. . . .

Mrs. Coleman Drayton was standing by her mother, calmly helping her to receive her guests.

.   .   .   .

The annual ball at the Astor house was the greatest social event of the year. It was also the occasion for much heartburning. Several weeks beforehand Mrs. Astor and Harry Lehr, as her lieutenant, would sit in solemn conclave scanning the columns of the Social Register, deciding who should and who should not be invited. The Astor ballroom only held four hundred, therefore New York society must be limited to Four Hundred. One name after another was brought forward and rejected. Mr. and Mrs. X——? No, they were too blatantly in trade. . . . "I buy my carpets from them, but then is that any reason why I should invite them to walk on them? . . ." said Mrs. Astor.

The process of elimination went on. The lists were written and rewritten at least half a dozen times until the guests had been brought within the limits of the four hundred. Then the invitations were sent out. This was always done by Maria de Baril, who acted as a sort of social secretary to all the great hostesses of New York and Newport, where she took up her abode during the season. The moment an envelope addressed in her delicate handwriting, embellished with the Gothic scrolls which no one dreamt of imitating, appeared on the breakfast tray, one knew that here was an invitation of importance. For Maria de Baril was exclusive, as befitted one who claimed descent from the Incas. Her handwriting

was by no means at the disposal of anyone who could pay
for it. She had to make certain that invitations emanating
from her pen would only be received by people of eminence before she would condescend to despatch them.
She would arrive at the great houses of Fifth Avenue, a
stout dumpy little figure always bedizened with a weird
assortment of bead necklaces and amulets, receive her list
of guests and depart to send out her invitations, perfectly
worded to suit the occasion.

Weeping and gnashing of teeth on the part of those
who did not receive the coveted slip of cardboard, "Mrs.
Astor requests the pleasure . . ." Life could hold no
more bitter mortification. There remained only one
course open to them—to hide the shameful truth from
their friends. They did it at all costs. Doctors were kept
busy during the week of the ball recommending hurried
trips to the Adirondacks for the health of perfectly
healthy patients, maiden aunts and grandmothers living
in remote towns were ruthlessly killed off to provide ali-
bis for their relations . . . any and every excuse was re-
sorted to. Not a man or woman in society who would let
their friends jump to the dreadful conclusion that their
absence from the greatest social event of the year was due
to lack of an invitation!

Even after all the acceptances had been received there
remained another problem whose solution almost demanded the judgment of Solomon: Who should sit on
"The Throne."

Even after all these years I have only to close my eyes to conjure up a vision of the Astor ballroom in all its splendours. The massive candelabra that William Astor had brought back from Italy, the walls lined with pictures of the nineteenth century French school, New York's last word in European culture, the long rows of chairs tied together in pairs with ribbons, the musicians' gallery with the band in the familiar Astor blue liveries. And on a raised platform at one end was an enormous divan—"The Throne." No one ever dreamt of calling it anything else. But alas, capacious as were its depths, it could only accommodate a limited number on those ample red silk cushions and there was acute disappointment every year when the seats were allotted. Once I remember Mrs. John Drexel ("Cousin Alice" as Harry Lehr christened her, and everyone else called her thereafter) bursting into noisy tears when she saw the names on the Throne list and found her own not included among them. Sobbing, she seized upon Mrs. Orme Wilson. . . . "Your mother doesn't like me. She has given me the most dreadful humiliation. . . . Oh, I have never been hurt so in my life. . . ."

"But what has Mother done?" asked Mrs. Astor's daughter in astonishment. . . . "My name is not on the Throne. . . . She does not love me. . . . I won't stay one minute longer in a house where I am not loved. . . ."

And she rushed out to the entrance hall in her white satin ball dress and ran to the cloakroom pursued by

Harry Lehr. It was several minutes before he succeeded in bringing her back to the ballroom and persuading her that no slight had been intended.

The occupants of the Throne outside the family were generally chosen in consideration of their social claims. One lady, however, was debarred from the privilege on account of her enormous hips. . . . "How can I have her when you have to allow at least two ordinary seats for her?" asked Mrs Orme Wilson plaintively. There was a harrowing legend of how on the one occasion when she had sat in the row upon the seat of honour her neighbour had been a young Englishman. Feeling her massive hips in their tight steel corsets running into him he turned to her and asked in all innocence . . . "I wonder if you would mind taking that book out of your pocket? . . ." She rose in outraged majesty. . . . "Young man, you are being grossly impertinent . . ." and left the house mortally offended.

There was an amusing incident at the ball which Mrs. Astor gave in Newport immediately after the Spanish War. As usual she had left all the arrangements in the hands of Harry—he had chosen the cotillion favours, issued instructions to the caterers and musicians. When she arrived in the ballroom she was amazed to see the members of the orchestra wearing, in place of their smart blue and gold uniforms, travel-stained suits of khaki. . . .

"What is the meaning of this?" she asked Harry. He was just as puzzled as she. Suddenly the explanation

dawned on him. He had wired instructions to the orchestra, "Wear regular uniform . . ." and as they had
all been serving with Colonel Jack Astor in Roosevelt's
Rough Riders they had interpreted his instructions as a
command to appear in their military uniforms!

CHAPTER VII
"THE UNKNOWN QUANTITY"

FOUR YEARS PASSED. I HAD LEARNT TO ACCEPT MY DESTINY, and the smouldering flame of rebellion in my heart had almost died when I met X—— if I can call anyone so vital, so full of the joy of living by such a dull, impersonal letter! Yet I remember that from time immemorial X—— has represented "the unknown quantity," and so it is not so unfitting to my story after all, for the unknown quantity, the uncalculated factor which changed the whole world for me again, was love.

Shall I ever forget our first meeting in New York, and how the dinner party that had seemed to me so boring, so flat, was transformed by the sunshine of his presence? There were many guests, and we sat on opposite sides of the table, but all through dinner our eyes kept meeting. There was some intangible bond of sympathy between us.

Harry Lehr brought him across the drawing-room to me afterwards. . . .

"Bessie, I want you to meet Mr. X——. He has been away in Europe for over two years. That's why you have never seen him around anywhere. . . ." His eyes as he made the introduction were so full of mockery that I turned from them sharply to encounter the clearest, the most candid eyes I had ever seen. . . .

We had not very long to talk together. X—— was the handsomest man in the room; he was being lionised on his return to the States. Someone claimed him to play bridge. But before he left me I had given him my permission to call on me.

That night I was very silent as I drove home. For once Harry's continuous flow of criticism of my dress, my appearance, my conversation at the party fell on unheeding ears. Some lines of Elizabeth Barrett Browning were echoing in my head:

"Such a starved bank of moss on that May morn.
Blue ran the flash across, violets were born. . . ."

I remembered that she had written them after her first meeting with Robert Browning.

.   .   .   .

How can I write of the days that followed? Of the summer to all outward appearances like so many that had preceded it, and yet how different because of this new, infinitely sweet friendship that had come into my life? Not for one moment did I think of it then as anything else, neither, I am sure, did X——. We talked of so many things, of ourselves most of all, but by common consent neither of us spoke of love. We were always together. How could it have been otherwise since we knew all the same people, went to the same houses? Harry showed him the greatest cordiality, insisted that I should invite him to all my parties. We drove in the Park together, danced at a variety of balls, went with all the rest of our friends to Newport early in August, played tennis together, spent long mornings sailing in his yacht.

For the first time since I had become Harry Lehr's wife the joy of living came back to me. Hope dawned in my heart once more; I ceased to be a spectator of other people's happiness. Without ever putting it into words X—— made me realise his understanding, his sympathy. I felt that he divined the truth behind the pitiful pretence of my marriage, but we never discussed it.

So the weeks slipped by and the Newport season came to an end, as did all Newport seasons, with Mrs. Fish's Harvest Festival Ball.

How vividly the scene of those balls comes back to my memory! I can picture it that night. "Crossways," the fine, solid Colonial house which Stuyvesant Fish had designed himself, with its spacious dining-room, where two hundred guests could have supper at once, and its enormous hall which served as ballroom decorated on this one night of the year not with the lovely flowers on which Mrs. Fish prided herself, but with a great array of fruits and vegetables of the fall. Sheaves of corn and garlands of yellowing leaves adorned the hall, giant watermelons and pumpkins, whose centres had been hollowed out country-fashion and replaced by candles, hung in rows in the garden; huge dishes of luscious pears and apples formed the centrepieces of the supper tables.

After the last dance the lights were lowered in the hall

and there was a sudden hush as the orchestra broke softly into the first bars of Tosti's famous "Good-bye." Melba was to sing it and she came into the hall, stately and beautiful in a corn-coloured dress, while showers of leaves, crimson and brown and gold, were scattered down from the galleries above us.

"Falling leaf and fading tree, lines of white on a cloudy sea . . ."

The glorious voice rang through the hall. Familiar words, I had heard them so often, yet that night they seemed to strike a chord of sorrow in my own soul. . . .

"Hush, a voice from the far away. Listen and learn it seems to say.
All the tomorrows shall be as today . . ."

sang Melba, and the words seemed to hold a message for me. How could I face a loveless lifetime of empty days, a marriage that was built up on deception?

"Good-bye to hope, Good-bye, Good-bye. . . ." Whyte Melville's last cry of despair. Must I too give up hoping, cease to fight against my destiny?

"Good-bye for ever. . . ." The last notes of the song died away. . . . "It's beautiful, but it isn't true," said a voice beside me. I turned, jarred out of my reverie, and found myself looking into the eyes of X——.

"We need never say 'good-bye,'" he said. . . . In that moment I knew I loved him.

· · · · · · ·

Afterwards he told me that he had loved me since the very beginning of our friendship, but that he too had never realised it until that night. He begged me to divorce Harry Lehr, to marry him. . . . "Darling, your marriage as it stands is no marriage. You would not have the slightest difficulty in getting a divorce. Even the Catholic Church would give you an annulment. You can be my wife without having to face any scandal. . . ."

I knew that it was true. I was bound to Harry by no ties except those of the law, which could be easily severed. Why should I endure a life of misery when I could find happiness with the man I loved?

But although I asked myself the question impatiently a dozen times a day, I always found the same answer: my mother, to whom divorce was an unbearable disgrace, who would not even allow it mentioned in her presence. How could I break the news to her? Tell her that I intended to leave my husband for ever? I shrank from the pain I should have to inflict on her. But there was X—— who had grown dearer to me every day. How could I give him up? The weeks passed in a conflict which seemed to have no issue. I was facing the hardest decision of my life.

At length I decided to go and see my mother, to tell her the whole wretched story of my marriage, of my love for X—— and ask her advice. It would hurt her cruelly, I knew, but she could not fail to understand. I would throw myself on her sympathy.

It was a wintry afternoon when I drove up to Pen

Rhyn, the beautiful house she had bought on the Delaware River, and Mother was sitting by the fire. I thought that she looked very small and very frail; she seemed to have grown so much older in the last year or two. But her welcome was as warm as ever; her cheeks were flushed with the pleasure of seeing me again, and I remember that she took such delight showing me the improvements she had made to the estate. She scarcely spoke of New York, was only mildly interested when I described new plays I had seen, balls and receptions I had been to. Her mind was full of the little things of every day, of the country people around her, her garden, drives.

As I was dressing for dinner on the evening of my arrival there was a knock at my door and the trained nurse who had been with my mother ever since her previous illness came in. . . .

She had guessed that I would be anxious to have her report. . . . "Madame Drexel has really made a wonderful recovery, Mrs. Lehr," she told me. "The doctors have been surprised at the way she has rallied. But of course we have to remember that her heart is in a very serious condition. Any sudden shock now or any worry would probably have fatal results. . . ." Perhaps she read the distress in my eyes for she added hastily, "But we need not trouble about that for she is not likely to have any shocks. It's for us to see that she doesn't, isn't it?"

It was with a very heavy heart that I went down to dinner. That evening as we sat together over the fire, my mother and I talked of the past and of the days in Saratoga Springs. She had put on a new pair of pearl grey hand-sewed gloves, and I remember that I teased her over this little vanity of hers, for she was inordinately proud of her hands which were very beautiful. They were the whitest hands in the world and she could never bear to expose them to the heat of the fire, so that she nearly always wore gloves in the house. I have often seen her change them seven or eight times a day, for she would not have them even slightly soiled, and, as she never wore the same pair twice and refused to have them cleaned, she was obliged to buy hundreds of pairs at a time. It was her only extravagance, and a very human one. She told me quite seriously that she felt herself justified in it as she gave away all her gloves to a society for aiding reduced gentlewomen, so that others benefited by them.

Presently she began to speak of my father. . . . "You know, my dear, I was so happy with him. There is nothing in the world like having the love of a good man. I cannot tell you what a relief it is to me to know that your marriage is so happy. I prayed God to make it a success and I am so grateful to him. If you had been one of those women who cannot remain with their husbands, and had dragged the name of the Drexels through the mud of the divorce courts I think my heart would have broken. I should not have wanted to live. But how could I even think of such a thing. You would never do that; you have always made me so proud of you, Bessie. . . ."

I could not speak because I feared my voice would betray me. I could only smile, hoping that she would not guess the effort it cost me. For I knew now that the story I had come to tell would never be told. I must safeguard the happiness of the years that remained to her, even at the expense of my own.

That night I wrote to X—— telling him I had made my decision. I could not face a divorce, even for him. It was only a brief letter. I dared not write more for fear he might read the truth between the lines, might know that my whole heart went out to him in longing.

I stayed with my mother for a few weeks. I did not want to go back to New York until I was quite sure that I should have the resolution to face a future that could hold no hope of marrying the man I loved. Gradually the peace of Pen Rhyn rested me, gave me back my courage. The edge wore off my sorrow.

The days slipped by so uneventfully, so different from the whirlwind of life in New York. We went to bed early —played cards—did embroidery—drove out in the phaeton.

Mother was very proud of her coachman, Thorne, because he was an Englishman and had been in service in some of the great English households. An incurable desire to see the world had made him cross the Atlantic. He soon found that the way to Mother's heart was to talk to her of Queen Victoria, whom he had once driven when she had visited the family of his employers. I fear many of the conversations he was supposed to have had with her existed only in his imagination—nevertheless they gave him immense prestige in the servants' hall.

When my mother told him that she had heard reports of his drinking too much he drew himself up with dignity. . . . "Madam, Her Most Gracious Majesty the Queen of England would not have called me drunk—so drunk I could not have been!" When, however, a week or two later he was found trying to harness the horses into the phaeton with their heads the wrong way round, Mother would take no excuses. . . . "Thorne, you are not going to tell me that that is the way the Queen of England drove out!"

.   .   .   .

While I was at Pen Rhyn Archbishop Ryan of Philadelphia came to address a meeting at the neighbouring Convent of St. Elizabeth and my mother invited him to stop at her house.

His impending visit was a source of anxiety to her on account of a picture which hung in her best guest-room. It had been painted by a comparatively unknown young artist, but my father, who had bought it in Europe, had loved the delicate beauty of its drawing and had valued it; so Mother, although she knew practically nothing of art, loved it for the memories it represented. Secretly its subject shocked her. She considered that a satyr in hot pursuit of a naked nymph was not a suitable ornament for a bedroom wall. Supposing it should offend the Archbishop!

For days we discussed the question whether to take it down or put a curtain over it for the Archbishop's visit. . . .

"Everyone will say afterwards that my pictures were so improper that I had to remove them when the Archbishop came to the house!" my mother exclaimed and, knowing the gossiping propensities of Philadelphia, I agreed with her. Finally it was decided to leave the picture where it was in the hope that the Archbishop would not notice it. Vain optimism! We observed next morning that he had turned his chair round to shut out the offending sight!

Soon after I encountered a young Philadelphian artist on the stairs. . . .

"He's come to see about the picture," explained Mother. "I am having him fix it so that no one will need to feel embarrassed over it any more. . . ." Under her instructions he painted a neat little chemise to cover the nymph's unashamed nakedness and dressed the satyr in a tiger skin. Mother surveyed it critically. . . . "Still something ought to be done. . . ."

So a few more strokes of the brush transformed the satyr's lustful expression into one of placid stolidity!

.   .   .   .

Harry Lehr wrote devotedly to my mother every few days, never forgot to send loving messages to me. One day he wrote—as I had subconsciously known he would write—"Bessie will be very sorry to hear that X—— has sailed for Europe again. He will be very much missed. What a globe-trotter that man is! He tells me it will probably be years before we see him again. . . ."

Two days later I went back to New York. There was

no longer anything to dread! X—— had gone out of my life. The words of Tosti's song which we had heard together that evening in Newport had been true—it was "Good-bye for Ever. . . ."

I would not have permitted myself to write this story of our love had not X—— been dead for many years.

CHAPTER VIII
BACK IN NEW YORK

I WENT BACK TO NEW YORK APPARENTLY THE SAME, IN reality a different woman. There was no longer any place for bitterness in my heart, my love for X—— had driven it out. Never again would I envy others their happiness. I had held mine within my own hands and deliberately put it from me, but the soft glow of memory remained to me. In the past women who had renounced a love like mine had gone into convents to safeguard its memory. I would virtually do the same. In the perpetual swirl of gaiety around me my secret life would be lived like that of a nun, chaste, inviolate. For the first time I was grateful for that locked door which stood between me and the man I had married. I could dedicate myself body and soul to X—— for ever and ever.

I began to think more kindly of Harry—perhaps love had taught me understanding. I tried to follow the workings of that curious, brilliant brain of his, twisted and warped as it was, ruled by strange, deep-seated complexes. I discovered that social ambition was the breath of life to him; he gloried in it, laughed when the journalists nicknamed him "The King of Snobs." . . . He had no use for people who could not advance him socially, no respect for any gathering of people that was not "representative," his favourite word. He would apply it to everything. . . . "Mrs. Orme Wilson gave a dinner, a very select, representative party," he wrote in his diary, and it was the highest praise he could bestow. Once he gave Jimmy Cutting a pompously-worded invitation to dinner, reeled out a list of the guests, all names taken from the very cream of society. . . . "I want you to appreciate that this is one of our representative parties . . ." he concluded, to emphasize the importance of the invitation. . . . "Representative of what?" said Jimmy bluntly. . . . "Embonpoint, I should think, judging from the list you have given me!"

I knew that I could never get any pleasure out of being a snob, I was far too much my father's daughter for that, but I tried to adapt my own personality to a tolerable degree of harmony with Harry's standards, and the result was fairly successful. Although he still avoided me and remained in his own suite he made more of an effort to be polite to me when we were alone, did not criticise me so much. Once or twice he even complimented me. . . . "You see my work is bearing fruit. You are becoming a smart woman, Bessie." And he would radiate triumph when my clothes were admired. After his death I found a whole series of newspaper cuttings which referred to me. He had kept them all carefully. . . .

"It is most apparent that Mrs. Henry O. Havemeyer, Jr. is imitating Mrs. Harry Lehr as nearly as possible, and Mrs. Havemeyer might go further and fare worse for a model.

She had recently acquired a pair of huge turquoise earrings, with a circle of diamonds to bring out the blue tones. Her hats are either the tiny marquise affairs or the slashing black plumed picture chapeaux that Mrs. Lehr has introduced, and they might be taken for twins except for Mrs. Havemeyer's auburn hair. Mrs. Lehr is certainly the first of the modish women to realise the beauty of turquoises in profusion, and she had the huge breastplate, collar and earrings long before Mrs. Dick Gambrill purchased her blue gems. Mrs. Havemeyer is booked for Newport this year, and she is a woman of increasing popularity. Her recently accentuated resemblance to the slender Mrs. Lehr may be unintentional, but even at that she had the credit or discredit of being a faithful replica. . . ."

"Mrs. Harry Lehr arrived so early for the Sands-Minott wedding that rather than face the empty pews and the rail-birds in the gallery, she took refuge in a furniture shop across the way. She was the most remarkably dressed woman in the church, and when the time arrived for the grand arrival, which however was not made with Mr. Lehr, everybody stared at her and then turned for another stare. She was in black mousseline de soie printed with bluet flowers, and trimmed with an abundance of white Alençon lace. The corsage was cut high, which heightened the effect of her wonderful, tapering nineteen-inch waist. She wore a smart Virot hat. In her ears were the conspicuous diamonds so often seen at the Metropolitan. Her entrance, everything considered, caused a subdued sensation. . . ."

"Throughout that summer at the Horse Show, the tennis and numerous other functions, Mrs. Lehr's entrance, thanks to Harry's eye for things sartorial, was awaited like the rise of a curtain. In the years following Mrs. Lehr's command of fashion continued. . . ."

To please him I gave a series of dinner parties. One was at the St. Regis Hotel on the night of Mrs. Astor's ball. My guests numbered a hundred and fifty and we all dined at one gigantic table, a record even for New York! The preparations were most amusing, for the waiters telephoned their directions from one end of the table to the other; while the florist's men, in special shoes of white felt, walked about on the surface of the table to arrange their trails of roses and carnations.

Afterwards we all went on to the Astors' ball, where Mrs. George Gould, in a dress of silver brocade shot with green and wearing her magnificent emeralds, looked so beautiful that she created a sensation.

Her husband was proud of her. He told Harry Lehr that he had just bought as a surprise for her some of the finest jewels in the world, the eight famous "Peacocks' Feathers" of emeralds and diamonds which had once been the property of the Emperor of China. She looked regally handsome when she wore them the next winter, reset by Cartier's; five as a superb tiara while the remaining three formed an enormous brooch which she clasped on one shoulder. Harry forthwith christened her "The Queen of Sheba" and indeed there was rather a barbaric quality in her beauty.

George Gould—who had adored her ever since the day when he saw her on the stage, fell in love with her, and

took her out of Augustin Daly's troup to be his wife—
thought no extravagance too great for her. I remember
that on one occasion when she was appearing as Cathe-
rine of Russia in a charity performance of tableaux vi-
vants at Sherry's, she ordered her costume from Redfern.
Redfern himself, who loved designing for her, created a
wonderful dress of velvet set with jewels and having a
ten-foot train of brocade lined with ermine. She was delighted with it but she quite forgot to stipulate that the
ermine must be imitation, with the result that the bill
which came in after the pageant made even George
Gould raise his eyebrows in dismay. But he only laughed
good-naturedly at her explanation, and refused to let her
ask Redfern to take it back. I believe that it ended as an
evening cloak for Vivien.

We spent many week-ends at "Georgian Court," Lakewood, the George Goulds' New Jersey home, for Edith
was a delightful hostess, and the house and gardens were
magnificent. I was always given the "Purple Guest Room"
as it was called, and slept in the enormous marriage bed
which George Gould had caused to be designed for his
bride. It was a particularly hideous example of the artis-
tic ideas of the 'eighties, and I believe Marcotte had been
paid a tremendous sum to embellish it with golden
scrolls, lover's-knots, entwined hearts and other appropriate devices. It reared an ungraceful head somewhere
near the ceiling, apparently without rhyme or reason
except perhaps the better to display its lavish coating of
gold. Edith laughed as she drew my attention to the de-

sign of the painted frieze on its centrepiece, eight cupids tending an altar of love on which hearts were melting in sacrificial flame. . . . "I shall never forget my feelings when I first saw it," she said. . . . "I just knew I should have eight children if I slept in that bed . . . and so I did!"

She brought up her large family on a wonderful system of efficiency. In spite of their father's colossal fortune they lived very simply in many respects; the nursery menu was composed of the plainest dishes, no candies were permitted, not too much liberty. They scarcely ever went outside the grounds of the estate. Not that they had any necessity to do so, for they could indulge in any sport to their hearts' content, had everything they could possibly want. There was a perfectly equipped gymnasium and riding school, tennis courts, squash courts, polo grounds where George and his sons practised, miniature golf links for Edith and Margery.

George Gould used to say, "I am sure no emperor's weekly bills cost him as much as mine do. . . ." He taught the parrot to say whenever Edith appeared, "Oh, what an extravagant girl you are! . . ."

Mrs. Gould, much in advance of most of the mothers of her generation, studied infant psychology, said that the average child was thwarted, and searched anxiously for the slightest evidence of any special talent in her sons and daughters so that it would be developed to its fullest extent from the start. When she found five-month-old Georgie waving his arms rhythmically she instantly de-

cided that boxing would be his future sport and as soon
as he could walk had a champion boxer brought out from
England at enormous cost to give him lessons. Jack For-
ester, the famous English tennis champion, was brought
over and installed in a cottage built for him and his family on the estate so that he could coach the children and
play tennis with the guests. When Vivien started dancing
to the music of the nursery piano, Edith telegraphed to
New York for the best ballet teacher available and arranged for her to have a three-year course.

The schoolrooms occupied a whole wing of Georgian
Court. The Gould children must have been among the
most highly educated in the States, for they seemed to
study every imaginable subject. They had English, German and Italian governesses. At seventeen Vivien wrote
Greek poetry, studied Latin with her brothers, and spoke
five modern languages fluently. She danced beautifully
(Edith's development system had been justified in her
case at least) and was altogether lovely with her tiny slender figure and curling dark hair.

Her marriage was romantic like everything else about
her. Harry Lehr told me the story of her engagement.
Edith decided that Vivien had finished her education and
and took her on a tour round the world. In Switzerland
they met Jack Beresford. He was attracted to the beautiful little American girl from the moment he saw her
sitting demurely with her mother in the lounge of their
hotel. Someone introduced them. They danced together
that evening, the next, and the next after that. Every

time he found her more irresistible. In less than a week
he was hopelessly in love. When the Goulds left for
Venice he spent two miserable, lonely days and then followed them. They went on to Rome; stayed there a week;
so did he. He wandered round Germany with them,
through the Tyrol. By this time he had made up his
mind that if he could not marry Vivien he would never
marry at all. But he had not the courage to propose to
her. Charming and unspoilt as she was he could not
forget that she was the daughter of one of the richest men
in America, that her parents were ambitious for her,
while he was a comparatively poor young Army officer,
with remote prospects of succeeding to the title. He decided that it would be unfair to ask her to marry him,
and forced himself to say "Good-bye" to her when she
sailed for New York without letting her know how much
he cared for her.

Then the unexpected happened. Lord Decies died
suddenly from heart failure at Newmarket and Jack
Beresford came into the title. After he had recovered
from his grief over his brother's death his first action was
to cable Vivien, "Will you marry me? . . ." He waited
impatiently for her reply—tore open the envelope. Only
one little word: "Yes." . . . He caught the next boat to
New York.

Harry Lehr led the cotillion at the magnificent ball
which Edith Gould gave to celebrate the engagement.
I still have the gold vanity-box which I received as a
favour.

Vivien's was not the only romantic wedding in the Gould family. I remember one week-end I spent at Lakewood when Edith and I had tea alone in her boudoir. She was unusually silent and preoccupied and after we had finished she said, "Do stay with me, Bessie. I've got rather a disagreeable duty to perform. I am going to talk to the children's Italian governess on the subject of Kingdon. You know he has been having a desperate flirtation with the poor girl, and I am so afraid she may be taking it seriously. I don't want to have any broken hearts here. . . ."

A few minutes later Signorina Lucci came in, a handsome girl with beautiful dark eyes and a graceful figure. She stood very calm and unemotional before Edith, and listened in silence to all she had to say. Then she raised her head proudly. Her eyes flashed fire. . . .

"So you say you tell me this for my good? You tink he not mean it, that he not love me? You are wrong. I will marry heem!"

Very much embarrassed Edith tried to reason with her, pointed out that such a marriage for her eldest son would be impossible, warned her that Kingdon was only trying to learn Italian. The girl only repeated more firmly than before, "I will marry heem . . ." and thereupon walked out of the room, leaving Edith beaten in the field.

Signorina Lucci was dismissed. She left Lakewood and returned to New York, but a few days afterwards a little procession of four closed cars left the Goulds' town house at the corner of Sixty-seventh Street. In one of them sat Kingdon with his brother Jay. They drove to Saint Bartholomew's Church where Signorina Lucci waited.

Half an hour later the Italian governess had become Mrs. Kingdon Gould.

CHAPTER IX
NEWPORT NEWS AND VIEWS

EVERY SUMMER HARRY LEHR AND I WENT TO NEWPORT like everyone else in our world, for in those days so much prestige was attached to spending July and August at the most exclusive resort in America that to have neglected to do so would have exposed a definite gap in one's social armour. It was an accepted fact that only those whose position in society was unstable never went there. Let them vaunt the charm of a country holiday, of a summer spent in Europe as much as they would, they deceived no one. Their acquaintances knew that they stayed away because they were afraid. For Newport was the very Holy of Holies, the playground of the great ones of the earth from which all intruders were ruthlessly excluded by a set of cast-iron rules.

"Avoid Newport like the plague until you are certain that you will be acceptable there," Harry Lehr would counsel ambitious newcomers who sought his expert advice. "If you don't it will be your Waterloo. Above all, don't take a house there and launch out giving parties. Try to get invited for a week or two on someone's yacht as an experiment to see whether you are a success or not. In that way you will leave your retreat open to you, and you can always pretend that the climate does not suit you and go back to New York without anyone having witnessed your defeat. . . ."

Dire indeed was the fate of those who were not "acceptable" if they had been unwise enough to take a villa for the whole season, for in so small a community there was no escape for them. Every week their humiliation was brought home to them more and more as one after another the all-powerful queens of Newport chose to ignore their existence. Splendid balls and dinners every night, but not for them. Bathing parties on Bailey's Beach, yachting at Hazard's, but both these sacred precincts were closed to them. Their men were not permitted to join the Reading Room or the Casino Club; their women had not the entrée to a single drawing-room. They might play an admirable game of tennis, their thoroughbreds might carry off the best prizes at the Horse Show . . . in other places these distinctions would have availed them something, never in Newport. They could only sit in the palatial villa they had so rashly acquired and accept their defeat with what grace they could. They seldom had the temerity to last out the season. A month of ostracism would usually send them over to the less aristocratic but more hospitable pastures of Narragansett, where they would try to console themselves with the big summer hotels on the water front, the smartly dressed crowds on the Pier, the friendly holiday atmosphere which they had sought in vain at "The Millionaires' Playground."

Even those acceptables who had triumphed had to walk warily for the first season or two in Newport. . . . "The battle isn't won yet," Harry Lehr would warn them. . . . "You have still got to be careful . . ." And if he were advising a woman he always gave her three golden maxims, "First, Be modest. Go quietly at the start; don't try to be original in your entertaining or your equipages. . . . Follow the lead of the others instead of striking out your own trail. Second, Never try to take any other woman's man, whether husband, lover or well-wisher. . . . Third, Never try to out-dress or out-jewel the other women."

None knew better than he that Newport Society was composed of a series of cliques presided over by the reigning queens, and that to offend any one of them was to court disaster.

If pitfalls beset the path of aspirants to villa honours the casual visitor fared even worse. Not even an hotel to accommodate him—the élite of Newport despised such plebeian buildings. Whenever one threatened to make its appearance the kings of trade, jealous of their privacy, banded together and nipped the project in the bud by buying out the interlopers. They would only look with favour upon the discreet little hotel with its dependent cottages owned by Mrs. Amanda Meunchinger; in fact they were glad to lease the charmingly furnished little cottages themselves while their own palatial villas were being got ready. But then Amanda Meunchinger was as exclusive as Newport itself; she would never dream of harbouring anyone not already admitted to the sacred inner circle. The only other hotel, the "Aquidneck House," a picturesque old place dating from colonial days, was tolerated for another reason. It was given over to commercial travellers, and the representatives of New York shops come up to open branches in the Casino block; and the fashionable colony of Newport recognised dimly that these beings from another world were necessary to minister to its comfort. Their modest baggage contained the latest thing in watches and cravat-pins from Tiffany's; the most exclusive models which the great Paris houses had created to add to the season's splendour.

The line of sumptuous villas—"The cottages," as they were ironically called by their inhabitants—which stretched the length of Bellevue Avenue along the cliffs and over Ochre Point, was Newport's glory. Here were the homes of its millionaires, the settings for that brilliant chain of balls and parties which made its season the gayest in two continents.

One splendid villa after another, each owned by men whose names made history in the world of finance, who thought nothing of spending ten million dollars for a house in which they lived for six weeks in a year. . . . "More riches to the square yard in Newport than you would find in miles anywhere else," Harry would say.

"Stone Villa," James Gordon Bennett's house, headed the line in Bellevue Avenue and faced the Casino, with its bronze owls on the gateposts. But it was always empty or leased to distinguished foreigners. Since the scandal that had driven him to Europe, Newport had almost forgotten the young man who had once been the leader of its "Jeunesse Dorée."

"It's a shame the way people have treated James Gordon Bennett," Harry Lehr who had known him and liked him in Baltimore would say hotly . . . "Why should a man's life be ruined because of a stupid practical joke?"

From him I heard the story of James Gordon Bennett's quarrel with his Baltimore fiancée which ended in his being turned out of all his clubs. It ought never to have arisen. Any modern girl would have known how to handle the situation, and would have passed over the offence. But she belonged to another generation, and she was provincial to her finger-tips. She swooned in the classical manner of the 'nineties, and called upon her brother to throw her fiancé out of the house. Within a few hours the story, greatly exaggerated, had become a first-class scandal.

Near to James Gordon Bennett's villa was "The Elms," a fine old brick house where lived Mrs. Burke-Roche and her twin sons, Maurice (now Lord Fermoy) and Frank, who were so alike that it was impossible to tell them apart, a fact of which they never failed to take advantage. They were constantly getting each other out of scrapes, and always took turns at entertaining bores.

"Say, Boy"—Maurice would call on the beach— "I had to sit next Miss X at dinner last night, to oblige you, so will you replace me at the Clam-bake Club luncheon today?" So "Frank" would be "Maurice" for the rest of the day.

"Elm Court" came next, the E. J. Berwind's palatial mansion which had cost five million dollars to build, and was filled with the masterpieces of French and Italian art for which "The Coal Baron" had ransacked Europe. The Berwinds had been to England, admired Buckingham Palace, and tried to reproduce some of its salient characteristics in the architecture of their own palace; consequently they had the only house in Newport which boasted three massive entrance doors so that three carriages could discharge their loads of guests simultaneously.

Opposite "Elm Court" was "Arleigh," the house which Harry and I rented from Mrs. Ruthven Pratt. It was the scene of my calvary. How often its walls would echo to the bitter reproaches, the recriminations hurled at me, the incessant demands for more money.

"Isn't it enough that I have to endure your presence here? I hate the sight of you—you are hideous to me. The only thing that you can do is to provide me with money which I at least have the taste to spend properly. . . ."

Sick at heart I would give in to him, sign endless cheques. . . .

One June day we lent our house to Reggie and Kathleen Vanderbilt for their marriage. Everyone had expected them to have a fashionable New York wedding and those who were not in the secret were astonished at their change of plan. The reason was an amusing one. Reggie Vanderbilt with all the vast wealth at his disposal was in flight from the Law! He dared not appear within the State of New York for fear of being served with a summons to give evidence at the Canfield trial.

For a long time there had been complaints of the manner in which the smartest gaming house in New York was being run, but as Reggie Vanderbilt said plaintively it was rather hard luck that the police should have chosen to raid it on the very night that he had lost $150,000, and should thereupon insist on his giving evidence for the prosecution. He left New York the next day, resolved to stay out of the State until the whole affair had blown over. But he reckoned without the tenacity of the police. The more determined he was to avoid the unwelcome publicity of the trial, the more determined they became to have him as a witness at all costs. They must prove to the world that even a Vanderbilt could not flout their authority. They put plain-clothes men to watch the house of his fiancée, Kathleen Nielson, knowing that sooner or later he would be bound to slip back to New York to visit her. Once they had served him with a summons they could be sure of him, he could not disobey it under pain of arrest. Their supposition was justified. One afternoon he stole into the house. He had come alone and on foot, dressed in the most ordinary clothes he could find; he looked like a respectable young salesman. But even those precautions were not enough. Within ten minutes the house was surrounded. Escape seemed impossible. Then Kathleen rang up the most resourceful man she knew—Harry Lehr.

Harry went round to the house at once, heard what had happened, rushed down to the servants' hall.

Half an hour later the police saw the Nielson's stout Swedish cook leave the house and take the Sixth Avenue car, but they paid no attention to her. It was only after hours of fruitless vigil that they realised that their quarry had escaped them. Harry Lehr's genius for costumes had served its turn. The supposed cook was none other than Reggie Vanderbilt, dressed in clothes borrowed from the servants, and made up by Harry and Kathleen.

.   .   .   .

Elisha and Mrs. Dyer were our neighbours at "Arleigh" and then came "White Lodge," a beautiful villa whose Nile green ballroom and panelled dining-room ornamented with the delicate Gothic scrolls of Walter Crane were considered the last word in elegance. It belonged to Lispinard Stewart whom every single woman in Newport had been trying to marry for years. Tall, thin and courtly, he was famed for the perfection of his manners and for his conceit. He never forgave Mrs. H. O. Havemeyer for the slight she put upon him at one of Mrs. Oliver Belmont's dinner parties. He had been deputed to take her in to dinner and, as the procession of couples advanced at a stately pace into the dining-room, was congratulating himself on the impression he was making. But Mrs. Havemeyer was young, pretty, rich and correspondingly spoilt. She saw some friends at the other

side of the room and evidently preferred their company
to his. Without a word of apology she left him, seized a
chair and drew it up to the other table. Poor Lispinard
Stewart, left to sit where he would, fumed throughout
dinner. . . . "I was faced with two alternatives," he explained gravely in recounting the incident to me afterwards. . . . "Should I remember my birth, my training, my aristocratic family, and offer her my arm again
as we left the dining-room, or should I obey my natural
impulse and leave her to walk out alone? In the end my
breeding won. When we rose from the table, I bowed
stiffly to her, held out my arm without a word and es-
corted her back to the drawing-room. But I never addressed a single word to her, and I never will again. . . ."

One of the most beautiful homes in Newport was
"Rough Point," a grey stone Tudor house with a great
Gothic hall and lawns running right down to the cliffs.
There Mr. and Mrs. William B. Leeds entertained re-
gally as befitted "The Tinplate King" and his consort.

They had come to Newport tentatively enough at first,
like all newcomers, and for at least two seasons their fate
hung in the balance. At one time it looked as though
they were going to swell the numbers of those defeated
in the social lists. They leased Fairholme from the John
Drexels, who were much criticised for letting them have
it. . . . "It's not fair to the rest of us," proclaimed
Edith Wetmore who, as daughter of the Governor of
Rhode Island and owner of "Le Château sur Mer," was
the centre of one of the most exclusive cliques. . . .

"How can you lease to those horrible, vulgar people? Why, the whole house ought to be disinfected after them! . . ."

Alice Drexel, plump and placid, laughed. . . . "Well, we are going to Europe this summer, and I shall have the house redecorated while we are away, so I thought they might as well have it."

But the Leeds found a champion in Mrs. Oliver Belmont, that valiant warrior to whom opposition was as the breath of life. Nothing made her happier than the knowledge that she was pitting herself against the rest of the world. She loved to see herself as a pioneer, to make others bend to her will, to have them follow her in the end, meek, sheeplike. . . .

"I always do everything first," she would say. "I blaze the trail for the rest to walk in. I was the first girl of my 'set' to marry a Vanderbilt. Then I was the first society woman to ask for a divorce, and within a year ever so many others had followed my example. They had been wanting divorce all the time, but they had not dared to do it until I showed them the way. . . ."

She quickened to the sound of argument as to a clarion call to arms, and arguments broke out in Newport whenever the name of Leeds was mentioned.

One morning she summoned Harry Lehr to her. . . . "I like those Leeds people, and the wife is lovely. I am going to take them up and put an end to this silly nonsense about them, and you have got to help me. . . ."

So she issued invitations for a dinner and ball at her

house "in honour of Mr. and Mrs. William B. Leeds."
The recipients were in a dilemma. Many of them had
been strenuously opposing the advance of the Tinplate
King and his wife; they had voiced their opinion in no
uncertain tones, they could not very well go back on it.
On the other hand if they declined the invitation Belcourt with all its lavish hospitality would be closed to
them for the rest of the season. They hesitated, uncertain.
Meanwhile everyone was talking of the ball; the preparations were being made on a staggering scale of magnificence; Harry Lehr was planning a marvellous cotillion.

Of course they gave in in the end. Their letters of acceptance were carried into Belcourt in shoals.

The light of victory shone in Mrs. Belmont's eyes as
she stood at the entrance of Oliver's enormous armour
gallery to receive her guests on the night of the ball.

By her side stood Mrs. William B. Leeds, young then
and imperially beautiful in her white satin dress, her
superb diamonds emphasising the delicacy of her colour-
ing, the velvet darkness of her eyes. She too had her night
of triumph. Her charm was far more potent than her
husband's millions. Society took her to its heart from that
moment. William B. Leeds, young, handsome, and ambitious for his beautiful wife, gazed at her in adoration. Her
beauty had won the day for him.

. . . .

Dr. and Mrs. Henry Barton Jacobs had a fine house
at the corner where Narragansett Avenue and Ochre
Point Avenue meet. There they gave stately dinner par-

ties and musicales. They were both too old-fashioned and dignified to countenance balls and cotillions. Mrs. Jacobs had formerly been the wife of Robert W. Garret, President of the Baltimore and Ohio Railroad, who for many years before his death suffered from a disease of the brain which gave him a curious delusion. He was convinced that he was the Prince of Wales. From having been a hard-headed business man he lived in a world of make-believe. To everyone's astonishment his wife encouraged him, indulged his fancies. Her friends remonstrated. . . . "The man's crazy. You should have put him into an institution where they would look after him. . . ." She refused. . . .

"My husband has worked hard all his life to earn his large fortune. He shall enjoy it in the way he wants. Why should I not spend it in giving him pleasure?"

So thousands of dollars were spent in maintaining him in his rôle. Their house in Green Spring Valley was transformed into a miniature Court of England. A whole staff of actors was hired to impersonate gentlemen-in-waiting, court officials, Cabinet Ministers and Ambassadors from other countries, and an expert was brought over from London to ensure that each of the costumes was correct. Robert Garret was given copies of every order worn by the Prince of Wales; he had the uniform of the principal regiments of every country, so that he should greet each of his visiting ambassadors correctly attired. Every day his wife would come to him as the

Princess of Wales, go through hours of tragic farce in order that he might keep his cherished illusion.

Harry Lehr used to tell me of how he had once gone to visit Robert Garret at his Baltimore house in Mount Vernon Place, and found him dressed in full regalia of British Field-Marshal's uniform, while half a dozen orders glittered upon his breast.

Harry rose to the occasion by having himself announced as the "Crown Prince of Germany" and delighted the poor old gentleman by talking broken English interspersed with German throughout the afternoon.

.   .   .   .

Mr. James Van Alen, handsome and elegant, was Newport's most eligible widower. A lover of all things English, he called his house on Ochre Point "Wakehurst" and had it designed to look as much like an Elizabethan manor as possible. On his visits to England he rummaged among the antique shops of Chelsea and Bloomsbury, toured through villages off the beaten track in Devon and Warwickshire in search of "period furniture" to add to his collection. His English tapestries were famous, his hall bristled with oak settles and dower chests, grandfather clocks and pewter tankards; every bedroom had its copper warming-pan, its Hogarth engravings. He even carried his predilection for the Tudor period into his vocabulary, and his conversation was so flavoured with . . . "Egad . . . Z'ounds . . . and prithee . . ." that one almost needed a special old English dictionary to talk to him. The highest praise he could bestow on any favoured lady was, "A most delectable wench, forsooth . . ." while an impertinent railroad car attendant would draw forth an indignant, "Yon varlet insults us! . . ."

Coaching was an old English sport, so nothing pleased him better than to be regarded as an authority on it. His turn-outs were always perfection, every detail correct to the last shining button on his grooms' liveries. He was such a stickler for the traditions that he maintained to the members of the Coaching Club that no guard in the United States could wind an authentic coaching blast, and brought over a man from England at enormous cost for the express purpose of teaching them how it should be done. Unfortunately the newspapers got hold of the story and published sarcastic comments, with the result that the star performer on the horn was interned on Ellis Island the moment he arrived, and it was some time before he was permitted to land.

The household at "Wakehurst" ran on oiled wheels; its hospitality was famous, for James Van Alen was a connoisseur of good food and good wines. His musicales were wonderful, for although he knew nothing of music he acted on his usual principle, engaged the greatest artists, paid the highest fees. During Yacht-week he invited the whole of fashionable Newport to one of them, given in honour of Pierpont Morgan. I received my invitation . . . it did not include Harry Lehr. Crestfallen he rushed off to consult Mrs. Fish. What could have happened? Mrs. Fish was equally chagrined. Stuyvesant had been

invited . . . but without her. She tackled Mr. Van Alen
on the beach. Adjusting the monocle he wore with such
lazy grace, he regarded her with Elizabethan gallantry.
. . . "Very sorry, my dear. . . . Upon my word very
sorry, but I can't have you and Harry Lehr at this party
of mine. You make too much noise. . . ."

"Oh, so that's it! Well, let me tell you, sweet pet" (her
invariable expression when she intended to say something
nasty) "that unless we are asked there won't be any party.
Harry and I will tell everyone that your cook has developed smallpox, and we will give a rival musicale. You
will see they will all come to it! . . ."

Sooner than rouse the enmity of one of Newport's
most powerful hostesses he gave in. "The two disturbing
elements" (as Mrs. Fish called them) were allowed to
come to the dinner provided they promised to stay on
the terrace during the music.

On one occasion James Van Alen managed to arouse
the concerted hostility of all the Queens of Newport.
Going over to Narragansett Pier on his yacht he encountered there a lady who was emphatically NOT acceptable to feminine Newport whatever she might be to
their menfolk. But she was young and very pretty, and
Mr. Van Alen, who was notoriously a squire of dames
(as he would have described himself) felt his heart melt
towards her loneliness. He invited her to return with him
to Newport and stop at "Wakehurst." The lady accepted
with alacrity, and they went on board the yacht
together. . . .

Later that evening May Van Alen (now Mrs. Griswold Thompson) encountered them in the garden of Wakehurst.

Mr. Van Alen's eyes fell before his daughter's stare of surprise. She was the one person of whom he stood in awe. She ran his house perfectly, made an ideal hostess to his friends, but she had a disconcerting habit of saying exactly what she thought.

He cleared his throat. . . . "May, this lady is to be our house guest for the week-end. I want you to see that she enjoys herself." He was relieved when his daughter held out her hand and made a non-committal reply.

He went to call on Mrs. Richard Gambrill, that majestic widow whose word to him held sway in all social matters. He was regarded as one of her most favoured cavaliers; she now greeted him coldly. . . . He fidgeted nervously. . . .

"Mrs. X—— is stopping with me. . . ." The widow's glance was ice. . . .

"So I heard on the Beach this morning,—but I denied it."

After a little fragmentary conversation he rose to go. . . . "I shall look forward to seeing you at my luncheon party tomorrow," he said as he was leaving the room. . . .

"I am afraid that I shall not be able to come."

"But you accepted three weeks ago . . ." he exclaimed in surprise.

"Yes, indeed, and I was looking forward to it, but I have such a bad attack of neuralgia coming on that I dare not risk going out. . . ." He could do nothing but accept the excuse with the best possible grace. It was the first of many!

That evening every woman among the twenty or so he had invited to his luncheon party sent some excuse or other . . . a headache, illness in the family, an imperative journey to New York. Whatever it was it made her presence in his house out of the question. And in many cases the husbands came without their wives!

One of his men friends called him up. . . . "Awfully sorry about your luncheon, but to tell you the truth my wife made such a fuss when I suggested coming without her that I shall have to call it off. You have offended all the ladies, my dear fellow. I should advise you to propitiate them as quickly as possible before they spoil any more parties. . . ."

So he was faced with the prospect of luncheon with his beautiful house guest and nine or ten men friends.

He sought out his daughter May. She listened in stony silence to the recital of his woes. . . .

"In other words, Pop, you want me to whitewash you. Well, I'll do it, but only on certain conditions. If you want me to come to your lunch and be your hostess it will cost you five thousand dollars. . . ." He pleaded with her but in vain. Neither arguments nor entreaties would move her.

Resistance was useless. He resigned himself to the inevitable, sat down and took out his cheque book. . . . "Oh, by the way, Pop," said the relentless young voice from behind his shoulder, "don't make out the cheque till you hear the other condition. For five thousand dollars I'll come to your party; but if you want me to talk to your guest and be polite to her, you'll have to make it ten."

Mr. Van Alen was beaten and he knew it. Without another word he filled in the cheque and handed it to his daughter. . . . She took it calmly. . . . "This is going to get me those earrings I saw in Tiffany's. . . . Now just leave the party to me. . . ."

It was a great success. Everyone enjoyed it except the host. May was a perfect hostess; no one guessed that the situation had been saved at the last minute.

But the next day Mrs. Fish met Mr. Van Alen face to face. There was no escape for her. She greeted him icily. . . . "Oh, I understand you have someone staying with you as a house guest. How is she?"

"She left this morning," replied Mr. Van Alen, lamely. . . . "The sea air did not agree with her. She could not keep her hair in curl. . . ."

"What a pity," Mrs. Fish responded, adding grimly, "She should have come to us women. We would have curled it for her. . . ."

And meanwhile May Van Alen was proudly displaying her cheque to a little group on Bailey's Beach. . . . "I guess Pop will let me choose our house guests next time. . . ."

CHAPTER X

"KING LEHR"

ᏳᏝ

Harry Lehr's empire of laughter extended throughout American society, even spread to Europe. But it was in Newport that his throne was most firmly established; its exotic atmosphere was the perfect setting for his eccentric escapades, the endless drolleries that made him famous. He was easily the most popular man in each of the little cliques, the first to be consulted when a party was in prospect, the centre of whatever group he happened to join on the Beach.

But, although he had the tact of an ambassador, even he was unable to keep quite free of the quarrels which invariably broke out towards the end of every season. Too many parties, too little exercise and too much rich food had had their inevitable effect on tempers, and a general visit to the Hot Springs was imperative to prevent half New York society being at loggerheads for the coming winter.

"When the Queens start fighting among themselves I always make for the nearest fence and sit tight on it," he would say. . . . "Nothing tempts me off it until I feel that it is the psychological moment for a truce. Then I do what I can to pour oil on the waters." It was part of his charm that he was always ready to act as peacemaker. He would listen patiently to the confidences of both sides, never betraying either.

Generally the quarrels broke out over the desertion of some favoured courtier who had been spirited away by a rival queen. James de Wolfe Cutting was a constant bone of contention. Tall and handsome "with just that dash of Jewish blood that enriches and makes beautiful a human being," he was one of the most popular bachelors in Newport, but his allegiance had so long been considered as belonging exclusively to Mrs. Stuyvesant Fish that all the unmarried girls had abandoned the chase in despair. So dire indeed was the consternation when it became known that he had transferred himself and his manly beauty to "Ochre Court" where Mrs. Ogden Goelet who, as an enormously rich widow, had more suitors than she could count, lived in an atmosphere of luxury and magnificence that far eclipsed "Crossways," the Fish's fine colonial house.

Thereafter was a state of armed neutrality between the two queens. Mrs. Goelet, cold, arrogant, clever, had the advantage. She had been born a Wilson and, said Harry Lehr, "The Wilsons are deadly opponents, their minds work like oiled steel. . . ." She flaunted her triumph in the face of her unsuccessful rival. Mrs. Fish, vivacious, impulsive, shallow, witty rather than clever, hid her mortification under an air of bravado. She affected to despise her former courtier, only invited him to one or two unimportant parties, where she and Harry Lehr held him up to the ridicule of the other guests. Everyone watched the situation with interest, certain it would have some dramatic development.

The climax came when Mrs. Goelet had the Grand Duke Boris of Russia and his suite stopping at her house, a fact which gave her enormous prestige in the eyes of feminine Newport. Magnanimously she invited Mrs. Fish to a luncheon party to meet her royal guest. Mrs. Fish, not to be outdone in generosity, sent out invitations for a dinner and ball "In honour of the Grand Duke Boris of Russia."

The preparations went forward on a truly regal scale of splendour. Two hundred guests for the dinner alone, hundreds more for the ball. It was Yacht-week—all the members of the New York Yacht Club had been invited. Harry Lehr was evolving a wonderful cotillion with Russian music.

On the day before the party the first shot was fired. Mrs. Fish and I were just leaving her house for an afternoon drive in my victoria when Mrs. Goelet was announced.

"Dear Mamie, I was thinking about your lovely ball this morning when I realised that you had quite forgotten to send an invitation to Jimmie Cutting and you know he is stopping with me at 'Ochre Court.' "

Mrs. Fish's eyes flashed. . . . "Oh, no, sweet pet. I didn't forget, but I have no intention of having Jimmie at my party. He has been to my house too often already."

Mrs. Goelet's smile was dangerously sweet. . . . "I am

afraid you don't realise, dear, that I cannot possibly come
to the ball if a member of my house party is not included
in the invitation, and, what is more, no other guest of
mine will be there."

"In that case we shall miss you so much, sweet pet, but
I cannot change my decision."

Mrs. Goelet played her strongest card. . . . "I hope
that you have not forgotten that you have sent out your
invitations 'to meet the Grand Duke Boris'? What are
you going to do about that? Besides, he has five gentlemen in his suite, so that will mean you will be six men
short at dinner. Very well, you must make your choice.
Have Jimmie Cutting at the party or sacrifice the Grand
Duke. . . ."

"I will not have Jimmie if I am reduced to the Training Station for men," replied Mrs. Fish with spirit.

The young officers from the Naval Training Station
were in great demand when extra men were required
for dances or bridge parties. Harry Lehr would ring up
the Commanding Officer . . . "Can you let me have five
bridge players for tomorrow at Mrs. Hamilton Twom-
bly's? . . ." "Will you send a dozen dancing men for
Mrs. Oliver Belmont's ball? . . ." and they would be
delivered in time, smiling, impersonal, always dressed in
their neat uniforms. . . . "So that no one should waste
any efforts on them," explained Harry. But no one ever
thought of asking them to dinner, least of all to a dinner
of such magnificence.

We did not go for our drive. Mrs. Fish had no heart

for it. She wanted time to think. Harry Lehr came round, heard of the impending calamity, sympathised.

"You have got to get me out of this, Lamb. . . . You must do something. . . ."

"Mrs. Goelet will keep her word; she won't let the Grand Duke come," said Harry thoughtfully. . . . "The only thing you can do is to turn the whole thing into a joke. You must make people laugh so much that they will not be quite sure of what has really happened."

Suddenly Mrs. Fish had an inspiration. . . . "I know. Lamb, you will have to impersonate the Czar of Russia. . . ."

There and then they drove down to Collins who supplied the favours for all Newport cotillions. . . . "Costume for the Emperor of Russia, Mr. Lehr? Yes, of course. . . ." The Imperial Crown, sceptre and various Russian orders were all delivered at "Crossways" the next morning. Mrs. Fish produced her emerald-green opera cloak lined with ermine. Turned inside out it made a splendid royal robe.

Meanwhile Mrs. Goelet was ringing up all her friends. . . . I'm giving an informal little dinner party in honour of the Grand Duke Boris this evening. . . ." None of them could understand what had happened. On their writing desks reposed Mamie Fish's elaborate invitation for the same night, also worded "in honour of the Grand Duke. . . ." Their acceptances had been posted long ago; regretfully they told Mrs. Goelet that they were already engaged.

That evening Mrs. Fish was radiant with triumph as she received her two hundred guests in the hall of "Crossways." Not one had deserted to the enemy camp. Senator Chauncey Depew, Pierpont Morgan, Lord Charles Beresford—they had all resisted Mrs. Goelet's blandishments. There was a thrill of expectancy in the air as they waited for the royal party to arrive before going in to dinner. Five minutes passed . . . no Grand Duke. Was he not coming? Some of them remembered the strange invitation they had received from Mrs. Goelet a few hours before. There were hastily smothered whispers. Mrs. Fish heard them. She raised her voice, "His Majesty is a little late? . . ." "His Majesty?" echoed those standing near her. . . .

"Yes, His Majesty! I could not get the Grand Duke Boris after all, but I have got someone better—the Czar of Russia!" She turned to Mrs. John Drexel . . . "Dear Cousin Alice, do help me. You are so familiar with the court etiquette, and I am so afraid I may not be equal to the occasion. Will you go out to the porte-cochère and receive His Imperial Majesty? . . ."

Slightly self-conscious but delighted at the honour that had been done her, Alice, who loved nothing better than to recount her entrée into Europe's royal circles, was about to leave the room when the doors were flung open. . . .

"His Imperial Majesty, the Emperor of Russia. . . ."

The ladies nearest the entrance, in varying degrees of hesitancy, sank in a court curtsey, only to recover themselves with shrieks of laughter when they realised they were paying homage to Harry Lehr! The whole room rippled with merriment as in his royal robes he made a solemn circuit on the arm of his hostess, pausing here and there to talk to people, in exact imitation of a stately royal progress. Mrs. Fish's party was saved!

The next morning the Grand Duke Boris came up to Harry on the beach . . . "I hear you represented the Emperor last night. It's a good thing you were not in Russia, but I only wish I had been there to see it. It must have been most amusing. Our party was poisonous. We shall have to call you King Lehr in future!"

The name clung to him.

.   .   .   .

CHAPTER XI
BAILEY'S BEACH

"I HAVE NEVER EVEN DREAMT OF SUCH LUXURY AS I HAVE
seen in Newport," said the Grand Duke Boris. . . . "Is
this really your America or have I landed on an enchanted island? Such an outpouring of riches! It is like
walking on gold. We have nothing to equal it in Russia.
Mr. Lehr, you will have to come over to Europe to show
us how you conjure up all these visions of splendour. . . ."

We were standing, the three of us, in the garden at
"Beaulieu," the Cornelius Vanderbilt Juniors' house,
and the scene around us was one of almost fairy-tale
beauty, for it was the night of Grace Vanderbilt's great
"Fête des Roses." A big harvest moon hung low in the
inky velvet of the August sky; the lawns were lighted by
myriads of shaded fairy lamps, while fireworks played
their glittering cascades of gold and silver. Red roses
everywhere, massed in gigantic baskets, hanging in festoons. Their fragrance perfumed the ballroom; they lay
crushed under the feet of the guests on the velvet-car-
peted avenue which led to the house, lined with the tents
of fortune-tellers, booths containing a dozen different
side shows, cocoanut shies, miniature rifle ranges and all
the rest. But the prizes, instead of being the ordinary

137

showmen's trumpery, were all beautiful presents, gold and enamel vanity-boxes for the women, cigarette-cases for the men.

In one part of the grounds a miniature theatre had been constructed. A hundred builders and carpenters had worked day and night for a week to have it ready for that one evening, fitted it out with a full-size stage and perfect lighting. The entire company of "Red Rose Inn" which was then having an enormous success in New York had been engaged and transported with scenery and baggage to "Beaulieu" to present the play to the guests. An expensive proceeding, this, for it had involved closing the theatre in New York for two nights, but the Vanderbilts could afford to entertain royally. Their balls were among the most famous in Newport.

Strange now when the social world has known so many changes, when the era of opulence and leisure seems to have passed forever, to look back on the brilliance of those pre-war seasons! America will never again, I think, see entertaining on such a lavish, such a luxurious scale. Into those six or seven weeks were crowded balls, dinners, parties of every description, each striving to eclipse the other in magnificence. Colossal sums were spent in the prevailing spirit of rivalry. I remember Mrs. Pembroke Jones telling me that she always set aside $300,000 at the beginning of every Newport season for entertaining. Some hostesses must have spent even more. A single ball could cost $100,000, even $200,000. No one considered money except for what it could buy.

The summer passed in a veritable pageant of wealth. Mornings spent on Bailey's Beach, or on the Horse Shoe Piazza at the Casino, where women, who prided themselves on their ultra-feminine pose and despised the sports girl whose era was fast dawning, sat arrayed like Solomon in all his glory, listening to the strains of Mullalay's orchestra. Such clothes! How they swished and rustled! Petticoats of satin, of lace, of taffeta; petticoats embellished with elaborate designs of plump cupids playing gilded lyres, true-love-knots interspersed with doves embroidered in seed pearls. Parasols to match every dress, enormous flopping feather hats assorted to every costume. White gloves to the elbow, three or four new pairs every day, priceless lace ruffles at throat and wrists, yards of lace flouncing on underskirts, thousands of dollars' worth dragged over the Casino terrace. Different dresses for every occasion, eighty or ninety in a season, worn once or twice and put aside. On the Casino Courts the "moderns" represented by Edith Wetmore and Mrs. John Jacob Astor played a strenuous but inefficient game of tennis in sports costumes considered the last word in daring—white tennis shoes and black stockings, white silk blouses, pleated skirts which fluttering in the breeze exposed . . . oh, horror, bloomers! Sailor hats to which were attached double veils protected their faces from the outrages of the sun.

Down on the Beach the bathers disported themselves in the propriety of full-skirted costumes and long black stockings. Mr. Van Alen always went into the sea in the full glory of a monocle and white straw hat which glimmered in the sun, thus proclaiming his whereabouts. Mrs. Oliver Belmont bought a green umbrella to preserve her complexion, carried it belligerently into the water. Harry Lehr and her son Willie Vanderbilt approached from behind. . . .

"You engage her in conversation, Willie, while I close the umbrella under the water. . . ." The manœuvre was executed with such success that Mrs. Belmont set upon them both with the remains of her ruined umbrella.

Only the élite could bathe at Bailey's Beach. It was Newport's most exclusive club. The watchman in his gold-laced uniform protected its sanctity from all interlopers. He knew every carriage on sight, fixed newcomers with an eagle eye, swooped down upon them and demanded their names. Unless they were accompanied by one of the members, or bore a note of introduction from an unimpeachable hostess, no power on earth could gain them admission. If they wanted to bathe they could only go to Easton's Beach—"The Common Beach" as the habitués of Bailey's were wont to call it. There they would have the indignity of sharing the sea with the Newport townspeople, referred to by Harry Lehr, who was fond of quoting the sayings of Louis XIV, as . . . "Our Footstools."

Between "The Footstools" and those who availed themselves of them there waged a continual guerilla warfare.

The townspeople despised the "cottagers," the summer colony of millionaires, and boasted of their ability to make them toe the mark. What harm was there in charging the idle rich prohibitive prices for two months and then living in comfort for the rest of the year on the proceeds? The millionaires must have their luxuries? Well, let them have them, but make them pay ten times the proper value. The "cottagers" on their side were only concerned in excluding the townspeople from any of the pastures which they considered their own. They themselves might wander at will in the lovely old town with its quaint little old-fashioned streets nestling down by the water front. But the inhabitants must not dream of returning the compliment. Not for them the sacred purlieus of Bellevue Avenue and Ocean Drive, where they might catch a glimpse of the forbidden splendours of villas which were only occupied for six or seven weeks in the year. Even their humble mode of transport, the street car, was not permitted to invade the privacy of the Avenue, for after one or two tentative attempts the offending lines were always uprooted at the instigation of W. K. Vanderbilt, Jack Astor or other autocrats.

Only once during the whole season was it possible for the despised "Footstools" to enter into the Elysium of the Elect and that was during Tennis Tournament week. Then they could, in company with smart visitors over from Narragansett and others temporarily placed within the social pale, climb to the dizzy heights of the Grand

Stand, on an equal footing with men and women whose very names, grown familiar through the medium of the newspaper social columns, inspired them with awe. While the men followed ardently the play for the championships, their womenfolk sitting beside them would be far more intent on the fashion display around them. Their costumes bought for the occasion, copied from the latest mode, must have represented terrifying sums to them, but not for worlds would they have forgone this annual pleasure. The expense it entailed was their libation poured out on the altar of snobbishness. In the same spirit they paid twenty-five dollars each for tickets for the Tennis Ball which brought the Tournament to a close. Those who attended it were divided rigorously into two camps—the observed and the observers. The latter were perfectly aware that they had come for the express purpose of watching the smart people on parade, and they made the most of their opportunity. They stared at them unashamedly as they clustered together in little aristocratic groups, trying to pretend that they and their friends were the sole occupants of the ballroom. It was a curiously uncomfortable evening for all concerned, yet no one would have missed it; it was one of the rituals of the season, this solemn parade of social conventions. And the whole fabric of Newport life was founded on social conventions; Newport, where even political greatness was of no avail, and where President Chester A. Arthur, over for the day, had to call his own carriage. No one except a handful of tittering grooms appeared even to hear him as he stood on the steps of the Casino yelling: "The President's carriage! . . ."

.   .   .   .   .   .

Lunch in Newport might be many things. It might be a pleasant and informal affair at the Gooseberry Island Club with one's row boat moored to the charming little landing stage, or at the Clam Bake Club where elegant women wearing the latest French models took off their long kid gloves to eat the clams cooked in the same stones the Indians had used, and brought to the table in tin basins.

Or it might be a magnificent luncheon party at Mrs. Fish's beautiful house, "Crossways."

Bobby Van Cortlandt, annoyed at being left out of one of her parties, said languidly, "I never can remember the name of your house, Mrs. Fish. Isn't it the Cross Patch? . . ." "Well, anyhow it's a patch you'll never cross, young man," was the sharp reply.

Her invitations were eagerly sought after. Her cook was a genius, her cellar a noted one. Her luncheons were served in stately splendour by her English butler Morton and his satellites.

Morton was a great character. He was also a great autocrat. Everyone acquainted with the Fish household (including his employers) was more or less in awe of his superb impassivity, his eagle eye for any breach of etiquette. He could wither the most brazen offenders with one glance of superiority. He had served in English ducal families, a fact which he never failed to impress on all with whom he came in contact. Even Mrs. Fish could find no suitable retort to his calm, "Just as you wish, Madam. But I can only assure you it is not done in the best English households. . . ."

Once, to his infinite disgust, she good-naturedly lent him for the evening to officiate at a dinner party which was given by some new-rich people. The hostess drove him to the point of frenzy by fussing over the arrangements of the table. Finally she gave him minute instructions as to what wines he was to offer with the different courses. He bore it in silence until she came to the Apollinaris water. . . . "I suppose you know how to serve that; you won't make any mistake?" she asked anxiously. . . .

Morton drew himself up to his full height, which was somewhere about six foot two. . . . "Madam, I have had the care of some of the most noted wine cellars in the British Isles. Apollinaris should be boiled. I have always seen it boiled. . . ."

Morton had only one failing. He had acquired, to use his own phrase, "through much aristocratic service a fine taste in wines." Once when he had rather overindulged he grew noisy and truculent. The climax came one morning when Mrs. Fish had invited a number of friends for luncheon. The last guest had just arrived when he burst into the hall, flourishing a napkin. . . . "I suppose that because you happen to be Mrs. Stuyvesant Fish you think you can drive up and down the Avenue inviting who you like to the house. Well, let me tell you, you can't. Sixteen is my limit, and if you ask any more they go hungry! . . ."

The next day he was dismissed, unfortunately on the eve of one of Mrs. Fish's biggest dinner parties. His revenge was subtle. With amazing ingenuity he unscrewed the whole of the gold dinner-service into three hundred separate pieces and mixed them in one heap on the dining-room floor, so that they resembled the parts of a jigsaw puzzle. As none of his satellites had mastered the secret of putting them together a wire had to be sent to Tiffany's and two men dispatched post haste from New York to have the service in readiness for the dinner.

. . . .

Mrs. Oliver Belmont, too, gave wonderful luncheon parties in the handsome setting of "Belcourt," with its wide Gothic arches and massive staircase, a replica of the famous one in the Musée de Cluny. From the point of view of Oliver Belmont, coaching and racing devotee as he was, the stables were by far the most important part of the house. Nothing was too good for them. They were steam-heated in winter, fitted with all the latest devices. The whole ground floor was given over to them and to the quarters of the eight smart grooms whom he had brought over from England. For the rest of the palatial residence he studied the Gothic period, and many and beautiful were the objects it contained. He brought his personal researches and taste to bear upon it. Tourists from Narragansett Pier over on day trips used to crowd round its doors hoping to catch a glimpse of its far-famed splendours. Every week the excursion char-à-banc would draw up outside it, much to the annoyance of the Belmonts, while the driver with the aid of a megaphone pointed it out to his passengers as "one of the sights of Newport," commenting with embarrassing freedom on the house and its occupants. At one luncheon party which Mrs. Belmont gave shortly after her marriage to Oliver, the char-à-banc arrived just as we were finishing dessert. . . . "Oh, here's that dreadful man with the megaphone," exclaimed Mrs. Belmont. . . . "He's going to tell all the tourists about our staircase. Do listen to what he says; it really is too funny for words. . . ."

We stopped the conversation to listen. But the next moment we were regretting it, for the man had changed his usual formula to: "Here you see before you the new home of a lady who is much in the public eye," he yelled raucously. . . . "A society lady who has just been through the divorce courts. She used to dwell in marble halls with Mr. Vanderbilt. Now she lives over the stables with Mr. Belmont. . . ."

No visitor ever called at "Belcourt" without making the acquaintance of Azar, Oliver Belmont's famous Egyptian valet who had been with his master since his bachelor days. On gala nights they made a strange exotic tableau, Oliver, sitting enthroned in a huge carved armchair to receive his guests, Azar, standing behind him, tall and handsome in his picturesque Zouave jacket and embroidered fez.

When his master married and "Belcourt" had a hostess,

Azar was promoted to the rôle of major-domo. In a costume glittering with gold and eclipsing in grandeur any of his previous ones, he would stand in the entrance between the two English footmen in their court liveries and powdered hair and welcome the guests with all the pomp and ceremony of a Grand Vizier. His air of conscious superiority was unrivalled. He rose to every occasion with superb complacency. Only once did his composure desert him and that was when on a train journey Mrs. Belmont asked him to take charge of her French bulldog. With tears in his eyes Azar drew himself up to his full height and folded his arms majestically across his chest. . . . "Madame, Madame, do not ask such a thing of me. Sooner would I leave my master's service for ever. Never in all my life has such an insult been put upon me. In my own land I have been a chief of camel drivers. Rather will I die than walk a dog on a string. . . ."

.   .   .   .

Between Mrs. Belmont and Mrs. Ogden Mills there existed a perpetual state of feud which extended itself to their respective courts. In temperament they were diametrically opposed. Mrs. Belmont, warm-hearted, impulsive, aggressive. . . . Mrs. Mills, who prided herself on being born a Livingston, descendant of one of the oldest Colonial families, cold, sarcastic and aristocratic. Always faultlessly dressed she was one of the most elegant women in New York; she had a set of jewels assorted to each gown, rubies, emeralds, diamonds, turquoises, sapphires . . . her furs were superb.

"Ocean Lawn," her house in Newport, was the centre of the bridge-playing crowd, her balls were perfectly organised; she had her own cotillion leader, Chappie Novarro. But she limited her guests to two hundred, her conception of American society, for she was infinitely more exclusive than Mrs. Astor. . . . "There are really only twenty families in New York," she would say in her drawling, supercilious voice, but we never found out precisely who they were.

Harry Lehr detested her, but he respected her poise. . . . "She has reduced rudeness to a fine art," he would say. . . . "She has discovered that most people respond to the lash. . . ."

She made a cult of rudeness, and it was extraordinarily successful. The ruder she was to people the more they courted her favours. She would invite them to her New York house on Fifth Avenue, to "Staatsburg," her place on the Hudson, or to "Ocean Lawn," greet them with a limp hand, languidly extended, and a far-away expression, and then apparently forget their existence. They were chilled but impressed. Only a woman who was supremely sure of herself could be so ill-mannered. The ambitious preferred snubs from her to kindness from more human hostesses.

She was one of the most ardent aspirants to the social throne left vacant after the abdication of Mrs. Astor, but she was defeated by her own exclusiveness. Her circle was too small, her influence too narrow and restricted to make her the accepted leader of the "Four Hundred."

Although the actual arena for this all-important contest was New York the preliminary skirmishes were fought out in Newport. It was tacitly acknowledged that she who succeeded in reigning there would reign later in the wider sphere of New York. There was an undercurrent of speculation for two or three seasons while Mrs. Astor, grown old now and failing in health, withdrew herself gradually more and more from social life, and the claimants to the succession vied for the distinction of giving the best entertainments, having the most beautiful clothes, the finest horses, the richest jewels—all weapons in the struggle for supremacy.

Then began a process of elimination. Mrs. John Jacob Astor was well-born and beautiful with that quality of insolence that either repelled or attracted; "nonchalante et froide," Robert de Montesquiou had described her with his flair for coining an apt phrase. She had the advantage of being Mrs. Astor's daughter-in-law, and the vast Astor fortune at her disposal. But she had no talent for social leadership; she lacked discrimination in choosing her acquaintances, preferred Bohemian gatherings to stately dinner parties.

Mrs. Mills had too few friends, Mrs. Belmont too many foes. She could not learn to be diplomatic. Mrs. Burke Roche invited her to a luncheon party, placed her at the table between two men neither of whom interested her. To their consternation she would not address a single word to them all through the lunch. Their attempts at conversation were repulsed with a stony glare and complete silence. By the time the uncomfortable luncheon was over she had made two fresh enemies. Impossible to have a Queen of the "Four Hundred" who could only sign declarations of war.

Mrs. Stuyvesant Fish might have attained to the most coveted position in American society had it not been for the "Monkey Dinner," which created an enormous sensation.

I came in from driving one afternoon and met Harry Lehr in the hall. . . .

"Joseph Leiter has just rung up," he told me. . . . "He wanted to know whether he might bring a friend to our dinner party tomorrow night. I told him I was sure you would not mind as it is not to be a big, formal affair. . . ."

"Who is the friend?" I asked. . . .

"Prince del Drago who is staying on the yacht with him. Jo says he is a charming fellow, and comes from Corsica. I asked him whether he was any relation of the del Dragos whom we met in Rome, and he said that certainly he was. They all belong to the same family, only the Prince's is a distant branch. Jo thinks we shall like him immensely, but he warned me that he is a little inclined to be wild. He doesn't want us to give him too much to drink, because he is not used to it. Anything goes to his head, and then apparently he is apt to behave rather badly. . . ."

"Of course I shall be delighted to see him," I replied, "and I will tell the butler not to fill up his glass too often. . . ."

The story of our aristocratic guest spread like wildfire. Everyone wanted to meet the charming Prince from Corsica.

The next evening, all the guests were assembled eagerly expecting a thrill, and they got one, but not the sort they were looking for. . . . Promptly at eight o'clock the doors were flung open and in walked Joe Leiter holding by the hand a small monkey correctly attired in full evening dress.

Of course, as the Prince was to be the guest of honour, there was nothing to be done except to treat him with befitting dignity. He was given the seat on my right with Mrs. Fish, who, like Harry Lehr, had been in the secret all the time, on his other side, and throughout dinner he behaved admirably. I hardly like to write that his manners compared favourably with those of some princes I have met, but it would be no less than the truth.

The dinner party was a great success, but somehow the story, absurdly exaggerated, got into the hands of the newspaper reporters and the result was a deluge of sarcastic comments. Harry and Mrs. Fish were stated to have "held up American society to ridicule. . . ."

One newspaper in referring to the competition for the social throne wrote:

"It is simply appalling to think of Mrs. Stuyvesant Fish becoming the leader of our society. In that case social life would be a long succession of monkey parties and equally undignified entertainments. I suppose our balls would all be more or less like Indian war dances! It is dreadful to think of distinguished foreigners coming over here and judging us by Mrs. Stuyvesant Fish's entertainments, arranged with the assistance of Mr. Harry Lehr. New York society represents America in the eyes of the foreign world, and we should behave with a becoming sense of dignity. . . ."

Eventually it was Grace Vanderbilt upon whom the mantle of Mrs. Astor fell, the lovely Grace Wilson who years before had so captivated young Cornelius Vanderbilt that he quarrelled bitterly with his family and gave up the greater share of his inheritance to marry her. Born with a flair for social intrigue, with all the qualities that make a ruler, she gradually assumed the leadership of New York society, despite the opposition of her husband's family.

She was firmly established on her throne when Harry Lehr encountered her at Ciro's in Monte Carlo. She was dissatisfied with the table allotted to her, summoned the maître d'hôtel. . . .

"Why have you given me this table? Let me have that one over there. . . ." She was told it had been reserved by Prince Danilo of Montenegro. . . .

"Well, then I will have that one in the corner. . . ." The maître d'hôtel was profoundly regretful, but the table was being kept for an English Duchess. . . .

"Then," said Mrs. Vanderbilt, much displeased, "see that you give me a better table than the Duchess's in future. . . ." Turning to an Englishman of her acquaintance:

"It is only here in France that I am treated in this way. In America I take a rank something like that of your Princess of Wales. . . ."

"Oh," replied the Englishman, "then who is your Queen? . . ."

CHAPTER XII

THE FAVOUR OF WOMEN

"S AMSON'S STRENGTH LAY IN HIS HAIR . . . MINE LIES IN the favour of women," Harry Lehr would say when he was congratulating himself on some fresh social conquest. . . . "All I have to do is to keep in their good graces and everything comes to me. . . ."

To this end he spent all his time in their company, listened to their confidences, gave them (whenever they sought it) his advice with the same careful consideration, whether the problem was arranging a dinner or luring an erring husband back to the fold. He chose their dresses for them, planned their house parties, taught them how to manage their love affairs and found them husbands.

"You ought to be called the matchmaker, Harry Lehr," Mrs. Oliver Belmont would say, laughing. . . . "This is the fourth engagement you have engineered this season. . . ."

"Well, wasn't it rather clever of me? . . ."

"You know perfectly well I don't believe in marriage. I never shall until we have true equality of the sexes. The marriage ceremony itself shows the unfairness of women's position. When a woman can get up in the pulpit, mum-

154

ble a lot of words over a couple and say, 'Go away and
sleep together . . .' then I'll uphold marriage . . . not
before. . . ."

"But you have been married twice, dear lady . . ."
Harry would say with his most disarming smile. . . .

"Oh, well, I have had to fall into line with the customs
of my world, but that does not mean I agree with
them. . . ."

And Harry would shrug his shoulders, but he went on
just the same playing fairy godfather to beautiful but
penniless girls, bringing them out in society, introducing
their golden princes to them. Louise Cromwell and
Walter Brooks of Baltimore . . . Nancy Langhorn and
Lord Astor . . . Elsie Whelen and Robert Goelet. He
deliberately picked them out as suited to one another,
brought them together and watched the romance ripen.
He was always ready to act as Cupid's messenger, to
smooth out any quarrels that beset the path of love. His
unfailing knowledge of psychology stood him in good
stead; he would say exactly the right thing to both of
them. And on the triumphant day when he was the first
guest to be invited to the wedding he had sponsored he
would smile that curiously mocking smile of his . . .

"Well, that's another house I shall be invited to. . . ."

When the lovely Whelen girls came to Newport, poor
and unknown, to stay with their wealthy friends the
Thaws, Harry prophesied they would make brilliant
marriages. He invited them to parties, introduced them
to the most eligible bachelors; with the result that Bobby

Goelet, the richest of them all, fell desperately in love with Elsie, the beauty of the family. The Goelets were against the marriage from the very start and did not hesitate to put every obstacle in the path of the young lovers. They were forbidden even to see one another. Then Harry came to the rescue, connived at secret meetings, poured oil on the waters and finally played peacemaker between Bobby and his mother, who not only promised to receive Elsie as her daughter-in-law, but even attended the wedding. Harry wrote in his diary:

"I must say that I have a certain satisfaction at the thought of the Whelen wedding which would never have taken place but for me. I always knew those girls would do brilliantly, and I think that the marriage will be most suitable, for Elsie has both brains and beauty. I do not think that Bobby would have ever screwed his courage to the sticking point if I had not urged him on. . . . Elsie was indeed a lovely bride and wore a magnificent emerald and diamond necklace—from her husband's mother—at the reception, which was in the open air. She looked like a fairy-tale princess. . . ."

But unfortunately fairy princesses and their husbands do not always "live together happily ever after" and before very long the Goelets were seeking a divorce. Elsie, unhappy and distrait, found her life at a loose end.

Henry Clews was studying art. His enthusiasm fired hers. She began to take lessons in painting and sculpture too. Before many weeks they had converted the hayloft of the "The Rocks," the Clews' Newport house, into a studio. Mrs. Fish went to visit it. . . . "Elsie tells me that they share the same naked man as a model," she reported. . . . "It doesn't sound at all proper to me, but I am sure it is. . . ."

When Elsie obtained her divorce no one was surprised at the sequel. . . . She married Henry Clews.

The millionaire prince and the beautiful princess did not find happiness together, but the princess and the poor young artist have been married many years and are still sharing romance as once they shared a studio.

Which is a new ending to an old story. . . .

. . . .

Elsie was not the only Newport fairy princess.

No one in Newport could produce mint juleps to equal those Mrs. Pembroke Jones dispensed every morning before luncheon to a select little coterie of the younger set at "Sherwood." It was before the era of cocktails, and some people did not approve of them. Mrs. Cornelius Vanderbilt was one. "It encourages people to drink," she used to say severely, sipping Apollinaris water with a slice of lemon in the glass.

But everyone continued to go to "Sherwood." It was the most hospitable house in Newport; its owners were ideal hosts, they entertained on a splendid scale; their balls were famous. But no one imagined it as the scene of a fairy-tale romance, which is exactly what it was. It made the story of Cinderella come true.

Somewhere at the top of that enormous house, in a tiny room, Mary Lily Kenan sat and sewed. She never came down to drink mint juleps in the midst of a gay crowd; the nearest she ever got to one of the splendid balls was to peep over the stairs and watch beautiful women arriving in dresses so lovely they made her catch her breath in ecstasy. She was not beautiful, and she had never had many pretty dresses in her life. But for all that she was romantic. She always dreamt that a fairy prince would come into her life some day and take her away from the tiny room and the sewing-machine. She never told her dreams to anyone, at least not then. Years afterwards she told me about them with a little laugh at her own expense.

Mary Lily was small and frail. Her little oval face was covered with freckles, her big wistful dark eyes were always rather tired. Her smile was sudden and very sweet. No one ever dreamt of calling her anything but plain in those days when feminine charm was supposed to be opulent and highly coloured. No one had ever been in love with her and as she was nearly thirty-five no one probably ever would be. She was rather like a little mouse as she crept about the rooms and sat sewing so quietly that she was scarcely ever noticed.

One day Henry Flagler, multi-millionaire, elderly, disillusioned with life, arrived in Newport. Everyone knew that he had just been divorced, and that he had no heart for balls or entertainments, that he only wanted to forget. But the women were all interested in him, speculating whether he would marry again. He came to the Pem-

broke Jones' house. . . . "No, please don't ask anyone
to meet me. I don't want a crowd. I'm going to be a her-
mit for a while. Let me come to visit you sometimes when
you are alone. . . . Just treat me as though I was one of
the family. . . ."

He stayed to lunch. Mary Lily Kenan came down.
She flushed all over her pale little face when she saw the
visitor, and slipped into her chair opposite him. Once or
twice he glanced at her. Afterwards he asked whether she
would not join them in the garden. . . . "Who, Mary
Lily?" said Mrs. Pembroke Jones in surprise. . . . "Oh,
she would not come down. She has so much sewing to
do."

Henry Flagler visited them the next day, talked a great
deal to his host through luncheon. Mary Lily was not
there, and he never mentioned her. They rose to leave
the table. . . . At the door their guest turned. "Why,
the button has come off my coat. Will someone sew it on
for me? . . ."

Why, of course. Mary Lily was sent for. She came
down, very shy, took the coat in her little hands, her small
freckled face bending over the needle. . . . The millionaire watched it while she sewed. Twenty minutes passed.
What a time Mary Lily was sewing on that button! Mr.
Pembroke Jones went in search of his guest. He found
him alone in the room, staring out of the window. Mary
Lily had vanished, gone back to her own room.

But the next day she came to Mrs. Pembroke Jones,

still very quiet, mouselike, but a new Mary Lily . . . no longer a Cinderella, a princess come into her own kingdom, radiant. . . .

"I am going to marry Mr. Flagler. He loves me and I love him."

Harry Lehr and I had just finished breakfast when Mrs. Pembroke Jones hurried into the room. . . . "I had to come to tell you the news. The latest engagement, who do you think it is?"

We made several guesses. . . .

"Our dear Mary Lily! She is going to marry Henry Flagler!"

We were suitably surprised. Somehow no one had pictured Mary Lily getting engaged to anyone, still less a millionaire.

Mrs. Pembroke Jones was full of preparations for the wedding. . . . "I have had her taken out of the servants' quarters and put into the best guest suite with two footmen to wait on her. . . . Nothing can be too good for her now! The yacht has gone to New York to bring back dresses from Worth and jewels from Tiffany's. Henry Flagler says that she is to have everything in the world she wants, if it is in his power to get it. . . ."

A wave of the magic wand and Cinderella was arrayed in the silk and laces of the fairy story, or, to be more precise, in the latest Parisian creations which Worth's saleswomen and their attendant bevy of mannequins and fitters brought down to Newport. They showed her a misty blue tulle. . . . "This would be the ideal wedding dress for Madame. . . ." But Mary Lily was romantic. She would be married in the traditional white satin and lace veil. It might not suit her, but it was the wedding dress of her dreams.

She looked a little bewildered, dazed with the unaccustomed splendours of it all as she walked down the aisle on the arm of her bridegroom, but her smile was radiant.

CHAPTER XIII
HOUSE PARTIES

❧

THE FALL WOULD FIND US BACK IN NEW YORK, THE NEW-port house closed until the next season.

Harry and I were generally among the last of "the cottagers" to leave. Mrs. Fish, too, lingered on. She loved the quiet of the golden late September days, the respite from entertaining. Without even a groom beside her she would drive her spirited roans over the countryside, exploring its beauties, come back laden with branches of yellowing leaves and scarlet berries. Often Harry Lehr would accompany her and they would drive to the little church at Middletown, join heartily in the simple hymns there. "It's so restful, it soothes me so," she would say. Once when she was driving with me we passed an old beggar-woman sitting by the roadside knitting a coarse grey stocking. Mrs. Fish looked enviously at her . . . "Just think of having the time to knit. How lovely!" She never had time for anything; it was her constant cry. She was always quoting the lines:

> "Her life was turning, turning,
> In mazes of heat and sound,
> But for peace her soul was yearning,
> And now peace laps her round."

162

Her husband had them inscribed on her gravestone.

. . . .

Every fall brought its round of visits. We would go to Tarrytown to stop at "Ferncliff," Jack Astor's place on the Hudson River.

"One cannot imagine anyone simpler, kinder or more considerate than Jack," wrote Harry Lehr in his diary. It was true of him. The real Jack Astor was the man who faced death gallantly, unselfishly, on the "Titanic."

As a host he did not have much chance of appreciation for he scarcely saw his guests. Ava Astor invariably invited people like herself, ardent devotees of bridge, and from the moment they arrived they would have their noses glued to the card table.

Their host, who detested bridge and was far more at home going at top speed in his new racing car or at the helm of his yacht in a storm than in his own drawing-room, shambled from room to room, tall, loosely built and ungraceful, rather like a great overgrown colt, in a vain search for someone to talk to. He was not even permitted to enjoy the Mignon-Welte pianos which he had installed all over the house, for a few minutes after he had turned one on a footman would appear. . . .

"Mrs. Astor asks you to stop the music, sir. She says it is disturbing the bridge players. . . ." And he would sigh and turn it off. He was not particularly fond of music, but the mechanical system of the piano interested him; it offered a temporary diversion at least.

He would go up to his room and dress faultlessly for dinner, come down, prepared to talk and entertain his guests, and find everyone scurrying upstairs to make hasty, last-moment toilets. Of course they would all be late, which annoyed him intensely, for he made a god of punctuality, and the probability of a spoilt dinner in consequence did not serve to improve his temper, for he was a notable epicure. The house party would come down to find him, watch in hand, constrained and irritable.

Dinner was not an enjoyable meal for him. Never a brilliant conversationalist at the best of times, he would be wanting to discuss what Willie Vanderbilt's new car was capable of doing, or whether the chef Oliver Belmont had brought back from France was really better than his own. And, instead, he had to listen to interminable post-mortems—"You should have returned my lead. . . ." "I was waiting for you to play your queen . . ."—of absorbing interest perhaps to those who had participated in the game, but decidedly boring to their host. And immediately after dinner they would return to the card tables.

It was the same thing next morning. He would come downstairs ready for church in cutaway coat and immaculate topper, only to find rubbers in progress already. So he would sit alone in his front pew, come back to lunch off a tray in his study, and return to New York in the afternoon, a lonely man in spite of all his acquaintances.

Sometimes we would go down for a week-end to Wilmington, North Carolina, where the Pembroke Jones dispensed hearty, Southern hospitality.

"Pem," as everyone called him, was a very different host from Jack Astor; no constraint at his parties; his loud laughter would ring through the whole house; his high-balls and mint juleps were famous. A merry man, getting the utmost flavour out of life, liking others to enjoy it too.

"Bessie and I, Adele and Francis Stevens, and Tessie Oelrichs and Lispenard Stewart start off for Wilmington today," wrote Harry in his diary. . . . "We are bound to have a good time. Plenty of gaiety and laughter and fun. . . . The welcome that awaited us was so real, and the pleasure on our host's and hostess's faces so genuine, and the enormous hot supper so good that we forgot the fatigue of the journey. After I had been forced into several cocktails by Elisha and Pem I became strongly gay. . . ."

Even a wet Sunday could not spoil Wilmington house parties. . . .

"The only thing is that it brings us all indoors and some of the gentlemen seem to me to be hovering too near the sideboard in the dining-room," wrote Harry. . . . "But we had a fine big dinner that night. There were speeches and I made a fine one, and sassed everyone well. I am tired and exhausted from laughing. . . ."

After dinner there would be dancing with Pembroke Jones leading off with his old coloured mammy, and the next day we would go back to New York, taking with us something of the warmth and colour of the South.

Quieter week-ends at "Waldheim," the Speyers' house on the Hudson River. James Speyers was a pioneer, the first Jew to be accepted in the Four Hundred. His wife, the former Ellen Dynley Prince, had achieved the victory. She and Mrs. Leavitt were, I believe, the first society women to go into trade in New York. They opened "The Afternoon Tea Rooms" in the old Knickerbocker Building and all their friends flocked to the opening day to admire the pretty setting of the rooms decorated in Elizabethan style, the tables with their big bowls of violets from Mrs. Leavitt's country estate, the waitresses in their picturesque mauve and pink uniforms. Mrs. Astor, Mrs. Oelrichs, Mrs. Cornelius Vanderbilt had all brought parties; soon the rooms were so crowded that people were being turned away from the doors; those who were able to get in at all had to reconcile themselves to kneeling on the floor. Mrs. Prince was besieged with reporters . . . "Aren't you afraid all your smart friends will drop you now that you have gone into trade? . . ." "Is this going to be the latest craze? . . ." Her answer, "If they did, they would not be friends, would they? . . ." "No, of course it is not a craze. It's deadly earnest. I'm trying to earn my own living. I made every one of these cakes myself. . . ."

There was no question of anyone dropping her, for she had so many invitations she could have gone to parties at New York's most exclusive houses every day of the week; only she had not the time.

One day after the tea-shop had become an established success she went to see Mrs. Astor. . . .

"A man who has been in love with me for months wants to marry me. Please give me your advice. . . . I should like to accept him . . . but you see he is a Jew. . . ."

A Jew! Such a marriage would violate one of the fundamental principles of the Four Hundred's code. While half the ancient families of Europe had allied themselves with the race of Israel, while English aristocracy, following the lead of King Edward VII, not only tolerated but held out welcoming arms to its swarthy sons and daughters, American society had withstood the invasion. Not a single Jew could boast of an invitation to any of the houses of the Four Hundred. Not a hostess in New York would be the first to open her salon to one. Husbands might plead for them, urge extensive business relations, but in vain. They could give them lunches in restaurants, take them to the theatre if they chose, but they must not bring them home.

And now here was one of the most popular women in society actually talking of marrying a Jew! Mrs. Astor was silent in dismay. . . .

"Who is he?" she asked at length. . . .

"James Speyers. I want to marry him, but I can't if it will mean losing all my friends. That is why I have come to you. Will you make an exception for me? . . . Will you receive him as my husband at your house?"

Mrs. Astor considered the situation with due gravity. Then she smiled. . . .

"I don't think we have any alternative, for we are all so fond of you. Marry him, my dear, if you want to. I for one will invite you both to my parties, and I think everyone else will do the same. . . ."

They did. Before the end of the day Ellen Prince had paid at least half a dozen similar calls. . . . Mrs. Ogden Mills, Mrs. Oelrichs, Mrs. Belmont, and all the rest had followed Mrs. Astor's example. They would all receive James Speyers for his wife's sake. The battle was won.

But it was the thin end of the wedge. Gradually the old anti-Jewish prejudices were weakening. The Great War killed them outright.

·   ·   ·   ·   ·   ·   ·

We would often go to Garrisons to stop at "Glenclyffe Farms," Stuyvesant Fish's lovely old home on the Hudson River.

Mrs. Fish loved to refer to her husband as "The Good Man," in the phraseology of the Knickerbocker days. She could have chosen no more appropriate name for him. His career was meteoric. He was still under thirty when he flashed into power as President of the Illinois Central Railroad, yet in the age when success in business went only too often hand in hand with corruption and unscrupulous methods he was the soul of honour and integrity. He was proud of the fact that he could trace his

descent in an unbroken line from an old Puritan family
that had come over in the "Mayflower." In many respects
he still retained the simplicity, the austerity of his ancestors. I think in his heart of hearts he preferred their
standard of life to that of the social world in which he
lived. He would never play cards on Sunday, he hated
ostentation and loved "Glenclyffe Farms" far better than
"Crossways" at Newport or his fine house in New York.
He loved to take his guests up to the commodious, old-
fashioned bedroom, without running water of course,
which he and his brother had shared all through their
boyhood. . . . "None of the maids will sleep in it, it is
not good enough for them; yet I spent some of the happiest hours in my life here. . . ."
He never really cared for society, and only tolerated
parties for the sake of his wife, who could not contem-
plate life without them. Sometimes he would come back
tired out after a long journey over his railroad and find
the house full of a noisy crowd of guests, occasionally even
his razors and shaving-brushes commandeered by those
unexpectedly staying overnight. But he would only shrug
his shoulders good-naturedly. . . . "It seems I am giving
a party. Well, I hope you are all enjoying yourselves. . . ."
A big, silent man who never wasted words, he was a
great contrast to Mamie Fish who kept up a constant flow
of light chatter wherever she was. Sometimes she teased
him over his taciturn ways. . . . "Where would he be
without me? I made him. I put him on the throne," she
would say even in his presence and he never contradicted

her. Whatever she chose to do or say was right. There was something romantic in his devotion to her. Had he lived in the Middle Ages he would have ridden into battle at her lightest word. Which was actually what he did, or at least its modern equivalent. Everyone heard of the feud between Stuyvesant Fish and E. H. Harriman, for its results were far-reaching, but very few people knew of its cause. Harry Lehr was one of them and this is the story he told me:

It began like many events which have made history in a women's quarrel. Mary Harriman heard Mamie Fish make some disparaging remarks about her at a tea-party, and took instant and mortal offence. Literally a tempest in a tea-pot . . . but it was a storm which wrecked the business relations of two Titans of the railroads. Both the wives went home and told their husbands what had happened. E. H. Harriman was furious. . . . "I'll make those people suffer," he exclaimed and he kept his word. Stuyvesant Fish knew that it was war to the knife. Harriman was a bad enemy, ruthless and implacable. He began his campaign carefully, sowed the seeds of dissension in Stuyvesant Fish's own company. He chose as his chief ally Harahan, a man who owed everything to Mr. Fish, who had raised him from a switch-tender to a position of trust in the company. Together the two laid their plans. There was a stormy scene at the next Board meeting of the Illinois Central Railroad Company. Harahan came out into the open, publicly attacked the man who had befriended him. After his first start of surprise Stuyvesant

Fish listened in silence until he had finished speaking. Then he swung round, shot out a massive fist and with one blow felled Harahan to the floor. "That is my answer. . . ." In that moment he had the sympathy of the entire meeting.

The next morning Stuyvesant Fish's daughter, Marion, had a visit from one of New York's most eligible bachelors. He was waiting for her in the library. He explained that he had come to ask her to marry him. She stared at him in astonishment. . . . "But you were one of the people who voted against Father yesterday," she exclaimed. "They told me you had hurried back from Europe specially to record your vote. Can you possibly believe that I should marry you after that?"

It was quite useless for him to explain that he had not anticipated that she would regard his hostility to her father in business from a personal angle. She asked him to leave the house and refused even to see him again.

.   .   .   .

Once Stuyvesant Fish had to go on a long tour of inspection over the whole of his railroad, and, as Mrs. Fish was to accompany him, Harry and I were invited to join them in their private car. To me there was endless fascination in the long hours thundering over the iron roads, watching the ever-changing panorama of scenery whirling by while we sat in our comfortable drawing-rooms or on the platform of the observation-car. I loved the variety of small towns and village stations at which we stopped, with their platforms decorated with flags and garlands of country flowers in honour of our visit, the deputations of local officials of the company and their wives dressed in Sunday clothes. But Mrs. Fish and Harry were bored. They decided they must do something to relieve the monotony of the train. At one small town they started off together on a sight-seeing tour. Before they had gone very far they were overtaken by a mule-drawn street car, and as neither of them had ever travelled in such a vehicle it became the one desirable thing. They hailed it and climbed into its rickety depths, proceeded past a station or two and then discovered that it would be the greatest fun to drive it. As a preliminary Harry started pulling the bell. He was so intrigued with its rusty note that he continued to pull. The aged driver turned round . . . "Here, Mister, you can't do that. It'll cost you something every time you pull that bell. . . ."

Harry took out a hundred dollar bill and waved it before him . . . "You can earn all this if you will let us have your street car for an hour. This lady is going to drive, and I am going to ring the bell and punch the tickets. . . ."

The old man's eyes bulged with astonishment. Probably he had never seen so much money in his life before. He fairly scrambled out of his seat, handed the reins to Mamie and after hurried instructions disappeared, clutching his hundred dollars.

Mamie whipped up the mule, Harry rang a peal upon his bell and off they started, much to the consternation of the passengers who had not anticipated this end to their journey. Harry's shout of "All aboard for Woodlawn Cemetery" did not reassure them. They clamoured to be set down, but Mrs. Fish who was shaking with laughter protested that she could not stop the mule, which in response to her liberal use of the whip had got going at a lively pace. As one after another saw their stations passed without the remotest chance of getting out they grew more and more alarmed and huddled in an indignant group round the door, probably expecting to be pitched into the roadway at any moment. When eventually the mule, obeying the impulse of exhaustion at the unaccustomed pace rather than the will of its driver, stopped dead, they hurried out of the car only too pleased to be able to pursue their journey on foot.

Harry and Mrs. Fish continued their drive until they arrived at the railroad station where poor Mr. Fish was presiding over a dignified gathering of pompous officials and their wives, whose consternation on beholding the wife of their President arrive in such a fashion can best be imagined!

. . . .

Before we had been back in New York long we would be sure to get an invitation to "Brookholt," Mrs. Oliver Belmont's great colonial house on Long Island. I found one of her letters to Harry the other day. . . .

"I have just returned to Brookholt and find your nice letter. I don't like the tone of it, I like your old merry ring. Do, do exert yourself and let us all make the most of the hour with us. It can be done, it is hard work at times, and often seems as if 'le jeu ne vaut pas la chandel (?)' but even with a broken heart and all the joys faded out of the picture believe me, we can paint anew the old canvas, put it back in the frame that held the real one, hang it on the wall a little below its old place and write in big letters above it: 'God's sun still shines for others; give to them what once was ours.' And then will come a peace and something still and helpful. Don't think of yourself, it is the greatest medicine of it all. I hope to see you before you sail, can't you come to Brookholt? You must see the farmerettes. . . . When will you come? . . . I have been there all day, their joy, interest and their belief in a possible future has already dispersed some of the heavy gloom about this dear home. It is a joy to hand over to them what I have lost. So you think you are old! There are days when years mean nothing, the sun is so vivid, so warm, the sky so blue, the trees so strong and green and the air so full of life. We are not 40 or 50 then, just children, careless with joy, knowing nothing, forgetting to feel, smiling not knowing why. When you say poems to me or play some dear melody, what do we know of age then? . . . Do you remember how we laughed on the Rhine (not Nile). . . . We were young then, just for the hour and that was wisdom, so shall it be again. . . . Come to Brookholt. You will whitewash the black clouds hanging over you and grow warm in the reflected light, and I, in an endeavour to cheer you shall know the comfort I may give even if I fail to know it myself and thus your presence will bring its own blessing. What a sermon! I started to thank you for the cheque Bessie gave me and you have almost an epistle such as St. Paul might have sent to the Corinthians. He was a wise man in his generation but should he now return to us we suffragists could hardly receive him with open arms. However, that might conquer

him for he loved not women. Write now, cheer up, spring is
with us and life is full, full of work and rest. . . ."

Every time we arrived at "Brookholt" we were shown
some new addition to the property, for Mrs. Belmont had
a positive passion for building, and, as Harry told her,
"loved nothing better than to be knee-deep in mortar."
She was always altering and improving. One of her curious fancies was that she could not bear to have a bedroom
in which anyone had died. Superstition had been deeply
implanted in her during her childhood by her old coloured mammy, and she had a veritable terror of ghosts,
an alien streak in so strong-minded a woman. Discovering
that "Brookholt," lovely as it was, could not present a
clean sheet as regards mortality, she determined to have
a brand-new bedroom built on for herself. She helped to
draw up the plans, engaged the best builders and was delighted with the result. She wrote to Harry Lehr and me,
telling us she had got exactly what she wanted, and inviting us down to see it. But alas for her hopes. On the very
day that the new wing was completed one of the masons
fell off the ladder, sustaining terrible injuries. The poor
man was carried into the new bedroom where he died
half-an-hour later. Mrs. Belmont was deeply distressed;
pity for his fate and consternation that he should have
chosen her room to die in struggled for the mastery. She
sat down and wrote out a handsome cheque for the
widow, but as she signed it she lamented, "It really does
seem as though Fate had decided I am never to sleep

peacefully at night. All I asked was a room where nobody had died, and now the first thing I know someone goes and dies a *violent* death in it. . . ."

Mrs. Belmont loved anything that could, rightly or wrongly, be labelled "mediæval," but as her enthusiasm was not backed by any real knowledge she managed to collect a great many antiques which were scattered here and there in a heterogeneous collection of no particular period or country in her various houses. The general effect was charming under the spell of her own vivid personality.

When it came to the choice of a home she allowed her imagination full play. "Marble House," which she had built when Mrs. W. K. Vanderbilt and "Brookholt" were, respectively, French (Louis XIV) and "Colonial." . . . "Beacon Towers" and "Belcourt" were respectively Gothic and Renaissance. Her New York City house at Madison Avenue and 50th Street, which she had built to suit herself, was pure Georgian.

I remember once staying with her years afterwards in the same house party in Scotland at Blair Castle, the centuries-old home of the Duke of Atholl. I loved its stately beauty, its link with the past and the romance woven around it by time-honoured traditions. I thought she would love it too, but she exclaimed, "It's not correct. There are a lot of mistakes. My castle at Sandy Point is far more authentic!"

In the days of her first marriage she gave Richard Hunt carte blanche in the designing of the new Vander-

bilt Palace at the corner of Fifty-second Street. . . .
"You can choose any style you like, Norman, Italian
or Spanish. I don't care what it is so long as it is
mediæval. . . ."

He submitted plans to her. She approved of them . . .
"Oh, how lovely. Just what I want. A real Venetian palace like the Doges had. . . ." He was too ironically
courteous to contradict her.

So in due course she had a home after her own dreams,
an imposing erection in white marble, with culverin
towers and broad battlements whence invisible archers
could presumably let loose their shafts over Fifth Avenue. Clusters of acorns adorned the towers, acorns were
carved on the flights of steps. On the topmost pinnacle
was a statue of Richard Hunt as a master-mason. All her
friends came to admire it. . . . "So like Venice! Think
how beautiful it would look with the water all around
it!"

Not one in a hundred realised the irony of Richard
Hunt's choice of a mansion for the Vanderbilts; those
who did kept their opinions to themselves. They knew
that the most popular architect in the States was noted
for an impish sense of humour. In all probability he had
given rein to it when he made his design. Mrs. Vanderbilt had stipulated that her home must be mediæval. She
had her wish. Fortunately for her peace of mind she had
never been to Bourges, so she did not know that she had
a copy of the famous house of Jacques Coeur, the greatest
upstart of the Middle Ages, the richest man of the fif-

teenth century. That her towers were as he had planned his, her statue of Richard Hunt replacing that of the glamorous adventurer!

The question of the house being settled, there remained the problem of the Vanderbilt coat-of-arms. They chose acorns because, as Mrs. Vanderbilt said, "Great oaks from little acorns grow. . . ."

Its simplicity was a contrast to the elaborate devices adopted by some of her friends who were in the grip of an epidemic of heraldry. Tiffany added a special department, "Blazoning, marshalling and designing of arms complete. . . ."

You went in . . . "I want armorial bearings. . . ."

"Certainly, sir. Name?"

"Smith. A large selection please. . . ."

A massive book would be produced. Illustrations of the arms of every known English family. The assistant would run his finger down the index . . . S. . . .

"Now which Smiths would you prefer, the Herefordshire Smiths, the Yorkshire Smiths; we have a great many to choose from. . . ."

"I like this design best, but could you not mix it with something? How about this?"

"That is the coat-of-arms of the Duke of X——."

"Never mind. I'll have half the shield like this, and half the Smith arms. . . ."

The results were decidedly original and quite unknown to the laws of heraldry, but the owners were delighted with them. If they coveted some other family's arms, they simply quartered them with their own.

Oliver Belmont emblazoned the arms of Dunois, the Bastard of Orléans, on the stained glass windows of "Belcourt." Harry Lehr, seeing it for the first time, drew his attention to it: "My dear Oliver, why proclaim yourself illegitimate? . . ."

CHAPTER XIV
YEARS OF TRAVEL

❧

"H ENRY SYMES LEHR, BALTIMORE, MARYLAND (VALET, wife, maid and dog) . . . ."

I have seen it so often written in Harry's neat precise handwriting in a dozen hotel registers all over Europe. It was his invariable manner of describing himself and his "entourage," to use his own word. Once I remonstrated with him over it, pointing out that friends who looked casually at the register would not know that I was travelling with him. He stared at me in astonishment. . . .

"How can you possibly expect me to write 'Mr. and Mrs. Symes Lehr'? Don't you realise that such a thing would detract from my reputation? All Europe has heard of me, but never of you. I am the one people want to meet, not you, so why advertise your presence?"

The humiliation of it! The miserable subterfuge of explaining to friends who happened to see the register and comment on it that it was one of Harry's jokes! To hear constantly, "Why, we never knew you were in Paris, Bessie. We thought Harry was alone—that is why we never asked you to our dinner party!"

I would never even have heard of the party but I

would lie valiantly. . . . "Oh, I couldn't have come. I
had such a frightful headache. . . ."

"And Harry forgot to tell us! How careless of him!"

And I would be left wondering whether they had
guessed. . . .

Years of misery made endurable only by the knowledge that my mother was happy—that she at least suspected nothing!

.   .   .   .

Panorama of those years of travel! Breathless rushes
across Continents . . . . One country blending into another . . . journeys by car, by boat, by train . . .
Paris . . . Newport . . . New York. Paris again. . . .
London . . . Vienna . . . Berlin . . . the Riviera . . .
Italy. Champagne years, colourful, sparkling, ephem-
eral; one skimmed lightly over the surface, not daring
to look beneath. Always entertaining . . . being entertained . . . the same scene in a new setting, for Harry
dreaded solitude above all things. He must always be the
centre of a crowd. He craved admiration and applause—
deprived of it he was flat, lifeless. He who could be the
gayest of companions to others, whose wit could enliven
the dullest gathering, was bored and miserable in his own
society.

Paris in the spring, like all good orthodox Americans.
We would be certain of finding a little coterie of acquaintances, women come over to buy the latest models
before the Newport season, men intent upon sampling
the distractions of Europe's gayest capital.

Mr. Van Alen would be stopping at the Hotel Bristol. He preferred the Ritz but King Edward VII always stopped at the Bristol, and as the resemblance between them was supposed to be remarkable, he got a great deal of pleasant anticipation out of the thought that someone was sure to mistake him for the King of England. His stately dignity was always more in evidence in Paris than anywhere else.

He invited us to an enormous dinner party which he was giving at Armenonville. His guests were to include some of the most distinguished people in Europe. He was very anxious that all the arrangements should be perfect and enlisted Harry's help over the orchestra, the choice of favours and table decorations, and the two of them drove off to Armenonville where poor Mr. Van Alen harassed the manager, the maître d'hôtel and the chef to the point of frenzy, before the menu was finally drawn up to his satisfaction. In the meanwhile Harry Lehr interviewed the chef d'orchestre.

When the night of the party arrived Mr. Van Alen was delighted with the preparations. The table had been beautifully decorated, everything was precisely as he wished.

We had just taken our places at the table when the orchestra, with beaming faces, struck up "The Star Spangled Banner," and we all got up again and stood while it was played through twice. Mr. Van Alen was gratified . . . "Charming compliment, eh, what? Most thoughtful of them. These French are always so polite. . . ."

We were beginning to eat our fish when the familiar strains rang through the room again, and we all rose once more to stand solemnly while the delicious hot soles cardinals congealed on our plates. Mr. Van Alen did not look quite so pleased this time. Patriotism was all very well, but he did not believe in letting it interfere with the enjoyment of his food. He sat down with pardonable irritation. The dinner was excellent, the conversation flourished. The orchestra was playing a dreamy Viennese waltz.

Then just as we had begun to appreciate delicate little poussins cooked to perfection the stirring notes of "The Star Spangled Banner" burst forth once more, and up we all got again. The foreign guests, though puzzled, were politely smiling; the Americans who had begun to think they were the victims of a practical joke were rather annoyed.

When the offence was repeated for the fourth time Mr. Van Alen summoned the chef d'orchestre and wrathfully demanded an explanation. The man looked astonished . . . "I have only carried out the instructions of Monsieur Lehr. . . ."

Then the truth came out. Harry had told him that the dinner was a patriotic reunion of Americans, and that as a compliment to the host and his guests he must be prepared to play the American national anthem whenever the signal was given him by Harry raising his glass level with his eyes!

Mrs. William B. Leeds was one of the guests at that dinner. She was stopping at the Ritz as usual. No longer the slim lovely girl whose beauty had taken Newport by storm. She had put on weight, coarsened, grown a little spoilt in possession of so vast a fortune. It was scarcely to be wondered at. She spent money like a child, without any idea of its value. I remember her husband laughing as he told me that she could never keep within her forty thousand dollars a year dress allowance. Her entry into the salon of one of the great dressmakers was the signal for the vendeuses to bring out the most expensive models in the collection. They used to try to persuade her into all sorts of absurd extravagances, dressing-wraps bordered with chinchilla, boudoir-caps sewn with real pearls. Often she would make the mannequin a present of the dress she displayed if she thought it suited her. I once saw her take two lovely diamond bracelets off her own arm and clasp them on that of her favourite vendeuse at one house, just because the girl had admired them.

She loved shopping and used to come back to the States after each visit to Paris laden with trunks and trunks of clothes of every description—a hundred new evening dresses, a dozen fur coats, crates of new hats. All the customs officials knew her. It always took them hours to examine her baggage.

One summer she arrived in New York in a state of distress. There had been an outbreak of fire on the liner, and although the flames had been extinguished before any serious damage was done, the hold had been flooded and the greater part of the passengers' baggage drenched with sea water. The result was that when the trunks were opened a sodden mass was revealed in place of the collection of beautiful frocks that had left Paris. Colours had run one into the other, an exquisitely lovely dress of blue and gold sequins had melted into a sort of jelly, skirts which had been in one trunk were ruined, while their corresponding waists, packed in another, were left intact. Poor thing, she had not one single garment out of the enormous number she had brought that could be worn. Worst of all, there had been some mistake in insuring the baggage, and although she sued the steamship company she could get no compensation. But she took the disappointment philosophically and only ordered a new consignment of models.

She loved England. When her husband died she took a house in Grosvenor Square, entertained royally. London did not appreciate her as a hostess, for English society either welcomes Americans effusively to its heart or remains aloof, unfriendly. In spite of all her money Mrs. Leeds found many doors closed to her. Her lavish generosity was often misinterpreted as ostentation, her natural exuberance as vulgarity.

Lady Arthur Paget, who acted as her social sponsor, drew her onto the committee of the great Shakespeare Ball which Lady Randolph Churchill was organising at the Albert Hall in honour of the Coronation of King

George V. . . . "Mrs. Leeds would like to help us. I am sure she will be such an asset, and she is so interested in the ball. . . ." The aristocratic ladies of the committee received her with enthusiasm. . . . She was given a seat between two duchesses.

"Such wonderful costumes! You really must see them, Mrs. Leeds. And of course you must take part in the quadrilles. You would make a lovely Cleopatra. . . ." She was delighted. How friendly and charming they all were!

Before the end of the meeting she had committed herself to pay the entire cost of the ball so that the charities for which it was being organised might benefit more substantially.

"So good of you, so generous. You Americans are always so sympathetic. . . ." They overwhelmed her with thanks.

She wrote to Harry Lehr and me in Paris. . . . "I am having a marvellous success in London! . . ." Invited us over for the ball.

The splendid pageantry of those quadrilles! English tradition backed by American dollars! Mrs. Leeds had that morning handed over to the committee a cheque for $80,000.

Weeks had been spent in rehearsals, months in the preparation of the costumes. Prince Youssoupoff who was paying his first visit to London, was a radiantly handsome young Henry V; Anthony Drexel appeared in the same quadrille as a French courtier in a wonderful

suit copied from an old engraving. Lady Arthur Paget
as Mistress Page danced in "The Merry Wives of Windsor" quadrille. But the most splendid figure of all was
Mrs. Leeds, who, as Cleopatra, led the dancers of the
"Antony and Cleopatra" quadrille, in a costume sewn
with rubies, emeralds and diamonds.

Lady Randolph Churchill had placed at her disposal
one of the boxes in the Albert Hall, requesting her to
bring her own party to occupy it during the ball. Apparently this did not meet with the approval of some
other members of the committee, for when Mrs. Leeds
arrived there with her guests she found the entire box
occupied by an English Duchess whose friends had taken
possession of all the best chairs. . . . "I'm afraid there
must be some mistake. This is my box," said Mrs. Leeds.
. . . "As you see, my name is on the door." The Duchess
surveyed her in apparent surprise. . . . "Oh, really?
Well, then, Mrs. Leeds, you can have those two
chairs . . ." indicating the only remaining ones at the
very back of the box. So poor Mrs. Leeds was obliged to
take her party downstairs to watch from a doorway the
quadrilles which had only become possible through her
generosity.

We were in Paris while Mrs. Leeds had her portrait
painted by Boldini. I was often present at the sittings,
which always took place at the Ritz Hotel as, much to his
annoyance, she refused to be painted in the more Bohemian setting of his studio. It was a full-length, life-size
portrait, and for part of the sittings Boldini used to perch

precariously on a pile of telephone books stacked one upon the other on top of the table. Getting him success-fully poised on top of them was a serious business for he was terrified of falling, and it took the united efforts of Mrs. Leeds's two maids, whom she always kept in at-tendance during the sittings, her own page, who re-mained on duty outside the door, and one of the hotel chasseurs. After about five minutes of suspense Boldini was generally placed to his satisfaction, and he would then turn towards his sitter, who was always convulsed with laughter while he was clambering onto his perch, with a vicious expression. . . . "Now, Madame, you are going to stand, while I am seated in comfort. . . ."

She was a very difficult sitter, for she could never be induced to keep the pose for more than five minutes; but Boldini had endless patience. I remember that when he was painting Mrs. W. K. Vanderbilt, Junior, she ar-rived in a different dress at every sitting, as she could never make up her mind which one she wanted to wear in the portrait. In the end he got tired of painting and repainting dresses of every colour, and when she ap-peared in a pale blue satin he exclaimed, "This is the dress you are wearing in my portrait, whether you like it or not. I will not paint another. Do you think I am a designer for the fashion papers?"

Boldini was a lovable creature in spite of his many eccentricities, a true Bohemian, child-like in his craving for praise. Once he spoke sadly to me of one of his Eng-lish sitters. . . . "She was so beautiful, but I did not

enjoy painting her at all. I never knew whether she was pleased with her work or no. Not once in all the time did she ever call, 'Bravo, Boldini; you are a great artist!' "
. . . I was able to assure him that she had been delighted with the portrait, which was one of his best, but she was a typical Anglo-Saxon, she had not understood his ardent Latin temperament. Great artist as he was it was almost impossible for him to work without a running commentary of compliments.

He loved music and when he was painting my portrait nothing pleased him so much as to have Harry Lehr come to the studio during the sittings and play his piano. . . . "Mr. Lehr, I do not like the things I read in your face—but on the piano you have the touch of an angel," he would say. He liked best the simple Italian airs—"Caro Mio Ben" . . . "O Sole Mio" and "Santa Lucia" and always asked for them by name. Once when Harry broke into "Funiculæ, Funicula," he turned round sharply and rebuked him. . . . "How can I paint to a jig like that?" But when he heard one of his favourites he would insist on its being played over and over again until I got tired of it. When he was painting he became so completely absorbed in his work that he scarcely noticed his surroundings; I have often seen him wipe his brushes on his scanty aureole of hair, until it had streaks of every colour of the rainbow. I think he rather gloried in being a Bohemian and in shunning society. He never accepted any invitations to parties, although he occasionally lunched quietly with Harry and me.

He was a great contrast in this respect to Helleu who did a beautiful dry point etching of me in New York. Helleu loved to be seen at fashionable gatherings and was very fastidious over his appearance.

He told us an amusing story of how he had once travelled on the Simplon Express with Boldini. They had not met for several years and were delighted to discover that they had been allotted the same table in the restaurant car. Over dinner they talked of the past, renewed old memories. Under the mellow influence of the wine they grew sentimental, became such good friends that they each started complimenting the other on his work. Finally Boldini suggested that in memory of such a pleasant evening they should exchange examples of their work, and begged Helleu to accept a couple of sketches which he had in his suitcase. Helleu was delighted and in return rummaged among his baggage until he too found some sketches which he presented to his friend. They parted on the most affectionate terms and retired to their respective lits-salons.

In the middle of the night Helleu was awakened by a thunderous knocking at the door of his compartment. He opened it, and found Boldini outside, a great-coat flung on hastily over his pyjamas.

"I had to knock you up," he said to the astonished Helleu, "because I could not remember which station you got out at, and I realise that I have given you some sketches which I cannot spare. I have not been able to

sleep thinking of it. If you will let me have them back
I will send you some others instead. . . ."

None too pleased at the interruption of his slumbers
Helleu climbed up to the baggage rack, got out the
sketches and returned them to their owner. But he waited
in vain for others to replace them, for Boldini forgot to
keep his promise. The only thing he kept was the souvenir parcel of Helleu's sketches!

. . . .

Then there was a young American millionaire who
generally spent the spring in Paris, and could be found
at this hotel or that, elegantly dressed, handsome with
that careless charm that so endeared him to women.

His visits to Europe had only served to develop his
passion for social climbing. He could talk of nothing but
the titled people with whom he had got acquainted, the
Princes and Grand Dukes whom he was accustomed to
address by their Christian names. . . .

"And I said, 'Mich-Mich, my dear old chap, . . .' "

"I really don't think you should talk of the Grand
Duke like that" . . . one of us would suggest, "I am
sure it is not done in the best circles in Russia. . . .'"

"How do you know, you have never been there?" And
the young man would burst into one of his uncontroll-
able fits of temper.

A well-known society woman took him under her
professional wing, and promised, if he was prepared to
spend enough money, to get him into the most exclusive
circles in Europe. She suggested that he should give a

big dinner, and assured him that she could get a Russian Grand Duke and Grand Duchess and a great many other distinguished people to come to it. He was delighted with the idea, and she sent out the invitations.

Unfortunately for her protégé, she was taken ill a day or two before the party and was unable to be present. Harry Lehr and I and the T—— B——s were the only Americans invited and immediately the Grand Duchess arrived she sought out Harry and asked him to sit next to her. . . . "I have heard so much of you, Mr. Lehr, from my son. He tells me you are the most amusing man he has ever met. 'King Lehr,' isn't that what he calls you?"

The dinner party was a most extraordinary affair. There was no one to receive us or to make introductions. The unfortunate pseudo-host was quite lost among his forty or fifty aristocratic guests, not one of whom was personally known to him, and nervousness made him disregard all the instructions of his absent sponsor. At last Olivier, with wonderful tact, grasped the situation, and eventually we were all shepherded to the dinner table.

But there confusion ensued. The young millionaire had given no instructions whatever beyond the fact that he was expecting a party. He had not known the number of his guests, and had completely omitted to mention the fact that they included royalty. He had not even taken the trouble to order a special dinner. The hotel staff rose to the occasion nobly. The table was prepared as though by magic. But there was no time to make a list of the guests or write out cards. People wandered round and round, wondering where they were expected to sit, until the crisp voice of the Grand Duchess called out, "Let us all sit down where we are." . . . And we sank into the chairs nearest to us.

Fortunately the dinner was excellent, the wine all that could be desired. Everyone began to talk to his or her neighbour, waiving the question of introduction. Harry Lehr and the Grand Duchess sat opposite to me. She was evidently finding his conversation amusing, for she laughed repeatedly. Presently she leant forward and said to her husband, who sat next to me, "My dear, it seems that that little man at the end of the table is paying for this dinner party. How very curious! Cannot we find out his name? We shall have to thank him for his kindness." . . . Apparently she had had no idea with whom she was dining!

Despite all this mismanagement, the "little man" was elated with the success of his party. The next day he was able to reel off a complete list of the guests. . . . "Now those really are NAMES for you" he concluded triumphantly.

After the Paris conquest he was fired with the ambition of adding to his laurels in London. His social guide, now recovered from her illness, again came to his aid. She suggested that she should take a house for him at Ascot, in which case it would be easy to get him into the Royal Enclosure, and even to take him into the Royal Box and introduce him to the King. It might even be

possible to arrange for the King to lunch at the house.
. . . "In that case money's no object," he said grandly.

Ascot week found him installed in a large house with
a full complement of house guests whose names included
some of the most famous titles in England. But even that
was not enough for his ambitions. He wanted to return
to America with the story of how he had sat in the Royal
Box. On the first day of the races he prepared to start
off for the course. . . . His mentor restrained him. . . .
"I really think it would be better for you not to appear
in the Royal Enclosure until I have paved the way for
you to be presented to the King. I shall be able to arrange it for tomorrow, but until then you had better
stay away from the course. It is so important to create a
favourable impression from the very start. You won't
miss anything, the first day is never very interesting."
Rather reluctantly, but in obedience to her superior
knowledge of the social conventions, he remained behind while she and the rest of his aristocratic house party
drove off to the races.

The next day the same thing happened again. . . . "I
am so sorry," she said, "but I did not get a favourable
opportunity yesterday of speaking to His Majesty about
you. However it will be quite easy for me to manage
today. You will not mind waiting one more day, I am
sure? After all, it is worth taking a little trouble, and
it is such a fatal mistake to rush these things. The racing
is really very poor this year, I don't think there will be
anything worth seeing today. But tomorrow when you

have your seat in the Royal Box you will really enjoy it all."

So the unfortunate man remained at home once again, watched his guests, most of whom were still strangers to him, drive off in the cars which he had hired for them, listened when they had returned for dinner to talk of the day's racing.

On the third morning he sought out the lady patroness and presented an ultimatum: "Am I going to be presented to the King today, or am I not?"

"Oh, Mr. ——, you know you *must* be patient. Just look at all I have done for you, the wonderful house party I have got for you! The best people in England, Lord X, the Duke of Z, Lady A, all staying under your roof! It takes time to get into English society. But today I really will be able to arrange for your presentation. I am going to speak to His Majesty immediately we get to the course, and then I will send one of the cars back for you so that you can come straight to the Royal Box, be presented to the King and Queen, and see the races."

He made no further demur, waved to his guests as the procession of cars started for the course. But when they returned in the evening there was no host. The millionaire—now disillusioned—had gone back to London, leaving his social cicerone to pay for the house which had been leased in her name!

.   .   .   .

Robert de Montesquiou, the most picturesque figure in pre-war French society, would often dine with us at the Ritz. Tall, slender, elegant, with exquisite hands and long tapering fingers, there was an incomparable air of distinction about him. He made a fine art of conversation, gave it the poise and dignity of another age. A great connoisseur of art and history, he was always looking out for Louis XV pieces to add to his collection. Once when he came to see us he was congratulating himself on having gained possession of the rose marble bath which had once laved the lovely body of the Pompadour at Versailles. He had been looking for it for years, and had at last discovered it in the guise of a fountain at the educational Convent of the Sacred Heart in the rue de Varenne.

He called on the Mother Superior, asked to be shown over the Convent. The good nuns entertained him with delightful old-fashioned courtesy, took him round the garden. Beside the fountain he stood still with an exclamation of horror. . . . "You cannot possibly be aware of what this was?" They shook their heads. It was their fountain, that was all. . . .

"Ah, I thought not! You could not have known that a woman of evil character bathed her sinful body in it. If you had heard its history you would not have permitted it to remain here in the presence of refined ladies like yourselves and the pure young girls who are trusted to your care . . ."

The nuns stared at it, horrified at the scandal within their midst. How terrible that they had not thought of it before; of course they could not keep it!

With an air of the utmost gallantry Robert de Montesquiou came to the rescue. . . .

"Ah, dear ladies, I well understand how distasteful it has become to you now that you know its unfortunate story. It distresses me too to think of these innocent young girls coming into contact with such associations. What would their parents say?"

The poor nuns almost shuddered at the thought. . . .

"Do not distress yourselves. I will present you with a beautiful cast-iron fountain, a perfectly new one which you can choose yourselves. And you need have no anxiety as to the disposal of the one you have here, for I will myself have it taken away, so that you will be put to no expense."

The nuns were delighted, overwhelmed him with their gratitude. In less than a week they had their fountain of blameless antecedents, and Robert de Montesquiou had the coveted bath of the Pompadour.

CHAPTER XV
REVOLUTION AT SHERRY'S

꧁

W E SPENT OUR WINTERS IN NEW YORK, HEARD THE
Christmas Mass at Saint Patrick's Cathedral, saw the New
Year in at the Plaza Hotel, because it was the accepted
thing to do, and as Harry said, "It is a good omen to begin the New Year well." He was surprisingly supersti-
tious, I discovered. "Friday and a New Year's Day! Could
there be a worse combination? I am sure that this will
be an unlucky year," he wrote in his diary. . . . "We
sat down thirteen to dinner last night, and never noticed
it until it was too late. What is worse, they say that at
Christmas, New Year and Easter this is specially unlucky.
I do wonder who it will be! . . ." Such an omen of evil
would make him miserable for days.

The old-fashioned family Christmas was already fading
into the past, the solemn New Year's Day ceremonial,
when my mother and every other hostess in New York
had sat in state in their drawing-rooms from ten in the
morning until late in the afternoon to receive the calls
of every bachelor whom they had entertained during the
previous year, had gone for ever. A new age was dawning,
an age of mammoth glittering hotels, restaurant parties,
rag-time tunes.

Mamie Fish and Frances Burke-Roche determined to be in the van of modernity, decided to inaugurate new customs. They had seen London society women dining in fashionable restaurants in low-cut evening dresses. New York must come into line! "Absurd that the general public should be deprived of the sight of a pretty neck just because an obsolete convention decreed that nice women could only appear in evening dress in the shelter of their own and their friends' houses," said Fannie Burke-Roche, agreeably conscious perhaps of the fact that her décolleté was said to be the most beautiful in New York. . . . "We really must broaden people's minds, but we must begin gradually. Next Sunday evening at Sherry's we will go without hats. You wear your dress with the bretelles, Mamie, and I will wear mine with the Dutch neck."

But it was some time before they could find cavaliers courageous enough to escort them, for one after another their male acquaintances, when invited to participate in the experiment, hastily excused themselves. Men are conservative creatures, and even in the interests of progress they had no wish to dine in the most fashionable restaurant in New York, and on the most fashionable night in the week, in company with ladies whose express purpose in going there was to flout tradition.

Eventually two intrepid pioneers were induced to come to the rescue and the little party of four arrived at Sherry's one Sunday evening when dinner was at its height. Attendants took their wraps from them, hastily averted shocked eyes from the shameful expanse of bare throats. The experiment had begun.

The restaurant was crowded and as they made their way to their table in the centre heads were turned in all directions to gaze at them. If they had come in naked they could hardly have caused more of a sensation! Incredulity, horrified condemnation, outraged virtue registered themselves in varying degrees on every face. There were audible comments of "bold," "shameless," "disgusting." Waiters drew back uncertain, musicians craned forward to see what was happening, even the very room with its walnut-panelled walls, its emerald green velvet hangings, scene of so many stately festivities, seemed a silent reproach to such a lapse from dignity.

Louis Sherry turned pale with indignation, but he retained his poise. Hurrying forward to remonstrate with the offenders, he faltered in his stride when he saw who they were. In silence he conducted them to their seats, summoned the head waiter. Only from two such celebrated leaders of society could he have tolerated so scandalous an infringement of the rules of etiquette. But his disapproval was evident.

The pioneers ate their dinner trying to appear unaware that the entire evening's interest centred round their table. They had gained their point, demonstrated that is was possible to dine in New York as one dined in London without loss of caste. The experiment had been a success.

On the next Sunday evening several white throats made their appearance, naked and unashamed.

Poor Mr. Sherry! His restaurant was always selected as the theatre for innovations. A year or two after the victory of the décolleté necks, Edith Gould, desiring further to modernise New York, gave him a terrible shock one day at luncheon when she took out the new vanity-case she had brought back from Paris and in full view of the whole room deliberately powdered her nose and rouged her lips! Trained diplomat as he was this was almost too much for Mr. Sherry's self-control! Hurrying forward to her table he asked her solicitiously whether she felt ill. Could he not assist her to the ladies' toilet room? When she assured his that she was in perfect health he could only retire crestfallen, probably to lament in secret the passing of once-sacred traditions.

But when Mrs. Frederick Havemeyer boldly lighted a cigarette at the table one Sunday evening and proceeded to smoke it in a leisurely fashion, she exceeded the bounds of his tolerance, for she was told politely but firmly that she must either extinguish it or leave the restaurant.

Those Sunday dinners at Sherry's! "Representative," as Harry Lehr always called them, and as indeed they were. They stood for the embodiment of wealth, luxury, refinement. They belonged to a spacious, leisurely age, unsophisticated in its pleasures for all its resources; an age that had no place in its vocabulary for boot-leggers and speak-easies, nor coined the phrase "sex-appeal."

Every table would be taken. People whose names stood at the very summit of the social peak, ambitious climbers who wanted to boast of having dined at the next table to them, distinguished foreigners visiting New York, the cream of fashionable Bohemia.

To the last category belonged Stanford White, the famous architect. Outrageously badly dressed, his untidy shock of red hair looking as though it had not had a comb passed through it for a week, he was not in the least embarrassed as he sat surrounded by some of the most elegant women in New York. A genius and an artist to his finger-tips he was quite indifferent to his appearance. Once he arrived very late for dinner at Mrs. Oelrichs' house and slipped into his seat when everyone else was half-way through dinner. . . . "It never takes me more than five minutes to dress," he remarked. "So I should imagine," said Mrs. Oelrichs rather coldly. . . . "But then just look at your idea of dressing!" He had merely flung on a dinner jacket over his ordinary morning trousers, and had not even taken the trouble to change his shirt.

.   .   .   .

One of the most romantic personalities of those Sunday night dinners at Sherry's would be Captain de la Marc, on the rare occasions when he dined there, for he rather shunned society. Half the fashionable marriageable women in New York cast wistful eyes in the direction of his table. But their efforts were in vain, for he had been a divorcé many years, and he continued to remain one. Tall, fresh-complexioned, stalwart, with vivid blue eyes, he always looked more like a sailor than a business man. When I met him he had made an enormous fortune as a ship-owner, had a beautiful house at the corner of Madison Avenue and Forty-first Street.

. . . .

The Duke of Manchester would sometimes dine at Sherry's with Harry Lehr and me. At that time "Kim," as everyone called him, was immensely popular in New York. No one had ever seen so democratically-minded an English duke—he upset all our preconceived ideas. One had only to walk into Childs Eating House to see him disposing of huge portions of corned-beef hash and doughnuts, sitting side by side with clerks and salesmen from the big stores, generally chatting amiably with them.

He was always hard up—and never cared who knew it. Harry once travelled on the same train to New York with him. "Kim" was broke—of course, but he took it as a good joke. He roared with laughter as he told Harry that he had no ticket—and no money to buy one. What would they do with him? . . . "I've always heard that American prisons are marvellously comfortable, now perhaps I'll get the chance of finding out for myself. . . ." Naturally Harry suggested that he should get the ticket for him, but Kim waved his offer aside . . . "No, no, no. I know a much better way out of the difficulty than that. . . ." He stood up in the car, divested himself of his overcoat and shouted at the top of his voice, "Who wants to buy a fine overcoat in excellent condition—made by the best English tailor—latest fashion, scarcely worn . . ."

Most of the passengers, several of whom knew him, laughed at what they supposed to be a joke. One or two men left their seats and walking over to him fingered the coat dubiously. . . . "Now then, here you are—look at it for yourselves—lovely material, really going very cheap . . ."

"I suppose the coat really is yours, no catch in this deal?" one man asked suspiciously.

"None at all, my dear sir, none at all—my own property, bought and paid for—well, perhaps not exactly paid for yet, but will be paid for—by myself. Now then"—to a travelling salesman who seemed the most interested—"my dear fellow, you really ought to take advantage of this opportunity, this handsome coat is just your style—slip it on and see how well you'll look in it."

The man was unable to resist such blandishments and finally returned to his seat wearing the coat! I do not know how much he paid for it, but it was certainly enough to enable "Kim" to purchase his ticket with an air of magnificent assurance.

CHAPTER XVI
THE KAISER AT HIS COURT

BACK IN EUROPE AGAIN IN THE FALL OF 1906, HARRY
Lehr and I were to be presented to the Kaiser and Kaiserin in January; we stopped in Paris while I bought
clothes.

We had good reason to remember our reception at the
German Court for it was the occasion of a violent campaign against us in the Berlin press. One of the principal
newspapers printed the following:

"AMERICAN MILLIONAIRES IN BERLIN

CONTRETEMPS AT A COURT BALL

The Kaiser's sympathies for America and Americans find
a ready response on the other side of the Atlantic. In the
leading circles of the Four Hundred it is considered ultra-
chic to be presented at the Berlin Court, which now has a
greater attraction for the millionaires of the New World
than the Court of King Edward. More and more 'Dollar-
Princesses' fly to Berlin, after having previously purchased
their dresses and jewelry in the Rue de la Paix in Paris.
Unexpected horizons loom before the marriageable youths
of our higher class nobility, who can now enter into successful competition with the nobility of France and England.

Court circles are interested in the presence in Berlin of a

certain Mr. Harry Lehr of New York. This interest is aroused
not so much on account of his highly satisfactory riches—he
must have a couple of solid millions—as on account of his
less satisfactory past. Mr. Lehr did not find his millions in
his cradle. Over in America he was an ordinary traveller in
champagne—but looked a picture. He found favour in the
eyes of Mrs. Astor and she introduced him into the circle of
the Four Hundred. His début was extremely lucky for despite his humble origin—and probably on account of the
nobility of his good looks—he obtained the hand and the
weighty millions of Miss Drexel and immediately afterwards
made himself talked about in New York society through his
eccentric behaviour. He gave a dinner where everyone was
supposed to appear in night-attire and showed his philo-
sophical outlook on life by giving a supper which, in addition to the ladies and gentlemen he had invited, united a
number of pigs and ponies around the festive board. His
other habits make him appear as the perfect exponent of
the 'Gentleman-Cowboy' type—the latest achievement of
American culture.

Mr. Lehr followed the trail of his compatriots to the East
and eventually arrived in Berlin accompanied by his wife.
Through the influence of the American Ambassador he managed to obtain an entry into Court circles. His début took
the form of appearing before the Grand Mistress of the Court
in a check grey suit, coloured shirt, brown boots and a bowler
hat, for he has the idea that, like the Prince of Wales, he is
perfectly capable of starting a new fashion. He wore the same
attire at a big reception given by Mr. Tower, the American
Ambassador.

His attitude at the Court Ball caused a certain amount of
half-amused annoyance. He decided that this was a suitable
occasion to introduce another new fashion and appeared in

baggy breeches, terminating a good four inches above the ankle, white silk stockings and patent leather shoes with diamond buckles.

When the time came for the ladies' défilé his wife, not having yet been presented at Court, had to take her place behind the other ladies of the Embassy. This seems to have provoked the anger of Mr. Lehr who appears to be filled with a sense of his own importance. Evidently under the impression that he was directing a free fight with whisky bottles in a New York bar, he became rowdy and announced that the combined price of all the trash worn by all the other ladies in the room would not pay for his wife's jewels and that he could not allow her to stand so far behind. In order to avoid a worse scandal he was given in to and his wife moved forward.

This is anyway the story as it circulates in American circles in Berlin, who appear to be well informed regarding the adventures of their remarkable countryman. At any rate he can now boast in New York that thanks to his American 'spunk' he was able to upset the precedence at a Berlin Court Ball. . . ."

There was not a word of truth in the whole ridiculous story, but it nearly ruined our visit to Germany. The article was reproduced in the New York papers with indignant comments. Harry was accused of lowering American social prestige by "clowning at foreign courts." Ambassador Charlemagne Tower, who was responsible for our presentation, was questioned. But although he did his utmost to trace the origin of the article he was unable to get any satisfaction whatever, even during a personal interview with the editor of the newspaper in which it had appeared. All he was able to learn was that it had been obtained from some outside source. The writer's name was not available.

Wherever we went during our tour of Germany we heard the echoes of that wretched article. When we wanted to be presented to King August IV of Saxony, St. John Gaffney, then American Consul General in Dresden, refused at first to make the presentation. It was only after Charlemagne Tower had personally written to him emphatically denying the story of Harry's supposedly outrageous conduct at the Court of Berlin that he agreed to present us.

.   .   .   .

Harry and I, Mrs. Cornelius Vanderbilt, Senior, and Alice Drexel (Mrs. John Drexel) all spent the autumn in Paris together, choosing our gowns for the Schleppen Court. A whole set of instructions was sent us from Berlin, and we were solemnly warned that if our costumes failed to comply with them to the letter we should not be admitted to the Palace—for the Kaiser, always a rigid disciplinarian in all matters of Court etiquette, would not tolerate the infringement of any sartorial traditions. Our dresses must be cut right off the shoulders; no straps or trimmings must break the line of the décolleté. Trains must be so many feet wide, and so many feet long, neither an inch more nor less, and they must be attached at the waist and not at the shoulders, the latter being a privilege reserved for princesses of the blood. Above all they must not be allowed to trail on the floor, as this again was a royal prerogative, accorded only to the members of the Imperial Family. Fortunately Worth came to our aid and undertook to design gowns that would fulfill all the requirements of the Court Chamberlain. Alice Drexel was quite excited over it all. For weeks she could talk of nothing else but her forthcoming presentation. She cultivated the acquaintance of Germans who "might be useful" as she explained, although in what capacity it was uncertain. At a reception at the American Embassy a tall good-looking young man was introduced to us as Prince Henry of Reuss. She was delighted; here was an opportunity to get first-hand information about the Court! She began by telling him about her presentation dress, and after he had been duly impressed with its magnificence said that she hoped to meet him at the Schleppen Court. He looked rather surprised. . . . "I shall certainly be in Berlin at that time," he replied, "but I never attend those courts." Alice was visibly disappointed at such an admission and began bombarding him with questions. A few days later she came to me . . . "That young German is going to be no use at all. I can always tell class when I see it. Believe me, he is just an upstart; I very much doubt whether he is a Prince at all."

I said he seemed nice. He had called on us and left us some beautiful flowers. Alice looked more disapproving than ever . . . "Yes, probably because he is an adventurer and has heard that we are rich Americans. I have found out all about him. He says he is here in Paris to study the language, and, I ask you, would a real Prince come over like that and stay at that cheap hotel where he is? Besides he admitted to me himself that he doesn't go to Court. No, Bessie, we must be careful. It will never do for us to get into the wrong set. If we make any mistakes in Berlin it might spoil everything. I mean to snub that young man next time he calls."

She snubbed him to such good purpose that she saw nothing more of him during the remainder of our stay in Paris. But when we arrived in Berlin and installed ourselves at the Grand Hotel he came to call on me. "I hope to have the pleasure of seeing a great deal of you and your husband, while you are here, Mrs. Lehr," he said in his usual pleasant manner. . . . "There are a great many things in Berlin I should like to show you. . . ." Alice pursed her lips when I told her of the visit . . . "I can't think why you waste your time on somebody like that. I tell you he has no social position, or he would go to Court."

The Schleppen Court at which we were presented was held in mid-January and I remember very vividly driving through the bitter cold of the streets to the Palace in the cortège of the Embassy and walking through an endless succession of corridors to take our places in the long file of women outside the Throne Room. Every few minutes while we waited the massive doors would swing silently open, giving us a glimpse of the room with its silver balcony and of the Kaiser and Kaiserin standing before their chairs of state surrounded by the members of the Imperial Family. Alice Drexel and I took up our positions behind Mrs. Tower (the doyenne of the Diplomatic Corps as the British Ambassador was a widower) and the whole line advanced slowly, each lady holding up the train of the one in front of her. At the door of the Throne Room our names were announced by one court official, while another with a long white wand adroitly flicked our trains into position so that they might trail gracefully behind us as each of us in turn crossed the room to curtsey to the Kaiser and Kaiserin. Immediately we withdrew they were caught up again by still another official and carefully arranged over our arms, where they were expected to remain for the rest of the evening. Alice Drexel, who had chosen a train of silver and blue brocade bordered with solid silver roses, was enduring agonies from its weight before very long and several times she let it trail in defiance of the regulations, thereby incurring the displeasure of the Chamberlain, who happened to notice the breach of etiquette and immediately sent over an equerry to draw her attention to it.

The rest of the evening passed uneventfully in an atmosphere of cold and formal splendour. We partook of an elaborate supper served in the Weisse Saal and then returned home. I felt vaguely disappointed as I got into bed. It had all been so dull, so different from what I had expected.

But I was yet to discover how delightful a side the Court life of Berlin could present on other occasions.

A few days later we received invitations to the Court Ball, a most coveted honour, generally reserved only to members of the great German families and to the Diplomatic Corps.

I shall never forget the brilliant spectacle of the crowd which awaited the entrance of the Kaiser and Kaiserin in the Weisse Saal. On one side of the room stood all the men, the foreign guests grouped behind their respective Ambassadors. On the other side of the Throne were the women. The wonderful jewels, the orders and decorations, the gold braiding on the uniforms scintillated in the blaze of the enormous candelabra. After a few moments of waiting the doors were thrown open and first the Kaiser and then the Kaiserin came in attended by their suites.

Immediately behind the Kaiser walked a little group, the Crown Prince, his brothers, one or two other princes. Alice Drexel, standing just beside me, nudged me violently and gave a gasp. My eyes followed hers. Right in the centre of the group, wearing a picturesque blue uniform, was her despised acquaintance Prince Henry of Reuss! "How could I possibly guess?" she lamented afterwards to one of our attachés. . . . "He told me he never went to the Schleppen Court!" The attaché laughed. . . . "That is because he is one of the mediatised princes, who are treated as brother sovereigns, and exempt from attendance at Court."

The Kaiser and Kaiserin made a circuit of the r   talking to many of the guests. When they arrived   he group of American men headed by Ambassador   er

the Kaiser insisted that Harry Lehr should come forward
to shake hands with him.

"I am curious to meet you, Mr. Lehr," he said, "because I am told that you are the man who makes America
laugh. I think we need someone like you in Europe. . . ."

During the dancing, which began immediately, the
royal party was seated. I talked to a young attaché of the
British Embassy who has since become a famous diplomat.
At that time however he was not characterised by his
diplomacy, for he was covered with confusion over a
faux pas which he had just made. He told me that a few
days before the ball he had been invited to tea at his Embassy and had sat next to a friendly and smiling little
Oriental who, he understood, was one of the secretaries at
the Japanese Embassy. After a variety of small talk they
began to discuss some forthcoming official celebrations
at which all the Embassies were to be represented. The
little Jap asked whether places had been allotted yet.
. . . "Oh, we shall not get any places given us!" replied
the Englishman. . . . "You must be very green if you expect anything like that. It's only the big bugs who have
them. Little fellows like you and me will be lucky if we
get a lamp-post to hang onto to watch the procession pass!
. . ." This levity appeared to annoy the Jap, who drew
himself up, haughtily muttered something unintelligible
and withdrew to the other side of the room. "Of course I
guessed I had put my foot in it. I ought to have remembered you can't joke with Orientals," concluded my
friend. . . . "But I wasn't prepared to make the discov-

ery I have just made tonight. It was the Japanese Ambassador I was talking to! All those damned Japs look so alike!"

After we had watched the lovely figures of the State Quadrilles, directed from the balcony by the Mistress of the Dance, we all went to supper in the various rooms assigned to us. I found my place in the Braunschweig Kammer and my supper partner Count Von Seckendorff, who was credited in the gossip of the Court with having been secretly married to the Empress Frederick. He was a handsome, elderly man, with a graceful figure and great charm of manner. To my relief I discovered that he spoke perfect English.

"Your husband is quite the most distinguished man at the ball," he told me. "Why?" I asked in some surprise. . . . "Dear lady, because of the originality of his costume. . . ." This was quite true, for there was no precedent for Americans visiting foreign courts, and Harry, on the advice of our Ambassador, was wearing the customary English court dress, such as is worn at Buckingham Palace, knee breeches, silk stockings and buckled shoes, while the other men were in long trousers. "And I am certain he has the finest pair of legs in the room," added Count Von Seckendorff. . . .

When we arrived at the ball I scarcely recognised Ambassador Charlemagne Tower in his magnificent Court dress of dark blue trousers and gold-embroidered coat; as he was a tall, handsome man I thought how well it became him. Incidentally he was the first Ambassador to break the tradition of Jeffersonian simplicity; and from Mrs. Tower I heard the explanation.

During his previous term of office in St. Petersburg he had been invited to attend the christening ceremonies of one of the Czar's children, and had arrived late at the Palace long after the other guests had been admitted. He had only recently been appointed to the Embassy and consequently none of the officials on duty recognized him. They exchanged incredulous glances when he announced himself the American Ambassador. He had been driven to the door in the very plainest of equipages, he wore no court dress, not even a solitary decoration. Coming as he did on the heels of a glittering procession of the representatives of every country in Europe in glorious array, it was hardly surprising that they regarded him with distrust. Politely, but firmly, they asked him to produce his credentials. He had none—not even a letter, and their instructions to admit no unauthorised persons to the ceremonies had been most explicit. The result was that the representative of the American nation had the humiliation of having the door shut in his face.

Naturally the matter could not be left at that. There were frantic despatches to Washington, contrite apologies from the Russian Ambassador there. But even after the storm had blown over Charlemagne Tower refused to be pacified until measures had been taken to ensure that such a situation could never arise again. All other nations, he pointed out, provided their representatives with suitable court dress. Why should the American Ambassador alone cut such a sorry figure before the rest of the world? After much discussion he was allowed to adopt a dress of his own choice. He designed its garlands of wheat himself; determined with the aid of his tailor the precise length of the trousers which were to raise the prestige of American diplomacy, and thereafterwards never appeared at any Court wherever he was appointed without it.

. . . .

In striking contrast to the splendour of the Kaiser's Court was the old-world atmosphere of the Palace of King August IV of Saxony to whom we were presented on our visit to Dresden. To me it was by far the most memorable part of our tour in Germany. The ancient Hoff, with its time-honoured traditions, its Court customs unchanged since the seventeenth century, seemed to breathe the very spirit of romance. The car that took us up to the massive doors seemed out of place; the Mistress of the Robes, who was being carried across the courtyard from her own apartments in a sedan chair, had chosen a mode of conveyance far more in keeping with the surroundings. The ceremony of presentation to the King was traditional, like everything else at the Hoff.

We walked down a succession of corridors between lines of soldiers in the picturesque uniforms of bygone centuries to the State Room where three tables were laid out for cards. At the centre table facing us sat the King, wearing a gorgeous uniform, a player on each side of him, and a fourth with his back to the room seated on a low stool so that His Majesty might have an uninterrupted view of all who passed before him. Behind each player stood an official who indicated the cards to be played.

Carrying our trains over our arms, we passed slowly in single file before the three tables, bowing to the occupants of each, while at the centre table we dropped a deep curtsey to the King.

After the ceremony His Majesty rose from the card table, and opened the ball, dancing with the Mistress of the Robes, while the courtiers in their elaborate dress chose their partners and followed his example.

The dancing was less formal than at the Kaiser's Court, for the King and his brother Prince Johann Georg danced with whom they would. The royal partners were summoned by the Master of the Ceremonies who presented himself before each lady in turn, tapping impressively on the ground with his long gold wand to inform her that His Majesty requested her to dance.

Unfortunately the King was by no means an expert dancer, and before the end of the evening his spurs were adorned with wisps of silk and tulle in every colour ripped from the skirts of his partners. Incidentally my own dress was so badly torn that I was obliged to retire to have it mended, but it was a very small penalty to pay for so delightful an evening.

The King was exceedingly gracious both to me and to Harry Lehr and seemed most interested in America. He was very anxious that we should enjoy our stay in Dresden and asked us whether we had seen the various places

of interest in the city. We found that we had been hon-
oured by being allotted places at supper in the first of
the many supper-rooms. In conformance with tradition
the guests were graded according to Court rank and importance. The menu was proportionately graded from
venison shot by the King, and chocolate pudding made
from a receipt given by Louis XV to Augustus the
Strong, which were eaten at the King's table, to humble
dishes at an enormous buffet in one of the ante-rooms.

The room in which we had supper might have been
taken from a seventeenth-century picture. The gold ves-
sels, which were arranged on one side of it on shelves in
tiers right to the ceiling and lighted by concealed lamps,
shed a beautiful soft glow on the scene.

During our stay in Dresden we were invited to a ball
given in honour of the King at the house of the Court
Chamberlain. Unfortunately, splendid as the ballroom
was, it had one drawback, for there was only one door,
and as it happened the King and his brother Prince Johann Georg chose to stand just inside it to hold a long
conversation. The space which was not filled by themselves was taken up by their voluminous coats and long
swords with the result that no one could either get into
the ballroom to dance or out of it to have supper for at
least half-an-hour, and agitated little groups waited patiently on each side of the door until the Court Chamberlain thought of the happy expedient of engaging the King
in conversation in his turn, and gradually edging him
farther into the room.

Later in the evening the King saw Harry Lehr and immediately bore down upon him. He had a habit of shooting out questions and scarcely waiting for the replies. He shot out one now:

"Oh, Mr. Lehr, have you seen my pottery at Meissen?" Harry replied that he had . . . and that he had thought it very fine. . . .

"Well, I hope you bought a lot of china?"

As a matter of fact we had not bought very much, just a few souvenirs of our visit. But the King's question had seemed so personal that we felt it obligatory to return the next day and come away laden.

As we drove home Harry remarked, apparently à propos of nothing, "I'm sure there are just as good salesmen out of America as in it!"

CHAPTER XVII
"THE STATUE AND THE BUST"

~❦~

"And the sin I impute to each frustrate ghost is
the unlit lamp and the ungirt loin. . . ."

How OFTEN IN THE LONG YEARS OF MY MARRIAGE I
thought of Robert Browning's poem "The Statue and the
Bust"! His condemnation of the unhappy Florentine
lady who had always meant to leave the husband who was
cruel to her for the man she loved, and had waited day
after day until years passed and at length death solved the
problem, seemed so applicable to my own case. How
many times I too had played with the idea of escape from
the misery of my marriage, made up my mind to apply
for a divorce, only to be held back by the thought of my
mother, the agony it would cause her. She had grown so
frail with the passing of the years, she bore the sufferings
of her long illness so bravely that I always came away
from my visits to her at Pen Rhyn with my resolve
strengthened. Come what might I would cause her no
sorrow. She should keep her illusions even at the expense
of my own.

"You are not happy with Harry Lehr," Mrs. Oliver

Belmont said to me suddenly one day, fixing me with her gimlet eyes . . . "You ought to leave him. I'll help you. I don't believe in marriage anyway. . . ." It was obvious that I had gone down in her estimation when I declined. . . . She shrugged her shoulders . . .

"You are the old-fashioned woman, Bessie. I am the woman of the future."

She was immersed just then in the cause of the Women's Suffrage Movement. None of her friends were very much surprised. They remembered that Alva had always been a fighter, that she had always championed her own sex, taken the woman's part in any discussion. There was the episode of Mr. James B. Haggin's will.

He had arrived late at one of Mrs. Belmont's receptions . . . "Please forgive me, but my lawyer kept me. I have just been making my will."

"Oh, really? Well, I hope you are leaving a nice fortune to that sweet wife of yours," was the reply.

"No, why should I? She is no relative. She is only my second wife. As a matter of fact I have left her practically nothing. I am leaving all my money to my own relations, my children by my former marriage. They have the first claim. . . ."

"What!" cried Mrs. Belmont, the light of battle in her eyes. . . . "You mean to tell me that you are going to disinherit Pearl after she has been such a wonderful wife to you, and put up with all your moods and your bad temper for years. I have never heard of such a disgraceful thing! Now listen to me: I won't allow you to do such a dreadful injustice. You can't die with it on your conscience; why, you would not rest in your grave! Unless you change that will right away I'm going to tell everyone I know about it, and they will all take Pearl's part. You won't have a friend left. Now just think it over and send for your lawyer and have him make a new will. It is the only way you can show your wife that you have appreciated all the kindness and affection she has given you."

His resistance soon gave way under the force of this attack. He carried out her instructions to the letter. Not only did he make a new will, but the next day he sent her a beautiful basket of fruit and an enormous bunch of orchids—an act of lavish generosity almost unprecedented on his part. . . . Pinned to the flowers was a little note. . . . "Thank you for opening my eyes," it read.

.   .   .   .

There was great excitement when it was known that Mrs. Belmont was to lead the great Women's Vote Parade in person. For days beforehand the newspapers were full of "this epic in the history of Womanhood," as some one wrote hysterically in a woman's paper; women old and young, from small towns and country districts, flocked into New York to take part in it. The line of march was to be from Fifty-ninth Street to the Washington Arch. . . . "I've ordered a white pleated walking-skirt and strong shoes," said Mrs. Belmont.

"My dear Alva, you'll never be able to do it," Mamie Fish remonstrated. . . . "It must be all of three miles and you have scarcely walked a step in your life. . . ."

"All the more reason why I should begin now. After all, my dear, I must have something to interest me in my old age. . . . I shall walk the whole way. . . ."

And she did too. She looked as serene and unself-conscious as though she had been in her own drawing-room when she stepped out proudly at the head of a long procession headed by brass bands and flanked by mounted police. Behind her walked serried ranks of women of all classes, of all ages, earnest and purposeful. Their banners floated above them. . . . A contingent of college women carried the legend, "Since we can be educated like men, why cannot we have a voice in the Government of our Land?" They were followed by the "Mothers' Brigade. . . ." "The Hand that Rocks the Cradle Rules the World. . . ." "We prepare the people for the Nation, we want to prepare the Nation for the people. . . ."

Delegates from the already feminine-enfranchised States, women workers of all types, grey-haired grandmothers, girls still in their teens. Thousands and thousands of them. Soon the head of the procession was out of sight.

Harry Lehr and I stood watching it from the new Hotel St. Regis, Jack Astor's pride. . . .

"The dear old Warrior has got something to fight for at last," said Harry.

Newport was distinctly annoyed when Mrs. Belmont announced her intention of violating its sanctity by lending "Marble House" for a great Women's Vote Meeting. This was really carrying enthusiasm too far! By all means walk in processions, or demonstrate your sympathies in any way that appealed to you, but why let loose a horde of fanatics on the stronghold of your friends, said everyone. The rumours of discontent reached Mrs. Belmont's ears, but she paid no attention to them, and the preparations went forward. An enormous tent was erected in the grounds, a platform was built for the speakers. Mrs. Belmont swooped upon her son Harold Vanderbilt . . . "You must help me. I want you to come on the platform and introduce the speakers." Dutiful son though he was he resisted violently. Nothing would induce him to identify himself with this new departure of his mother's mental activity.

The great day arrived. Governor Pothier of Rhode Island was enlisted to address the delegates. . . . "How on earth shall I begin my speech?" he asked Mrs. Belmont doubtfully. . . .

"Only one way of course, 'Voters and Future Voters.' . . ." She prepared him a speech full of warlike challenge. But at the last moment his courage deserted him. He wavered. . . . "Ladies and Gentlemen," he began, and filled ten minutes with mild and pleasant platitudes.

He was followed on the platform by an English militant suffragette. . . . "They say in London that I've the brains of a man. . . ." She began tapping her untidily dressed head impressively . . . "Well, I should like to see the man whose brains I have. . . ."

Poor Azar's consternation was boundless as hundreds

of women from New York, Boston, Chicago—every part of the country, swarmed into the house that had earned the reputation of being one of the most exclusive in Newport, and wandered in the garden in groups of three and four. Women in shirtwaists, their jackets hanging over their arms, women carrying umbrellas and paper bags. Man-hating college women with screwed-back hair and thin-lipped, determined faces; old country-women red-cheeked and homely, giggling shop-girls. Azar had never seen such guests. What a contrast to the elegant garden parties of former years, the splendid entertainments that had been his greatest pride. It was too much for him!

Only when the last guests had departed was it discovered that Mrs. Belmont's banner, bearing the device of the Women's Suffrage movement—four white stars on a blue ground—had disappeared. It was said that an enemy of the cause had stolen it.

A week or two afterwards we were all dining at the Elisha Dyers' when "Mrs. Carrie Chapman Catt" was announced and Mrs. Dyer turned in surprise at the entrance of a guest whose name was completely unknown to her.

Into the room walked a lady of noble proportions, majestically draped in blue with a flowing court train whose four white stars on a blue ground seemed vaguely familiar. Mrs. Belmont's eyes fell on it. She gave a cry of astonishment . . .

"Why, it's Harry Lehr! And *you* were the culprit who
stole my banner!"

.   .   .   .

Newport again! Another season; the same background
of dinners and balls, the same splendours. The same set,
the same faces, here and there a few lines on them carefully powdered out—no one could afford to get old, to
slip out of things. New jewels, new dresses, new quarrels,
new ambitions. Harry Lehr striving to surpass himself.
All the old forms of entertainment had been exhausted,
grown stale through repetition. Why not give something
quite different?

So we sent out invitations to a "Dogs' Dinner." All
our friends' dogs were asked (accompanied by their owners of course). There must have been at least a hundred
of them, big dogs and little dogs, dogs of every known
breed; many of them came in fancy dress.

The dinner was served on the verandah, leaves from
an ordinary dining-table placed on trestles about a foot
high. The menu was stewed liver and rice, fricassée of
bones and shredded dog biscuit. It must have been appreciated, for the guests ate until they could eat no more.
Elisha Dyer's dachshund so overtaxed its capacities that
it fell unconscious by its plate and had to be carried
home.

Under the trees a young man waited, holding a little
dog tied to a string, a paper ruffle round its neck. Harry
Lehr not recognising him as one of the guests went to
question him, ascertained that he was a newspaper re-

porter and had him put out of the garden. The result was that scathing columns appeared in the newspapers next day. We were said to have fed our canine guests on wings of chicken and paté de foie gras . . . and this in a time of trade depression. Harry Lehr was denounced by preachers throughout the States for having "wasted on dogs, food that would have fed hundreds of starving people."

After that everyone wanted to give a party whose keynote was originality, not extravagance. Henry Clews, Junior, gave "The Servants' Ball." Some days before it he issued invitations on which was printed, "No one admitted unless wearing servant's dress," with the result that the local stores were ransacked for the correct apparel of ladies' maids, valets, cooks, chauffeurs and footmen.

When the evening of the party arrived no one had the courage to face their servants dressed in what appeared to be clothes purloined from their own wardrobes, with the result that Freebody Park was thronged with maids and menservants who had been given an unexpected evening off so that they should not witness their master's and mistress's departure for the ball.

I donned the black dress and white apron of a ladies' maid; Harry Lehr was a pompous butler.

The door of "The Rocks" was opened by Henry Clews attired as a valet and holding a duster in one hand and a kitchen pail in the other. Behind him was Mrs. Oelrichs with a large mop, industriously polishing the floor.

Oliver Belmont, a little feather dusting brush stuck into his cap, was acting as cloak-room attendant, taking charge of coats. The funniest part of the evening was the dinner, cooked by the guests. Everybody made his own specialty, and the result was a weird assortment of dishes. Mrs. Fish made scrambled eggs, Mrs. Pembroke Jones a salad, Elisha Dyer cooked lobster à l'Américaine, Mr. Van Alen, spaghetti. Those who could not contribute to the menu spread tomatoes and sliced onion on toast and laid the table. Harry Lehr acted as butler and poured out the wine.

After that Nancy Leeds wanted to give a "simplicity party," and invited us all on her yacht, the "Noma," which immediately put out to sea. Our destination was Rocky Point, where the whole of the amusement park had been reserved for the afternoon at an enormous cost. After a sumptuous luncheon we spent the rest of the time on switch-backs, water-chutes and in the different sideshows, returning to Newport in time for dinner.

Mrs. Hermann Oelrichs was one of the hostesses who remained faithful to the stately traditions of Newport entertaining, for her beautiful villa, "Rosecliffe," lent itself to picturesque settings. Her lawn, with its white marble balustrade, looked right out over the sea, so she had a fleet of full-size skeleton ships of all types made, each brilliantly illuminated, anchored in front of the house to give the illusion of a harbour. In her magnificent ballroom she gave dinners for two hundred guests, transported the whole Russian ballet from New York to entertain them afterwards.

Paul Rainey, enchanted with the Russian dances, took several of the artists on his yacht for a cruise to amuse his guests. Every season he used to descend on Newport in a blaze of splendour. When his yacht was sighted in the distance, harbour-masters and their satellites used to rejoice, knowing that from no other, excepting perhaps that of Colonel Walters, Commodore of the New York Yacht Club, could such generous pickings be obtained. Wherever he went he took his orchestra of negro musicians, transferred them from his palatial house to his equally palatial yacht to play to him at any hour of the day or night. Once he arrived for a dinner party at Mrs. Fish's house . . . "I have brought my music with me. I hope you don't mind?"

"Of course I'm delighted, but I never knew you sang," said Mrs. Fish.

With a dignified gesture he indicated the eight grinning niggers who were staggering up the drive in his wake carrying their instruments. . . . "Those are the members of my orchestra. . . ."

Paul Rainey's generosity was so notorious that he was always much in demand at any charity fête. Remembering this, Mrs. Fish sent him an enthusiastic invitation to come to the bazaar and garden party in aid of St. Mary's Church, which was being held at the Reggie Vanderbilts' house, "Sandy-Point Farm." Mrs. Fish and I were in charge of the livestock stall, and spent the whole afternoon selling a succession of rabbits, cats, dogs, guinea-pigs, goldfish, doves and any other pets which had been donated by charitable members of St. Mary's congregation. Only half an hour before closing time and Paul Rainey had not appeared. . . . "Too bad of him," said Mrs. Fish. . . . "I've been saving this pair of foxes for him. I know he would have given me a good price. . . ." A well-known young American whom, for the purposes of this story, I will call Johnnie Jenks, who was standing near the stall, came forward. . . . "I'll take them off your hands if you like. . . ." After some bargaining he secured them for fifty dollars and departed carrying them in a basket. . . . "I wanted more for them, but I could not hope to get it so late," said Mrs. Fish with a sigh of resignation.

Ten minutes afterwards Paul Rainey's tall form was seen making its way towards us. . . . "So sorry I'm late, but I could not get here before. . . ." Mrs. Fish immediately swooped upon him . . . "I've got a lovely Persian cat for you. Have a look at him. . . ." He laughed . . . "No, thank you. No more livestock for me today. The foxes are quite enough, and by the way you did me out of a lot of money for them, but you and Mrs. Lehr have been so kind to me I felt I ought to do something for your pet charity. . . . All in a good cause, you know."

"The foxes! Where did you get them?" Mrs. Fish and I exclaimed in one breath. . . .

"Why, Johnnie Jenks has just sold them to me for a

thousand dollars. I understood he was helping you with your stall? That is why I bought them, though God knows what I am going to do with them."

Kathleen Vanderbilt and Mrs. Fish sped through the crowd without waiting for another word. They caught up Johnnie just leaving the bazaar and demanded that the thousand dollars should be handed over forthwith. There was a long and painful discussion. Johnnie Jenks insisted that as he had bought and paid for the foxes he was at perfect liberty to dispose of them as he wished. They, on the other hand, were equally certain that the money belonged to the charity, pointing out that Paul Rainey had only bought them because he knew Mrs. Fish to be in charge of the livestock stall. Eventually, after a long and acrimonious discussion, the ladies retired victorious, in possession of the thousand dollars (less the original fifty which Johnnie Jenks had paid) and Mrs. Fish proudly handed over to the committee the largest takings of any of the stalls!

But she spread the story of the foxes far and wide, much to Johnnie Jenks' discomfiture.

She and Harry Lehr were in the highest spirits that season. Their practical jokes were endless, they were like two children. They caught Mrs. Campbell's dachshund, floured it all over and turned it loose on the Casino terrace at the most crowded hour of the day to bespatter black lace dresses and satin petticoats in its efforts to wipe off its unfamiliar coating.

In Bellevue Avenue they discovered a public auction

in progress. They wandered into the sales rooms and seated themselves on a bench at the back, Mrs. Fish very elegant in a white lace dress and a shady hat which immediately distracted the attention of her neighbours. A fire-screen was put up for sale. . . . "Who will bid for this magnificent piece of furniture? . . . Genuine Chinese antique . . ." chanted the auctioneer. Hollow groans from Harry. . . . Mrs. Fish covered her eyes with her hands and turned away her head from the offending screen. Everyone looked round, one or two people tittered. The auctioneer fixed the newcomers with a stern glance and continued extolling the merits of the screen. Not a single bid . . . the screen was removed.

A china cabinet came next . . . the same procedure. Harry's groans grew louded and louder; Mrs. Fish seemed on the point of fainting. . . . The more the auctioneer praised his wares, the more they affected horror at the sight of them. After five or six lots had been carried away with no bidding, for the audience was far more engrossed in Harry's pantomime than in the sale, the auctioneer raised his hammer. . . . "The sale is suspended until the lady and gentleman at the back leave the hall," he announced. Harry and Mrs. Fish sat on smiling blandly, apparently unconscious that he had been referring to them until their neighbours urged them to go, threatened to remove them forcibly.

But they had their revenge. . . . They had no sooner got outside the door, which was wide open in the summer heat, than loud shrieks were heard from Mrs. Fish.

. . . "Oh, look, look . . . he can't get the horse to stop. He will be killed; there's going to be a frightful accident . . . oh . . . oh, how terrible!" The audience rushed in a body from the hall to behold the scene of horror, only to be greeted by peals of laughter as Harry and Mrs. Fish drove off. It was at least ten minutes before everyone realised that they had been hoaxed and the auction could be resumed again.

. . . .

Mamie Fish gave a party for the members of the New York Yacht Club which had put into Newport on its August cruise. She was very anxious to have something rather original, so she and I went to Narragansett Pier to hire the crystal-gazer there who had a great reputation. When the day of the party arrived he was attired in some marvellous flowing robes which Mamie had presented to him, and installed in a room which she had had specially decorated in Oriental style for the occasion. There was a lot of laughter as everyone compared notes on his predictions; all the guests wanted to consult him, even the sceptics. Only the young son of Senator Walsh was disappointed. . . . "The fellow would not tell me anything at all," he complained to Mamie. . . . "He stared into that crystal of his until I thought he had gone to sleep, then he said he could see nothing for me, and that it was no use going on trying. . . . I told him he was not much of a fortune-teller if that was all he could do. . . ."

At the end of the party Mrs. Fish and I went over to

the seer who was packing up his table and crystal with a most brisk and business like air. Mamie told him his performance had been a great success. . . . "Oh, by the way," she added, "you don't seem to be able to see the future for everyone. One of my guests told me you could tell him nothing. . . ." The man nodded. . . . "Was it a young gentleman about nineteen or twenty?" "Yes."

"Well, Madam, you would not have liked me to tell him what I did see. I saw no future for him, because there is none to see. His life is finished. He is going to die within the next few hours."

Mrs. Fish started in surprise. . . . "That young Walsh boy! Nonsense, it is impossible. Why, he is in perfect health. Do you mean he is going to die violently? . . ." The man nodded. . . .

"That young gentleman will die because it is his time to die. It is his destiny. I could not avert it. By this time tomorrow he will be dead. . . ."

Mamie laughed incredulously, but I was rather relieved the next day when we all went to lunch at the Clam Bake Club to see the Walsh boy at the table, looking the picture of health and high spirits. Mrs. Fish whispered, "It just shows that one should not pay any attention to the rubbish those fortune-tellers try to make you believe. . . . He said 'a few hours' and it's more than a few hours now, and the boy is perfectly well. . . ."

Alas! We rejoiced too soon. Evelyn Walsh and her brother were to drive home in their new sports car, taking a number of friends with them. We watched them all pack into the seats; their laughter came back to us on the wind as they started off.

An hour later a man drove up to the Club, white-faced and shaking . . . "There has been a frightful motor accident along the road. . . . Senator Walsh's son has been killed. . . ."

CHAPTER XVIII
LIVING IN FRANCE

I LOVED LIVING IN FRANCE. SO DID HARRY; IT WAS ALMOST the only thing we had in common. A few years before the War we decided to have a permanent pied-à-terre in Paris, and after a search lasting some weeks we found exactly the house we wanted in the rue de Lille, next door to the German Embassy. It was a beautiful old hotel dating from 1718, with a big shady garden sloping right down to the Seine. Into it we put the period furniture and objets d'art we had collected during our travels, my pictures, the grand piano at which Harry would sit playing for hours, sometimes far into the night. Listening to him as he drifted dreamily from Chopin to Liszt, from Liszt to Grieg, to Schubert, to Beethoven, completely absorbed in the music, unconscious even of my presence, I would wonder what quality it was in his playing that so stirred my heart. I have heard all the greatest pianists of the age, but not one of them has ever excelled that extraordinary finesse, that delicacy of touch which was his. Even after many years his music could still enthrall me. In those moments at the piano I forgave him many things. He knew it, learnt to take advantage of it. Whenever the situation was particularly

strained between us he would wander off to the piano
immediately after dinner, sure that I would remain to
listen. For an hour or more I would sit silent, enchanted.
Then he would swing round suddenly on the piano
stool . . . "Bessie, I want you to do something for me
. . . nothing of any importance, just a few bills . . ."
and the spell would be broken. But he had gained his
point.

I spent some very happy hours in the house in the rue
de Lille, for Harry and I had a great many friends on
both sides of the Atlantic and our social life was so much
wider than it had been in America. It was pleasant to
be rung up in the morning by some friends whom one
had believed to be thousands of miles away . . . "Oh,
is that you, Bessie? I've just arrived at Cherbourg. Can
you put me up for a day or two? . . ." And before night
one would be in touch with all the latest home gossip,
comparing notes on the newest fashions. Or a letter
would arrive, "Do let me know your plans for Ascot
week. Why not come over both of you? We would love
you to be our guests . . ." and a few hours later one
would be motoring through winding English country
lanes in the cool of the evening. There was always movement, always coming and going of guests, like the ripple
on a pond.

Paul Rainey, who had been spending several months
in England, came over to stop for a week-end with us before starting for South Africa to shoot big game. He was
full of his successes in London where he had become

tremendously popular. His parties were the talk of May-
fair, his yacht was one of the most envied at Cowes. He
had been invited to shoot in Scotland, to hunt in the
Shires, he had stayed at some of the most famous houses
in the British Isles. His satisfaction was so artless that
one could not resent it. There was something likeable
in his bluff sincerity, his Middle-West accent, his frankness. . . . "I don't understand folk that talk one way to
your face and another behind your back," he would
say. . . . "Way in Indiana when we say a thing we mean
it, and we don't care who hears us. . . ."

. . . .

One of our constant visitors was the Grand Duke
Alexander of Russia who came to us whenever he was in
Paris, which was often, for he longed for the gaiety of
the French capital and could never remain away from
it for long. He was the most human, the most natural and
the kindest of all the members of the Imperial Family.

Once when I was staying at the Ritz Hotel I was waiting to get into the lift (the only one the hotel boasted
in those early days of its career) when I was joined by
the Grand Duke Michael who was just as ungracious in
manner as the Grand Duke Alexander was charming. He
was evidently in a hurry, for after a few curt words of
greeting he was preparing to push past me into the lift
when the Grand Duke Alexander appeared on the scene.

"Where are your manners, Mich-Mich?" he exclaimed. "Have you forgotten that you are talking to a lady? Don't you intend to uncover your head?"

With that he seized the Grand Duke Michael's hat and hurled it as far away from him as he could; much to the horror of the group of hall porters and chasseurs who rushed forward in a body to pick it up and restore it to its owner.

.   .   .   .

We entertained the Grand Duke and Grand Duchess Vladimir of Russia whenever they came to Paris. The Grand Duchess, who only demanded of life that it should amuse her, soon came under the spell of Harry Lehr's personality, and delighted in his eccentricities. The most brilliant of all the women of the Imperial Family she was naturally charming and gay, with a flair for saying precisely the right thing at the right moment.

On their last visit to Paris Harry and I gave a big dinner for them at the Ritz, and at that dinner the Vernon Castles made their Paris début.

They had only recently been married when they came to see us, and explained that their European tour was combining work and a honeymoon. It was a courageous undertaking for they had scarcely any money, and were almost unknown when they arrived in Paris and set out to look for bookings. Harry Lehr wanted me to choose other dancers, artists who were already established favourites, but there was something in this young couple that appealed to me and for once I had my own way. . . . Perhaps it was their engaging frankness, perhaps the fact that they were so obviously in love, but whatever it was I wanted them to have their chance. From the first moment of their performance it was easy to predict that they would have a tremendous success. All our guests were enchanted with them, they recalled them again and again. Their art was a revelation. One felt instinctively that this was the dancing of the future. Paris had never seen anything like the rhythmic grace of Vernon Castle, the little sleek bobbed head of Irene, her freedom of movement in a day when the stereotyped classical ballet was considered the only interpretation of dancing. And so they danced to victory.

Years afterwards during the War Vernon Castle came to see me in his uniform of the Flying Corps. . . .

"I came to say good-bye to you because I have a feeling I shall not come back, and I want to thank you. You were our fairy godmother. You opened the door to the happiest years of my life. . . ."

. . . .

While the house in the rue de Lille was being redecorated for us we stopped at the Ritz, where we found others rendered temporarily homeless like ourselves. One of them was the British Ambassador, Sir Francis Bertie, who had at last succeeded in getting his Embassy decorated after his own taste. Immaculately dressed, distinguished-looking with an air of impenetrable reserve, he seemed a typical English diplomat of the old school. It was impossible to imagine him ever betraying any emotion, ever even looking perturbed. When one night fire broke out in a part of the hotel, and the guests were hastily aroused from their slumbers to congregate in the hall in various degrees of déshabillé, he was the only correctly dressed member of the group. He had even found time to put on a collar and tie. There was pained surprise in the glance which he turned on a young Englishman who arrived attired in a light blue wrapper and carrying a silk hat, succeeded by embarrassment as he beheld the apparition of the beautiful Countess Friedlander-Feld running downstairs, her chiffon nightgown billowing out behind her, clutching in one hand a gold purse, in the other two long gold plaits of hair which she had evidently snatched up from her dressing table.

Harry Lehr was one of the last to make his appearance, for he had run back to rouse Mrs. Leeds, who always slept heavily. Unable to get any response from her room he finally pushed one of her enormous cabin trunks, which was standing in the corridor, against the door and bore down upon it with his full weight, splintering it, and terrifying poor Lady Paget who was staying with Mrs. Leeds and who imagined that a burglar had broken into the suite. It was some minutes before she could be calmed and assisted downstairs and by that time all danger was over.

.   .   .   .

Mrs. Townsend Burden was one of the women staying at the Ritz, buying clothes for the Newport season, and she invited Harry and me to dine with her. We had no sooner taken our places at the table than she gave an exclamation of dismay and pointed to the inoffensive-looking occupant of a neighbouring table whose shining ebony skin almost matched his evening suit. She summoned Olivier. . . .

"Olivier, there's a nigger in this room. It is an insult to me and to every other American here. You have got to take him away or I leave this hotel and never come back to it again."

Olivier, whose tact would have raised him to unprecedented heights in the diplomatic service of any country, shook his head. . . . "I am afraid it is impossible to have the gentleman removed, Madam. He is the newly appointed Minister for ——."

"I don't care what Minister he is," replied Mrs. Burden. . . . "He's a nigger and you've got to get him out of my sight or I leave this room."

Olivier departed, but a minute later he approached the table of the offending diner followed by waiters bearing a large screen . . . "Excuse me sir, but I am afraid

you may feel the draught." The Minister was delighted
at such sympathetic consideration, and Mrs. Townsend
Burden finished her dinner secure in the knowledge that
"the nigger" was completely hidden from view.

•   •   •   •   •   •   •

One or other of the Burke-Roche twins always seemed
to be passing through Paris. They would drop in upon
us suddenly in the rue de Lille with all the latest news
from New York, London, the Riviera, wherever they
happened to have been. Once Frank arrived full of indignation against his brother, who had just let him in
for a most unpleasant encounter.

He told us that Maurice, who had been stopping in
Biarritz, had got engaged to a beautiful Spanish girl, the
daughter of the Duc d'Alcedo, with the entire approval
of both families. But the engagement was of short dura-
tion for almost immediately the fiancés quarrelled, and
Maurice left for Paris, from where he wrote to the Duc
saying that he considered himself unworthy of the hand
of his daughter and that he was returning to America.

The Duc was furious. Spanish tradition had been outraged. No family of the nobility could swallow such an
insult! He wrote to Maurice challenging him to a duel,
and adding that if he failed to meet him and give him
honourable satisfaction he would shoot him on sight.
Maurice's only reply was to leave for England imme-

diately, where he remained six months. During that time he grew a moustache. But he neglected to advise his twin brother of what had happened. Frank was amazed one morning when on crossing the Place Vendôme, he was pounced upon by an elderly Spaniard who was apparently thirsting for his life. As it was, he had the utmost difficulty in convincing the Duc d'Alcedo that he was not the American who had slighted his daughter, and it was not until he had dragged him into his bank, where the manager was able to vouch for his identity, that he was able to get rid of him.

.   .   .   .

Always on our visits to Paris we saw a good deal of Boni de Castellane and his wife, whom I had known since the days when she was Anna Gould, tiny, sallow-skinned, beautifully dressed. "Elle a les yeux d'un singe," said Robert de Montesquiou in describing her . . . "un singe qu'on a pris en captivité." Certainly I think her life with Boni was captivity to her; theirs was simply the tragedy of two people utterly unsuited to one another. Boni, elegant and charming, a poseur to the day of his death, could never understand Anna with her disconcerting directness of speech. It was inevitable that their marriage failed to survive the test of discovering one another's personalities.

Anna's real tragedy was her earlier love for Frank

Woodruff. To him she showed her true self. The love she gave him was all the greater because of the self-sacrifice it entailed. But old Jay Gould, ruling his children even from the grave, had left it in his will that if Anna married without the consent of her brother George she forfeited her share of the immense fortune he left. Anna pleaded to be allowed to marry the man she loved, but to no avail. George Gould wished for his sister a destiny other than that of an actor's wife, even though that actor might be the most famous in America. From the very beginning he refused his consent. Anna said she would marry without it, renounce riches for love. Then Frank Woodruff unselfishly stood aside. Anna had been brought up as the daughter of a rich man, he said. She would never be happy in the milieu in which she would live with him. He could not allow her to sacrifice herself for him. Their short engagement was broken off; Anna travelled in France, met Boni de Castellane . . . married him.

I remember very well the magnificent party which they gave at their house in honour of King Carlos of Portugal who was then in Paris. Boni had staged it superbly with an artistry worthy of him; never had their salons held a more distinguished gathering of royalties, statesmen, beautiful women, the noblest names in French society. Never had the music been more lovely, the menu, the table decorations more perfectly chosen. But it was the swan song of their life together. In less than a month Anna had left her husband for ever.

When I was in Paris I often went with Anna to the little chapel, "Notre Dame de la Miséricorde," she had built in the rue Jean Goujon on the site of the terrible fire which broke out at a charity fête and in which hundreds of lives were lost. The chapel was her thanksgiving for her own extraordinary escape. She was dressed and ready to leave the house for the fête where she was to have been a stallholder when the Duc de Luynes called to see her. His errand was not important, but as he was an old friend, the godfather of one of her children, she remained talking to him for ten minutes or so while her carriage waited at the door. That conversation saved her life. When she arrived at the scene of the fête she found the marquee a mass of flames, while firemen carried out one by one the charred bodies of the women who had been her friends.

.   .   .   .

We spent several winters at St. Moritz, where Harry would take skating lessons from the instructors at the rink and dazzle the spectators with the brilliance of his green and purple sweaters, the perfection of his sports clothes.

The Crown Prince of Germany, with his suite, always stopped at our hotel. Once he was chosen to captain a bobsleigh in the races, and picked his crew with great care. Among them was an American girl of solid proportions who was so elated by being chosen by the Crown Prince of Germany that she could talk of nothing else. She was boasting of her conquest one evening over cocktails in the lounge when the Crown Prince arrived on the scene, bowed casually to her and began to talk to a group of friends. Someone spoke of the trial run which was to take place the next day and asked particulars of the crew. What was the name of the American girl?

"How can I possibly remember their names?" replied the Crown Prince, quite oblivious of the fact that the girl was standing close to him. . . . "I don't choose her by name but by weight. Just the same way as you buy a sack of potatoes."

George Graham (now British Ambassador to Madrid) who was one of the members of the group turned to me. . . . "A perfect example of German gallantry," he murmured.

But after that we heard no more of the Crown Prince's choice of a bobsleigh crew!

George Lauder Carnegie, the nephew of Andrew Carnegie, was also stopping at the hotel with his wife. He had only recently recovered from a severe operation, and he told us an amusing story of how, while he was in the hospital, he had patched up his quarrel with his eccentric old uncle.

They had been the best of friends until George, shortly after his marriage, had decided to drop the name of Carnegie while he was travelling and describe himself and his wife as "Mr. and Mrs. George Lauder" on hotel reg-

isters. "I could not afford to live up to the 'Carnegie,' "
he explained, "I was not rich like my uncle, and the moment I arrived in any town there would be notices in the
papers about 'the multi-millionaire's nephew,' and I
would be deluged with begging letters."

The plan succeeded admirably until old Andrew Carnegie found out about it. He was furious. . . . "I have
made the name of Carnegie, and if you are ashamed of
it, then you are ashamed of your uncle. . . ." He refused to accept any excuses, and for some time they were
not on speaking terms.

But when George was taken to hospital very ill the old
man came to visit him, sat down by the bed, took his
hand affectionately. . . .

"Now, my dear boy, we are going to let the past be forgotten. I have brought you something that will do you
more good than any of the doctor's medicine! You must
have a little present to cheer you up. . . ."

"I had been lying there wondering how on earth the
hospital bill was going to be paid," said George, laughing
as he told us the story . . . "and my hopes rose as I saw
him fumbling in his pocket. I was just speculating how
big the cheque would be when he produced . . . an
apple! I am afraid I hardly listened to the lecture he gave
me on its health-giving properties!"

.   .   .   .

St. Moritz, with its keen mountain air, its scent of pine
forests, reminded me irresistibly of my father's house on

Mount McGregor where I had spent so much of my childhood. I had only to shut my eyes to conjure up a picture of the long sweep of the Saratoga Hills spread out before me.

General Grant spent his last days there at our house. My father was one of his staunchest friends and admirers, and refused to listen to the scandals which were spread about him during his term of Presidency. "The man's a soldier, not a politician," he would exclaim impatiently when the General was attacked in his presence, and remained unshaken in his loyalty.

When at length it became known through the newspapers that the man who had been Commander-in-Chief of the Union Forces during the Civil War was dying of cancer of the throat, my father was the first to answer the appeal. He immediately put his cottage on Mount McGregor at the disposal of the General, and within a few days the invalid was installed there with his doctors and nurses.

We were at Saratoga while General Grant was in possession of the cottage, and I often ran across to visit him. He was one of those people who have the art of gaining the friendship of children, perhaps because he was so simple and unassuming. He never talked of his triumphs either in the field or as President, but he would often tell me stories of his early days as an obscure store-keeper, or his childish escapades. He was the most generous-hearted man alive. I remember once hearing him tell my father of the surrender of General Robert E. Lee. "Of all the things in my life I hated the most it was accepting surrender from that man. It was awful having to humiliate so fine a soldier and so great a gentleman. I never admired him more than in that moment of defeat, and I made it as easy for him as I could. I turned out to meet him in my oldest uniform, wearing no sword or gloves, dressed anyhow. I knew that he would not expect me to look a gentleman, and I took care to live up to his expectations. He was such a splendid figure, so beautifully turned out in his spotless uniform. I knew how he must be suffering, and I wanted to make the whole ceremony as careless and informal as possible."

I saw my dear old friend for the last time just a few days before his death. He was sitting on the piazza in his big leather armchair gazing out far away into the horizon where the sun was sinking in a blaze of crimson and purple and gold behind the dark shadows of the hills. Even my childish eyes were impressed by the beauty of the twilight, and I grew silent. Suddenly the General stretched out a thin hand and pointed to the sunset. . . . "The Heavens declare the Glory of God and the firmament showeth His handiwork," he said, and his voice, which had been weak and broken in his illness, was loud and firm and young again. The sonorous music of the words remained in my memory for ever afterwards.

·   ·   ·   ·   ·   ·   ·

I was starting out for the skating rink one morning when a cable was put into my hand. I opened it. My mother had died very suddenly. Her last words had been a message of love for me.

After the first shock of grief had given place to that tender recollection with which we mourn those who are taken from us at the end of a long life, I began to readjust my own state of mind. The gates of my prison had been unlocked for me at last. I had safeguarded my mother's happiness to the end; she had never known the bitter truth; there was no longer anything to fear. I was free to throw off the shackles of a marriage that was no marriage in the true sense of the word. The need for self-sacrifice was over. I was still young enough to begin life again, to look to the future, not the past.

On my return to Paris I went to consult a lawyer—he was confident.

"Of course, Mrs. Lehr, you can get your divorce. You will not have the slightest difficulty. With the evidence I have here, there can be no possibility of your losing the case." Expressed polite wonder that I had waited for freedom so long.

On the way home I slipped into the church of St. Roch, knelt before the altar of the Blessed Virgin. She would, I felt sure, understand.

.   .   .   .

Almost unconsciously I found my thoughts turning to
X—— in those days. He had read of my mother's death in
the papers, sent me a letter full of tender sympathy. I
wondered whether he had guessed the truth; known why
I had sent him out of my life, for I could read between
the lines of his letter a message of hope. For the first time
in all those years he wrote of meeting me again, "I hope
to be in Europe in three months. Will you let me see
you?"

Ever since I had written "Good-bye" to him at Pen
Rhyn he had respected my wishes, had avoided me as I
had avoided him. There had been occasional letters, every
year flowers had been sent to me in his name on the an-
niversary of our meeting. But that was all.

My heart told me as I left my lawyer's office that I was
going to take up the threads again.

As I entered the house I heard the music of the piano.
Only one light in the salon; Harry was playing in semi-
darkness as he loved to play. He had been strangely subdued these days, quiet, unlike himself, almost humble.

He followed me up the stairs now. . . . "Bessie" . . .
he hesitated. All the arrogance had gone out of his voice.
It was almost pleading. . . . "I saw a lovely old diamond
and ruby cross in the rue St. Honoré this morning. I
thought it was just the sort of thing you would like and
I bought it for you." There was something childish in
the eager propitiating way in which he unwrapped it and
hung it round my neck, but I hardened my heart.

"I want to go away," I said. I could scarcely get out the words I had longed to say so often. . . .

"Yes, of course. We will go anywhere you like. Italy perhaps, the lakes are lovely just now; or the Tyrol. . . ." His eyes were on my face.

"You don't understand. I mean that I want to go away alone. . . ."

He turned very pale . . . his voice faltered.

"Bessie, you would not leave me? Not now after all these years. I know you have been miserable, I have not been fair to you. But I am not like other men. I told you long ago that I cannot love any woman. All women are repulsive to me, from a physical point of view. I have hated you, hated the scent of your hair, the sound of your voice, because you represent womanhood to me, and so I have tried to make you suffer. Don't you understand? Won't you understand?"

But I had endured too much in the past. I would not let my resolve weaken.

I left him and went into my room.

. . . .

A month went by. My lawyer rang me up.

"I have been going into your case, Mrs. Lehr. I think you had better let me begin the preliminary steps immediately. . . ."

"Very well." Tomorrow I would tell Harry.

I was still in bed the next morning when he came into my room . . .

"I have brought you the newspapers, Bessie. You will be interested to read . . ."

"Please leave them there for me," I broke in. The familiar mockery had come back to his eyes. I only knew that I could not read the news he had wanted to show me while he sat there to search my face.

I listened until his footsteps had gone downstairs before I took up the newspapers. A column on the front page was marked in blue pencil, "Death of Famous American . . ." The print swam before my eyes.

X—— would never come back to me. We had waited too long.

.   .   .   .

Later I rang up my lawyer . . . "I have changed my mind. I do not intend to apply for a divorce. . . ."

Of what use my freedom? Vain dream of beginning life again, now that I had no one I wanted to share it with! The man I loved was dead. What did the rest matter? I had drunk of the cup of sorrow so long. I would drain it to the end.

I went through the days numbed and apathetic, crept into dim churches to kneel in agonised prayer before altars blazing in the light of a hundred tapers, striving to find comfort in the sense of sanctuary, of remoteness from the outer world. But I sought it in vain.

CHAPTER XIX

THE WAR

THE WAR WOKE ME OUT OF THE APATHY INTO WHICH I had fallen after the death of X——. Impossible to remain selfishly wrapped in one's own grief when half Europe had been plunged into tragedy. America seemed far away now, the war zone very near.

Harry Lehr was taking the cure in Karlsbad during that fateful summer of 1914, and I was stopping in Venice with my son Jack. We joined the agitated little group of Americans who met at the summons of the Consul in the lounge of the Grand Hotel on August 5th.

Only a short week before the hours had seemed scarcely long enough for all the gaieties of the Venetian season, sunny mornings spent on the Lido beach, starlit nights given over to dancing in one or other of the beautiful old palazzos that offered a seemingly endless chain of hospitality. No one had realised the gathering storm until the first bolt fell.

We talked hopefully to reassure one another, but the faces of many of the women were haggard with suspense. Nearly all of them were waiting for news of friends and relatives travelling in one or other of the countries hurled so suddenly into war; some had sons who had already

joined the French Army as volunteers. All that day and
the preceding one there had been no letters, no newspapers; we were cut off from all communication with the
outside world, and the rumours grew more and more disquieting as they flew from mouth to mouth. At the hotel
Britannia where I was stopping the proprietor came to
bid me good-bye before he left to join the German Army
with half his staff. I held out my hand and his eyes were
full of tears as he took it . . . "Ah, Mme. Lehr, how can
I possibly have any happiness in going to this war? How
many of my patrons, my friends I might call them, people who have come here year after year, will now be
called the enemy! . . ."

I stood in the lounge and watched them depart, a for-
lorn little cluster of men, clerks and cashiers, German
waiters and valets-de-chambre; they piled their modest
baggage onto the hotel barge, and climbed in. At the door
they were met by the chef and his kitchen staff, French to
a man, who had also received their calling-up papers and
were to leave in a few hours. Silently the two little groups
shook hands, but it was a silence more eloquent than any
words.

August 7th came and I wrote in my diary, "The war
news is terrible, more than eight thousand Germans have
been killed. . . ." Newspapers and letters were beginning to filter through now. I got a wire from Harry Lehr,
who was doing his utmost to get back from Karlsbad,
but without success. Eventually he managed to persuade
someone to sell him a car, and in this he started off, tak-

ing with him the Duke of Alba and Berwick, who was in a similar plight and could get no news whatever from Spain. After a journey of seven days and a variety of adventures, which included being arrested twice as suspected deserters from the Austrian Army, they succeeded in crossing the Italian frontier, and arrived in Venice on August 18th. Two days later we received word that'Italy was on the point of mobilising, and all foreigners were advised to leave the country, so we decided to return to Paris, and secured the necessary passports and permits to travel.

I shall never forget that journey. The constant changes from one slow train to another, the stifling heat of the carriages, the long waits at tiny wayside stations; the uncertainty of ever getting anywhere, for no one seemed to know the destination of any of the trains into which we and other passengers were herded like sheep. We would no sooner settle ourselves in a compartment before we were all turned out and told to wait for the next train, which might be six hours late. Sometimes we were huddled into second or third class carriages; sometimes we stood in the corridors, threading our way from coach to coach, stepping over the prostrate forms of our fellow passengers who were so exhausted that they were thankful to fall asleep on the bare floor. Our food was a basket of rolls which we had brought from Venice and some grapes which we bought from an old peasant woman at one station. At the end of four days we presented a sorry spectacle, with our clothes crumpled and dusty, our faces streaked with grime.

When we got to Lyons we had an adventure which nearly ended disastrously. As no one could tell us when the next train for Paris left we made our way to a hotel hoping to get at least something to eat—the first meal since we had left Venice. The restaurant was crowded. Soldiers on their way to join their regiments, Red Cross workers, tourists stranded like ourselves. After great difficulty we managed to get a table in the centre of the room, and a harassed waiter appeared to take our orders. Harry Lehr took up the menu and . . . began to talk German! Afterwards he explained to me that he was so worn out with lack of sleep that he scarcely knew what he was doing; he had been talking German for weeks in Karlsbad; mechanically he continued to do so; he had always spoken it fluently since his childhood.

It was our undoing! From that moment all thoughts of a comforting lunch faded into thin air. Everyone at the surrounding tables had heard him; they began to whisper and nudge one another, the whispers grew into an angry murmur, "A party of spies. . . ." "They ought to be taken out and shot. . . ." Soon the whole restaurant was ringing with it, chairs were overturned; the room was in an uproar. Just when I was beginning to fear that we really might be lynched without a chance to defend ourselves, three or four policemen pushed their way through the crowd to our table. In a few sharp words they ordered everyone to return to their seats, the doors were closed, we were asked to produce our passports. Fortunately these were satisfactory enough to remove all serious doubt, but we were not allowed to proceed on our way until the American Consul had been summoned and had personally vouched for our identity. In the meantime we had not only missed our lunch but the only direct train for Paris, and hours passed before we managed to get another. We were hardly able to stand when at length we arrived in Paris and were driven to our house in the rue de Lille in a rusty old one-horse cab that looked as though it had been resurrected from the scrap heap.

We stayed in Paris two days, just long enough to collect our baggage and obtain permits to travel to England, then we left for Boulogne. There were no taxis to be had in the streets, and it was only after we had sent a messenger down to the Ritz Hotel that we were finally able to get a cab to drive us to the station. The train was crowded and during the greater part of the way we crawled along at the rate of twenty kilometres an hour. All that day we travelled through the theatre of war, an unforgettable journey. British columns on the march, hospital trains bearing their convoys of wounded to the base; the music of "Tipperary" mingled with the cries of the dying. Outside Amiens we passed one troop train after another bringing the British Forces up to the lines; along the country roads bordering the track we saw an endless chain of cavalry and infantry, winding along the dusty roads, while the aeroplanes hummed overhead.

And every now and then as the train drew up at some station we would catch glimpses of another army, a sad straggling procession, hollow-eyed and weary, hundreds of refugees flying from the devastated regions. Many of them were only half-dressed; we saw women in nightgowns, children wrapped in blankets. They crouched miserably on the platforms among their pitiful belongings, their eyes full of a dumb resignation more terrible to witness than any tears. Once while we waited a young peasant woman just outside our carriage broke into agonised sobs. Poor soul, she had just made the discovery that the baby she had pushed for miles in a little handcart under the grilling sun had died on the way. Two other children, a boy and a girl, clung to her skirts weeping in sympathy. An old woman stepped forward and patted her shaking shoulders, "C'est beaucoup mieux. . . . Comme ça il ne souffre plus," she repeated again and again as the poor mother rocked to and fro in the abandonment of her grief. We could only look on, helpless, unable to offer any comfort. I felt the tears running down my own cheeks. Suddenly I had a happy thought. Taking out all the money I had in my bag I thrust it into her hands . . . "Keep it; it will buy food for these two little ones who are left to you. . . ." Mechanically she took the roll of notes, thanked me chokingly. From the look of relief that spread over her wan face in the midst of her sorrow I knew that at least I had lifted one heavy burden from her mind.

At night we arrived in Boulogne, the train drew up at

the town station. Too late already to dream of catching
the cross-Channel boat, but somehow we must get to the
marine station, to be in readiness for the next day. There
was not a taxi to be had, they had all been commandeered days ago. Finally after an hour's search we found a
battered horse cab driven by a boy of about twelve. He
agreed with the air of one conveying an immense favour
to drive us to a hotel down by the port. We got in with
our baggage piled around us, our young Jehu whipped
up his decrepit horses and away we went. So tired were
we that we dozed in our seats to awake with a start as we
drew up at the door of the hotel. It looked neither clean
nor inviting, but it was the only one not taken over by
the military, and we were so glad to get in anywhere that
we were not disposed to be critical. An elderly waiter
brought us lukewarm coffee and some stale rolls and we
devoured them thankfully before turning into bed to get
a few hours' sleep. At dawn the next morning we managed to get a boat for England.

On our arrival in London we drove straight to the
Ritz Hotel and slept peacefully for the first time in weeks.
But although our own troubles were over for the time we
were racked with anxiety for our friends. Every hour
the news from France was more disquieting. The Germans were marching steadily on Paris; the city was preparing for what promised to be the grimmest episode in
its stormy history. No one could foresee what the issue
would be.

At the Morgan Harjes Bank in the Boulevard Hauss-

mann, the house which my father had been so proud of
when he had founded it half a century before, troops of
marines from the "Tennessee" guarded the doors. They
lined the entrance, their arms piled behind them, solid,
American, reassuring. Their presence gave an illusion of
security to Parisian mothers, distraught with fears for
their children, and they came as many of them as could
crowd into the building to encamp with their families on
blankets and mattresses which they spread out in the
waiting rooms and corridors, even on the staircases. No
one had the heart to turn them out and for three or four
suspense-filled nights the bank echoed to the sound of
crying babies, the growling of dogs, the miaowing of cats,
for even the family pets had not been forgotten in the
quest for shelter from the advancing Germans. Elderly
bachelor clerks heated coffee and dispensed rolls, and
strove to recall the games of their own childhood in an
effort to amuse the children. When at length the welcome news came that the German troops had unbeliev-
ably been turned aside from their goal, the little band of
refugees disappeared as silently, as unobtrusively as it
had come, and business was resumed with a semblance of
normality.

In the meantime every cross-Atlantic steamer was
crowded with Americans returning home. England would
find it hard enough to feed her own people, she did not
want foreigners in her midst. Harry Lehr and I decided
to sail on the "Olympic" on September 16th. We packed
our trunks, taking as little with us as possible. But there

remained the question of my jewellery, stored at Morgan and Harjes. I could not leave it in Paris, for at that time the bank had no strong rooms for customers, yet how was I to get it to London? Eventually I wrote to our Ambassador, Myron T. Herrick, and despatched the letter by special messenger, begging him to help me. I knew that I could count on him, for he was always the soul of kindness and consideration, and although he was desperately busy with affairs of far more importance than the disposal of a woman's jewels, he managed to find time to go in person to Morgan and Harjes and to write me a reassuring letter.

"Of course I will attend to it for you, my dear Miss Bessie," he wrote, "but you must not take too black a view of the situation over here. The morale of the Parisians is wonderful—they set us all an example in courage. Don't pay too much attention to what you read in the papers, or what people tell you, for that matter. France is not beaten yet—not by a long chalk, and in my opinion never will be. . . ."

He presented himself at Morgan and Harjes. Herman Harjes hurried forward to receive him. . . .

"No, I've not come on a diplomatic mission. I'm here as Myron Herrick, not as the American Ambassador, and I want to do a little personal errand for a friend of mine. It concerns a lady's jewels. . . ."

So my jewellery was given to him in an inconspicuous package which he handed to an employee of a prominent Paris jeweller, specially recommended by the firm for any confidential mission, who had undertaken to get the jewels safely over to me. The method he employed was ingenious, for he donned the worn clothes of a workman, mounted a bicycle that looked as though it had seen much service and on this rode to the coast, taking two days over the journey. He sustained his rôle perfectly, stayed at cheap wayside lodgings and lunched during the day on hunks of bread and cheese which he carried in his knapsack. How was anyone to guess that in many of the slices of bread were embedded diamonds, emeralds and sapphires worth a fortune? He reached the end of the journey without mishap and delivered the jewels to me in London. The reward I paid him was naturally a large one, but even so it scarcely seemed to me adequate compensation for the risk he had run of being murdered on the way by thieves. I told him so, but he only laughed . . . "One has to die sometime, Madame. A little sooner or later is not of so very great importance. As Madame sees, I am not a young man, too old for military service, but I have three sons in the fighting line. The money that I earn in this way keeps their families in comfort while they are with their regiments. It is little enough I can do for them and for France, but what I can do I do happily. . . ."

I wrote to thank Myron T. Herrick for the trouble he had taken. It was only one of the many little kindnesses I received from that great-hearted diplomat and loyal friend. He was always ready to help in any emergency, whether it was a national catastrophe or the individual dilemma of one of his friends.

In September 1914 when von Kluck was marching on Paris, Mr. Herrick saw M. Poincaré at the Elysée, where the President asked him eventually, and if necessary, to drive out and see General von Kluck in order to prevent, if possible, the destruction of the monuments and art treasures in the capital. At the same time the Norwegian Minister, Baron Wedel Jarlsberg, who had stayed in Paris with Mr. Herrick when the corps diplomatique left for Bordeaux, was asked by the Secrétaire Général of the Foreign Office to join Mr. Herrick if he went to see General von Kluck. Mr. Herrick and Baron Wedel Jarlsberg both promised to do what they could.

General Joffre's victory at the Marne did away, however, with any necessity of seeing General von Kluck in the matter.

.   .   .   .

We spent the winter of 1914 and the following spring in New York, staying at the Ritz-Carlton, where we found many other Americans who had just returned from Europe. Mrs. Leeds was among them. She had been spending the summer in England and had just taken a house at Harrogate when war was declared, and her house party broke up in confusion. One of her guests was Helié de Talleyrand and she told me that he had shut himself in his room for two days while he fought out his own personal battle, tried to decide whether he owed his loyalty to France or Germany. Both were his countries, both equally dear to him, the family ties in each one were equally strong. When he came downstairs his face was white and drawn. . . . "My dear friend, I am leaving today to offer my services to Germany, the land of my ancestors. It is to them I owe loyalty and I must put it before my personal love of France. . . ." There and then he took leave of her, and left that night to join the German Forces.

No one talked of anything but the War, and its personal reactions. Lily Martin, whom I had known since the days when she was little Lily Oelrichs, was jubilant because she had managed to smuggle Prince Borwein of Mecklenburg-Strelitz (whom she afterwards married) out of Europe. He was so averse to joining the German Army that he had begged her to take him back to the States with her. At her suggestion he had disguised himself in dingy threadbare clothes and got taken on in the stokehold of the liner on which she was a passenger. The plan worked so perfectly that no one had any inkling of his identity. She laughed very much as she described their stolen meetings on deck, she in her dainty evening gowns, he in his grimy stoker's overalls.

Mrs. Cornelius Vanderbilt had had the German Ambassador to Washington, Count Bernsdorff, stopping with her at her Newport house when war was declared. Before his arrival she had issued invitations for a dinner party which she was giving in his honour during the second week of August.

But by that time German troops were pouring into

France and Belgium, British ships were scouring the Channel, even America was divided into opposing camps in loyalty either to the allies or their common enemy. Naturally she supposed that Count Bernsdorff, knowing the position and appreciating the embarrassment his presence would cause her on account of the divided sympathies of her friends, would curtail his visit. To her consternation he did no such thing, possibly because he had decided that his absence would be tantamount to a confession that his country was in the wrong. She thought of the approaching dinner with many misgivings. However, she decided that she could rely on the tact of her other guests, and rang up several of them to remind them that under no circumstances must they make any reference to the War during dinner. She hoped that in spite of conflicting emotions the party might still be a success.

But she had forgotten to make allowance for the patriotic feeling of her servants, and as luck would have it her entire kitchen staff was composed of English, French and Belgians.

The dinner began in an atmosphere of cordiality. Count Bernsdorff, taking his cue from the other guests, talked upon every subject but the one which was nearest to his thoughts and those of everyone else in the room. The soup was served to the accompaniment of light conversation. There was no evidence of the undercurrent of tension. Then came a long wait. An almost unprecedented occurrence in a house that was famous for the perfection of its dinner parties. Mrs. Vanderbilt rang the bell. Nothing happened. She rang it again . . . again. Still without result. More waiting. By this time everyone was talking feverishly to hide what was beginning to be a strained situation. Ten minutes went by while the hostess was wondering what could possibly have happened. Then one of the chambermaids, a Swiss girl, appeared, very confused and tearful, and handed Mrs. Vanderbilt a note. She opened it and read:

"We the undersigned regret to inform you, Madam, that we cannot any longer serve the enemy of our respective countries. We have thrown the rest of the dinner into the dustbin and we have all left your service. There is nothing else to eat in the house. We hope you all enjoyed the soup, for we took good care to spit well into it, every one of us, before it went to the table. . . ." It was signed by the entire kitchen staff.

The dinner party broke up in confusion! The next day Count Bernsdorff took his departure.

.   .   .   .

Mrs. Leeds could talk of nothing but the patriotism of the British nation. She never tired of quoting the case of her heroic young English footman, William. It appeared that as a footman he was everything that was perfect, tall, handsome, of irreproachable manners, excellent at waiting at table. He went in her household from Kenwood to Grosvenor Square, from Grosvenor Square to Harrogate. A few weeks after the declaration of war he came to her . . . "Madam, my country is calling me. I regret that I must leave your service to join the British

Army. . . ." She tried to dissuade him from going, pointed out that there were many others to volunteer, that he was his mother's only son. But he shook his head . . . "My duty to England comes before anything else, Madam. God will provide for my mother if I am taken from her. . . ." Mrs. Leeds described the fervour in his eyes as "a beautiful sight." Impulsive and sentimental, she was deeply touched. She not only told him that she would keep his place open for him, but she insisted on his taking a cheque for two years' wages, as a present for his mother. Then she drove to the big stores and herself bought him blankets and mufflers, socks and a complete outfit of underclothes, pipes and tobacco, hampers of food, in fact every conceivable type of luxury which the salesman could suggest as likely to brighten the lot of a new recruit. Her enthusiasm spread to the rest of the household; from Mrs. Leeds' own maids to the gardener's boy each of the servants subscribed handsomely to the fund for the equipment of William. He was loaded with presents above and below stairs. His gratitude was touching. When he came to say "Good-bye" to his generous employer he begged her "for one small favour. . . ." Would she write him out a recommendation? . . . "But I am afraid my recommendation as a footman won't help you in the British Army," she said, rather surprised at the request. . . . Tears rose to her eyes when the reason was explained . . . "I want to send it to my poor old mother, Madam. If I should be killed it would comfort her to know you thought highly of me!" Of course she

gave it, written in the most glowing terms that came into
her head. After an affecting leavetaking in the servants'
hall William left, accompanied by the prayers of the entire household.

This was the story she told us, a fine example of British
patriotism. Unfortunately it had a sequel. One evening
soon after our arrival in New York we were all invited
to the Elbridge Gerrys for dinner. Mrs. Leeds happened
to look up and catch the eye of the tall handsome English
footman who was carrying round the soup. She gave a
gasp! It was the heroic William!

He had foreseen conscription for his country, and had
taken good care to avoid the possibility of it for himself
by entering into the service of an American family on the
point of leaving for the United States.

.   .   .   .

One of my most vivid memories of that winter is of the
magnificent party which Mr. and Mrs. E. T. Stotesbury
gave at Philadelphia. Whole floors of the Bellevue-Strat-
ford Hotel had been reserved to accommodate the hundreds of guests who came by special train from New York;
everyone had a luxurious suite decorated in rose pink
and gold, the colours of the fête.

We had been told that the dinner was to be a surprise
for Mr. Stotesbury, and as we assembled in one of the
salons we were all trying to guess what form it would
take. Suddenly the folding doors were flung open and we
found ourselves in Venice.

It was almost unbelievable; the whole room had been

transformed. Venetian scenes had been painted on the walls, the soft lighting came from lanterns swinging on the prows of gondolas; musicians seated in a "barca" sang the love songs of old Venice. The Stotesburys had spent their honeymoon in Venice, they had been happy there, and this fête was to commemorate it.

From dinner and dancing in Venice the guests suddenly found themselves transported to an inn in the Tyrol. Champagne was served at long trestle tables, surrounded by benches, Tyrolese singers appeared on the scene, beautiful Tyrolese maidens distributed favours.

The whole evening was one of unparalleled luxury. Nearly half a million dollars had been spent to make it so. And somewhere in France! . . . I tried to close the gates of memory, yet I knew I could not succeed. As we went up to our suite that night I said to Harry Lehr suddenly, "Let us go back to Paris. I want to help in the Red Cross. . . ."

To my surprise he agreed.

CHAPTER XX

LIFE GOES ON

꩜

In 1915 WE RETURNED TO PARIS, WHERE WE REMAINED until the end of the War. Americans were needed in France now. They were running Red Cross hospitals and field ambulances, caring for the refugees from the devastated areas, offering hospitality to the men on leave from the trenches. My son Jack enrolled as an ambulance driver. I gave my car to the Red Cross, sent $10,000 to Anne Morgan for her "Comité Américain des Régions Dévastées," which was caring for thousands of homeless women and children, and offered my services to the American Ambulance at Neuilly. There was so much to be done to help a courageous nation at war; every day more voluntary workers were needed.

Strange to look back on those memories of war-time Paris! The silent sobered people who crept about, the women almost invariably dressed in black. A joyless city with all its youth at the war, its children sent away to the safety of the Riviera or the Pyrenees. After nightfall the streets were almost deserted; everyone dreaded at any moment to hear the sirens announcing the advent of German aeroplanes, never knowing when the first bomb would fall.

Like all the rest of Paris we took refuge in our cellar during the raids. We made ourselves as comfortable as we could with piles of cushions, and books, for we were lucky enough to have had heating and electric light installed there when we first took over the house. The neighbouring cellar, which belonged to the Marquis de Nickolay, boasted of no such luxuries. It was dark and so damp that the moisture dripped from the walls so that the poor old Marquis and his brother nearly died from the cold until we insisted on their joining us. They never betrayed the slightest emotion even during the height of a raid with bombs crashing only a few yards from the house. The Marquis had only one complaint . . . the discomfort of leaving his warm bed in the middle of the night. He always protested that if it were not for the fact of worrying his brother nothing would induce him to come down to the cellar. . . . "After all, chère Madame Lehr," he would say . . . "we may be killed one day by a German airman, but I for one shall most certainly die of rheumatism if I have to remain for many nights in the cellar. . . ."

The fact that our house at 80 rue de Lille was next door to the former German Embassy caused us annoyance on more than one occasion, for in the earlier years of the War many of the lower-class Parisians were unfamiliar with the Stars and Stripes which flew from our house, and believing it to be some German emblem flying from the Embassy tried to invade our garden. Several times we found our flag stripped down and lying in the gutter where it had been torn and defiled. Once Myron T. Herrick, unaware of this confusion, was surprised to receive a message from some French acquaintances, "Harry Lehr is flying the German flag on his house. . . ." His informants were so emphatic that he decided to investigate for himself. He went off in his little runabout, which he drove himself, and of course discovered the mistake. But it nearly caused his death, for on his way home a squadron of German planes appeared without warning from out of a cloudless sky and the first bomb which fell in the Avenue du Trocadéro narrowly missed his car.

Every week I gave teas for the hospital staff and patients of the American Ambulance, and everyone who could spare the time off duty, surgeons, nurses, orderlies and ambulance drivers, would gather round the table to partake of doughnuts, cocoanut cake, hot biscuits and other wartime luxuries calculated to remind the exiles of home. Generally there would be visitors from the outside world, often the Duchesse de Vendôme, who would come amongst us, charming and gracious, with a kind word for everybody. She was a great favourite in the wards, and all the patients regarded her as a personal friend, for she took infinite trouble to find out not only their names and particulars of their families, but their individual tastes in books and chocolates, and other little gifts.

Mrs. W. K. Vanderbilt would glide sinuously down from the wards to join us, picturesquely attired in the white piqué uniform Worth had made for her with an impressive cap like a Russian headdress, and an enormous cross as her only adornment. She was quite the most zealous person in the whole hospital. I remember that when Mrs. Whitelaw Reid, who was visiting the hospital, having seen her walk up and down stairs at least a dozen times in the space of half an hour asked, "Are there no lifts, Mrs. Vanderbilt?" she replied with humility, "The lifts are for the wounded. . . ." Kind-hearted Mrs. Reid was so moved that she there and then presented the hospital with two new lifts, one for the patients, the other for the staff.

No more empty days stretching ahead of me now; no more long hours consecrated to brooding and vain regrets for the past. Instead there was so much to be done that the only problem was to find time for it all. Letters to be written for wounded men hungry for news from home. Anxious letters from America from one's own friends, every mail brought them . . . "Bessie dear, my boy is in France" . . . and then there would be leave-trains to meet at the station, young khaki-clad forms about the house, parcels to be sent to the trenches.

Days at the hospital, learning to sink one's own personality in a little community, a world in itself, limiting one's conversation to the small daily happenings in the wards. Impossible to remain an observer here, to stand aloof from the emotions of others. One might be tired, discouraged, but it was vital. The warm glow of pleasure one felt when some patient given up by the doctors made a miraculous rally, the amusement one got out of the petty quarrels and jealousies which were always breaking out among the helpers; the sorrow over other people's tragedies. I lived every moment of the day.

One of the volunteer nurses was as beautiful as an old Florentine picture. Strands of copper-red hair were always escaping from under her stiffly starched cap; an amber necklace made an indecorous appearance from under her uniform collar. One of the ladies in authority looked at her with disfavour, made enquiries. Someone discovered that she had been a well-known demi-mondaine. Virtuous eyebrows were raised in horror! She must be dismissed instantly before others learnt of the terrible scandal. All the doctors pleaded for her; she was the best nurse they had, the most conscientious, the most eager to learn. Her conduct at the hospital had been absolutely blameless. It was obvious that she loved her work. But the authorities were adamant. Her entreaties to be allowed to stay on were of no avail.

I met her as she was leaving the hospital. . . .

"I am sorry you are going," I said, holding out my hand. . . .

Her eyes were full of tears as she took it . . . "They might have let me stay. I was so happy here; happier than I have ever been in my life."

   •   •   •   •   •   •   •

When General Pershing came over as Commander-in-Chief of the United States Expeditionary Force he added considerably to the gaiety of the American colony in Paris. In this respect he was rather a revelation to the French, who found it difficult to understand that so great a soldier was not above seeking distractions in war-time. They looked rather askance at first at the informal dances and garden parties which he gave at his house in the rue de Varenne, not realising that his cheery optimism was invaluable in keeping up the morale of his troops.

He was the most indefatigable dancer at the ball given by Mr. and Mrs. Herman Harjes, and I have an amusing recollection of that evening. Harry Lehr and I took with us to the ball lovely Louise Brooks, daughter of Mrs. E. T. Stotesbury, who had recently obtained her divorce and was staying in Paris. The moment he saw her Pershing admired her enormously. He came over to Harry . . . "Introduce me to the girl in green. . . ." For the rest of the evening he monopolised her. They were part-ners in dance after dance, for none of the young officers there, however much they might want to dance with the prettiest girl in the room, had the courage to cut in on their Commander-in-Chief, in the full glory of his uni-form, and as he showed no sign of relinquishing his place beside her even at supper they could only look on en-viously.

But on the way home Louise, instead of being proud of her conquest, was full of misgivings lest she might have bored the General. . . . "I was so afraid he might feel that he couldn't get away from me," she explained. . . . "No one else came to ask me to dance, and I thought that probably he was too polite to leave me without a partner. . . ."

General Pershing, Mr. and Mrs. Herman Harjes, Harry Lehr and I and James Hazen Hyde were practically the only Americans who entertained in Paris during wartime, and our houses were always open to the men on leave from the Front. Later James Hyde gave over his house at 18 rue Adolphe Yvon to the Red Cross, who were delighted to have it for it was one of the most luxurious homes in Paris. He had designed it himself and had introduced into its construction all sorts of improvements of which he was very proud. He told all his friends that it was to be the home of an æsthete. So a special apparatus was installed to prevent any smell of cooking from permeating from the kitchen, and, as he detested noise, sand was laid under the floor of his bedroom to shut out sounds from below. He had selected the site for the repose it seemed to offer. He meant at all costs to secure complete tranquillity. But alas for his hopes! He was awakened on the first morning at dawn by the noise of bugles and drums! When he had the house constructed, he had quite overlooked the fact that just opposite him were the fortifications, which hummed from morning till night with the sounds of barrack life.

· · · · · · ·

In the early spring of 1916 we went to stay with James Gordon Bennett and his wife, who had been the beautiful Baroness de Ruyter, at their villa in Beaulieu-sur-Mer.

Our host was eager for the latest news from New York. Despite the fact that he had made Europe his permanent home, had his villa on the Riviera, his house and magnificent chasse that had been the property of the Duc de Bourgogne at Versailles, he never really lost his nostalgia for his own country.

During the War he did a great deal for the Allies, gave lavishly to the Red Cross and other charities. He even quarrelled with his wife over his sympathies, if indeed their disputes could be described as quarrels, for they were devoted to one another and their marriage, although made late in life, was one of true love. During the first year of the War Mrs. Bennett was distraught with anxiety over the eldest son of her previous marriage, Oliver de Ruyter, who had gone to Germany to consult an ear specialist and as a naturalised Englishman had been interned in Ruhleben when War was declared. As his letters from the prison camp became more and more despondent she grew nearly frantic and implored Gordon Bennett to use his influence to secure the release of her son, at all costs. She pointed out that as an international sportsman he had many influential acquaintances in Germany, and that the Kaiser had eviced his friendship on many occasions. Surely something could be done.

Terribly distressed at her grief, Gordon Bennett wrote several letters, despatched them to Germany. Weeks passed before they were answered. Then came a diplomatic intimation that Germany was badly in need of propaganda in the United States. If Gordon Bennett would throw in the influence of his newspapers he would be suitably rewarded. James Gordon Bennett indignantly refused, but his wife was heartbroken. She almost went on her knees to entreat him to reconsider his decision. He was an American, America was not in the War, she urged. How could there be any harm in making propaganda for Germany when her son's liberty was at stake?

But in spite of his love for her he was adamant. . . . "My loyalty belongs to my adopted country. I will not sell my honour, whatever the price. Not even for you. . . ."

Eventually Oliver de Ruyter was exchanged in the ordinary course of events.

Like everyone else who knew him, I always associated James Gordon Bennett with the birds he loved. He had owls everywhere. Owls engraved on all his cuff-links, live owls in the garden of the Villa Namouna at Beaulieu, painted owls on the panels of his house in Versailles. Even the bathrooms on his yacht the "Lysistrata" were decorated with scenes from the romance of two owls. When anyone teased him over his mania he always said that owls were lucky for him, as they had been lucky for his father. He had a curious streak of superstition, which was perhaps justified, for his life was full of strange coincidences.

Mrs. Gordon Bennett told me that some months before his death they went together to a charity fête on the Riviera and that a clairvoyante there had insisted on telling his fortune.

She told him amongst other things that his two dogs would die, and that the death of the second would be followed by the death of some member of his household. When a little later the two Pekinese died, as she had foretold, one within a short time of the other, James Gordon Bennett was convinced that the rest of the prophecy would be fulfilled. He gave up all hope of fighting his illness from that moment. . . . "It was my death she saw in the cards," he insisted. . . . "I know that it will happen as she said. I have lived out my life."

A week or two later he was dead.

. . . .

After leaving the Bennetts we went to stay with Mrs. Leeds who had taken the Villa Primavera at Cap d'Ail. She had just arrived from London where she was engrossed in a variety of War charities and was returning almost immediately to organize a bazaar at her house in Grosvenor Square in aid of the Red Cross. She told us of the last of these bazaars, which had been held as usual in the big black and gold ballroom on the first floor. The room was crowded when a burly convalescent soldier who had been lent from his hospital to guard the door was seen pushing his way through the throng to where Mrs. Leeds was standing trying to attend to a dozen things at once.

"Beg your pardon, Ma'am, but my pal and I have just caught a young fellow trying to get upstairs to your rooms on the floor above. He doesn't seem to be able to give a satisfactory account of himself, so my pal is holding him outside till you tell us what to do with him."

"Oh, telephone to the police, of course," said Mrs. Leeds, who had a horror of burglars.

Ten minutes later the crowd which had gathered outside the house to watch the arrival of the guests had the satisfaction of seeing a police van drive up to the entrance. Two stalwart policemen descended and rushed up the steps to emerge in a few seconds dragging between them a slender young man whose face, bowed over his handcuffed wrists, appeared to be convulsed with laughter. He was just being hustled into the van when there was a shout from the house. A footman stood at the door, eyes wide with astonishment . . . "Why, it's Master William you've got. . . ."

It was true. Mrs. Leeds' son, William B., Junior, being bored with the fête and in terror lest his mother should force him into helping at one of the stalls, had been sneaking stealthily upstairs to his own room when the zealous doorkeeper, supposing him to be a thief in quest of the famous Leeds jewels, had pounced upon him. The police arrived on the scene prepared to make an important arrest, and it was then that the supposed criminal began to enjoy the adventure. He determined to say nothing in order that he might have the story of his experience in an English prison to relate when he got back to America. Fortunately for everyone concerned the footman saved the situation.

CHAPTER XXI
BEGINNING OF THE END

❧

T HE END OF THE WAR FOUND US STILL IN PARIS. HARRY
had no inclination now to go back to America. Already
the first warning signs of the illness which destroyed that
brilliant, complex brain of his were beginning to mani-
fest themselves. Gradually he started to lose touch with
the very things that had once held the essence of life for
him. That radiant vitality was gone for ever. His friends
tried to cheer him by the raillery he had always responded to. Mrs. Fish wrote, "They say, sweet Lamb,
that you have lost your mind. Come back to New York
if you have, for I can assure you that the loss won't interfere with your popularity. You know quite well that you
won't need any mind to go with the people in our
set. . . ."

Mrs Gurnee Munn and Aksel-Wichfeld heard that he
was ill; arrived at the house laden with cages, baskets,
boxes of every sort, from which emerged a weird me-
nagerie—pigeons, guinea-pigs, rabbits, a monkey, a prize
rooster, lizards, tortoises—loosed them all in his room,
filled his bath with goldfish. . . . "The doctor told us
live animals are a certain cure for nervous breakdowns,

Harry. Hurry up and get well or we will loose the lions and tigers next. . . ."

Mrs. Leeds came to see us. She was very much perplexed as to which of her suitors to choose. An incessant rivalry went on among them and they followed her about the Continent. She arrived in Paris, had Worth design a splendid silver-grey dress, a long train trimmed with chinchilla. She exhibited it proudly to me . . . "My wedding dress."

"Ah, then you have made up your mind who it is going to be?" I asked, interested, because I knew that my cousin Anthony Drexel was one of the most ardent.

"I am not sure yet, but it will do for any of them. . . ."

She hurried off to Switzerland still undecided.

Before she went she gave a magnificent dinner party at the Ritz in honour of Prince Christopher of Greece. Harry Lehr and I were invited. On the morning of the party she rang us up . . . "Please, please come round, something dreadful has happened." We went round at once.

Lady Paget, who had been her chaperon for so many years, had died very suddenly. The undertakers had already arrived. . . .

"It seems so dreadful to give the party with her lying dead here," said Mrs. Leeds tearfully, "and yet I simply can't put it off."

"Then there is only one thing to do. Don't let anyone know she is dead until tomorrow," was Harry's suggestion. It was put into practice. No whisper of the tragedy was allowed to cloud the atmosphere of the dinner.

I sat next to the Grand Duke Alexander who had just arrived in Paris. Everyone was congratulating him on having escaped the fate of so many members of his family. Halfway through the dinner we both looked up simultaneously. Over the screen which shut off the room in which we were dining from the corridor, heads had bobbed up; their owners were standing on chairs to get a glimpse of the party. We recognised the Grand Duke Michael and the Grand Duchess Anastasia. . . .

The Grand Duke Alexander smiled his curious whimsical smile . . .

"Is that not a sign of the times? Imagine two members of the Imperial Family craning their necks over a screen to find out who is present at a dinner to which they have not been invited! Our star is on the wane; that of our hostess, as you see, is in the ascendency. . . ."

. . . .

Lady Sarah Wilson, that pilot of so many ambitious social craft, would come to see us. Slender, elegant, with the disdainful, aristocratic profile that had been so much admired in New York, sharp-tongued, keen-witted as ever.

She came on her way back from Switzerland to tell us all about Mrs. Leeds' wedding with Prince Christopher of Greece at Vevey, brought us a bag embroidered with an imposing crown and filled with christening dragées, a souvenir of Nancy's baptism into the Greek Church, which had preceded the marriage.

"The Queen of Greece arranged the whole thing," she said caustically. . . . "Mrs. Leeds was discussing the question with me at dinner one evening in her suite when the door opened and in walked a woman dressed all in black who gave me a *frisson* to look at her, she was so like a cross between Machiavelli and Mary Queen of Scots. I knew instinctively that it was the Queen of Greece. I left them together and within half an hour they had decided all the details of the wedding."

.   .   .   .

Four years passed by, years in which Harry grew steadily worse. His apathy had given place now to a feverish craving for gaiety. As he felt life slipping from him he tried to recapture it in the only way he had understood it. He sought it in crowds, in laughter, in the company of people who were amusing themselves. He would sit for hours at a time in crowded restaurants and bars, trying in a way that was infinitely pathetic to find himself again in the familiar background.

There were rare flashes of his brilliant wit, the light touches of satire which had been so characteristic of him. There was something of gallantry in the way that, in his sane moments, he would still laugh at life and at himself. The old spirit of mockery was in his eyes as he bade me "Good-bye" before sailing for the States, where he was to undergo treatment. I had wanted to accompany him but he had insisted on going without me. I tried to cheer

him, to talk to him of his return. At the last moment
he took my hand in his. . . . "No, no, Bessie. . . . La
commedia è finita. . . ."

They were the last coherent words he ever addressed
to me. When a week or two later I joined him after the
operation which it was hoped might save his life, I found
him a wreck of his former self, unable to speak except in
a jumble of meaningless sounds.

I brought him back to France with me. No longer any
thought of leaving him now. The chains of pity held me
far too strongly. Although he had four nurses he was
completely dependent on me. No one else seemed to understand him, to interpret the wishes he could never
voice. His eyes would follow me about the room; he
would not go out driving unless I was with him.

And so three more years slipped by until the day
came when he was taken once more to Baltimore for
treatment. He never recovered. . . .

.   .   .   .

After his death I went through his papers, came upon
the diary that he had kept always locked.

It told me everything. For the first time I understood.

"I can never love any woman," he had said to me so
often. "Women are actually repulsive to me. . . ."

It had been true.

Yet he had known love, had given an emotion of which
I had not believed him capable.

His diary was a love story.

CHAPTER XXII
RUE DES SAINTS PÈRES

I AM FINISHING THIS STORY OF MY LIFE IN MY GARDEN IN
Paris on a July morning. There has just been a sudden
shower. On the sun-splashed lawn the grass is still wet,
the leaves are still bowing under their burden of rain-
drops, but the whole garden is bathed in the golden
glow of the sunshine, and somewhere in my acacias a
bird is singing.

That is what my life has been as I look back through
the years. Sunshine and showers, the grey and the gold.
Overcast skies one moment, the next the radiance of
spring. And always in my heart there has echoed the
voice of a bird.

Life has been generous to me. The crowded years have
given me many things I value beyond price—love, friendship, romance, much travel. I have read a great deal,
thought a great deal, realised many dreams.

Some time after Harry's death I went back to America,
revisited the familiar places I had last seen in company
with him—New York where we lived so many years together, Newport the scene of his triumphs. Time had
robbed my recollections of all bitterness.

"King Lehr's" kingdom has almost disappeared; his subjects are dispersed.

Mamie Fish who shared so many jests with him died before him; Tessie Oelrichs, Edith Gould, Mr. Van Alen, Jack Astor, Elisha Dyer are only names, already half forgotten.

I watched the funeral of Mrs. Oliver Belmont from the St. Regis Hotel where years before I had stood with Harry Lehr to watch her lead the great Suffrage Parade. Once again the women's banners fluttered in the wind; the girls who had marched behind her in that first procession carried her coffin now . . . grey-haired women. But in death she was thwarted as she had never been in life, for in spite of the instructions in her will a woman preacher was not permitted to deliver the funeral oration at St. Thomas's Church.

I went to Newport, stayed with Mrs. Cornelius Vanderbilt . . . "Alice of the Breakers" as Harry had christened her years before, but Newport was changed. No more splendid dinner parties of eighty or ninety guests, no more cotillions, no more magnificent fashion parades. Their day was gone with the passing of the Gilded Age.

We went to a cinema together, the first time Mrs. Vanderbilt had ever been inside one. Took our tickets . . .

"No seats for another twenty minutes," said the man at the door.

Mrs. Vanderbilt, who had never heard of continuous performances, drew back, administered a gentle, digni-

fied rebuke, "Don't you think it is very wrong of you to
sell tickets when there are no places?"

One of the attendants, who had recognised her, smiled
indulgently, called out . . . "Here, Bill, shoot Mrs. Vanderbilt and her lady friend over here. We'll fix
them. . . ."

Mrs. Vanderbilt turned to me with a little sigh . . .
"I am afraid that socially Newport is not what it was,
my dear."

I went back to New York. Called on her daughter-in-
law, the other Mrs. Vanderbilt, that lovely Grace who
assumed the crown of Mrs. Astor with such dignity.

She was charming and gracious as always; her house
on Fifth Avenue was the perfection of taste, yet in my
fancy it seemed to be resisting something. It was like a
citadel of another age. The ever-encroaching skyscrapers
around it, the nearby Radio City were an advancing
army. Modernity on the march.

.   .   .   .

Here in Paris there are still the links with another,
statelier age. The beautiful old châteaux of my friends
are an unfailing joy to me. Grosbois, where the Princesse
de la Tour d'Auvergne entertains in an atmosphere that
recalls the great days of French monarchy; and where
Gabriel Louis Pringué, the only really picturesque figure
in modern Paris, seems also to belong to the setting of
the past. The Château Gallius, Ganna Walska's lovely
home; the historic Château de Maintenon which belongs to the famous family of the Duc de Noailles; the

regally splendid Château de Fontaine-Française where
the Comte de Chabrillan, one of the last of the Grands
Seigneurs, descendant of Henry IV, offers the gracious,
unbounded hospitality of another century.

My Paris home is an unfailing source of happiness to
me. I love it, this mellow old house that has known the
joys and sorrows of nearly four centuries. There is something of warmth, almost of tenderness in its atmosphere.
Its memories seem to enfold me. It has seen so many
spring mornings like this one, harboured so many generations of chatelaines before me. It is austere and tranquil
now as it stands back in its sun-splashed garden, shut away
from the busy world of Paris by massive gates.

I have lived in many places. I have known the sense of
exaltation which the air of New York gives, the elegance
of Newport, the gaiety of Florida. I have thrilled to the
voice of the past in the old-world cities of Dresden and
Nuremberg, I have watched the splendid pageantry of a
London season. I have stood on a Florentine balcony to
watch the unearthly beauty of a moon-bathed Fiesole; I
have gone to sleep in a Venetian palace to the gentle
plash of oars on the Grand Canal. But until I bought my
Paris house in the rue des Saints Pères I never knew
the feeling of having come home. Perhaps because it is
the house of my dreams.

Long ago, when I was a child and my parents brought
me to Paris, I was fascinated by the great portes cochères
of the houses of the old noblesse. I always longed to see
beyond them; they caught my youthful imagination. I

was a romantic child, always prone to dwell in the past rather than the present, and I conjured up visions of little high-heeled satin slippers tripping across the cobbled courtyards, of hooped skirts of taffetas rustling up massive oaken staircases, of stately minuets danced across shining floors by candlelight.

On later visits to Paris the longing to penetrate into those old houses returned with even greater force, strengthened now by a knowledge of French history and the lives of some of the personages who had lived in such settings. Perhaps for that reason I found myself in wandering about Paris most often attracted to the quarter that has been called the Faubourg St. Germain. Once across the Seine the rush of modern Paris life seems to be forgotten. The streets begin to narrow, façades lean a little this way and that, picturesque angles crop up and form interesting perspectives—and those fascinating portes cochères become like eyes in high walls. The rue des Saints Pères, even from the first, particularly appealed to me. It looked like one of the oldest of those narrow streets and was surely filled with romantic stories. At one corner was the chapel de Saint Pierre from which it received its original name of Saint Pierre. Before long careless pronunciation and worse orthography corrupted this name into its present form of Saints Pères. In the neighbourhood had lived many of the people whose lives and writing I had pored over with so much interest. Saint-Simon, the famous diarist of the 17th century, was born on the south-west corner of what is now the Boulevard St. Germain; a few yards away had stood the exclusive Abbaye-aux-Bois, to which many women who had held sway in their much-discussed salons retired after they had dismissed a final lover, married off their children, given away their jewels in dots and settled down to a peaceful life—perhaps one of penitence. It was there that Juliette Récamier retired after having astounded the world with her beauty and her luxury when she lived in her magnificent hôtel at No. 1 rue de Regard, which still exists, and yet who retained enough charm in her old age to attract to her simple quarters the renowned Chateaubriand and his following. Two doors away is the historic Hôtel de Cossé-Brissac in which such gorgeous entertainments were given; also near-by, in the rue du Bac, is the Hôtel Bernard, the house of the banker who was rich enough to buy himself a presentation to the Roi Soleil and marry into the noble family of de Villars.

I often passed No. 52 rue des Saints Pères and looked up at its heavy gateway—wooden doors painted a dark red with a big bronze knocker, set deep in an archway of crumbling stone with a partly destroyed coronet with two L's and an O to denote what it had once been and to whom it had belonged. It was deserted and neglected, but there was something of dignified silence and aloofness about it that spoke of past grandeurs. I remember so well the first time I made enquiries about it from a house directly opposite. I was told, with a shrug of indifference, that behind the old gate was a house that was rented out in apartments. As for its name, the local one was "La

Ruine des Saints Pères." It probably had some sort of history. No doubt it had once been the house of the noblesse. Who knew and who cared! It was nothing more nor less than a place where one could rent a few rooms cheap. They had to be cheap because they were old and had no modern conveniences. Could one see it? Why not? Another shrug. It was for sale.

For the next few days the neglected old hôtel remained in my thoughts. In a way it seemed to be pleading with me. At first I did not understand what the appeal meant; then, little by little, I began to think of it as being like some person who had known all the beauty and fastidiousness of life and had now fallen upon evil days. It was forgotten, abandoned, neglected—and called the ruin of the Holy Fathers (the Popes). And yet that one glance into the courtyard and up at the once handsome façade had given me a deep thrill. In spite of years of ill treatment there was beauty there still. Somehow it made me think of the sleeping beauty awaiting the touch of a magic wand to restore all its splendour.

Questions brought to light the fact that the ruin of the Saints Pères was for sale. The possibility of actually owning such a place brought back all my original emotions. More enquiries convinced me that what I had created in my imagination as its real life was actually true. A Frenchman, as sympathetic to this old quarter as I was, gave me some fragments of the history of the house and the people who lived in it. Its most important owner and inhabitant had been a certain Louis d'Oger,

Marquis de Cavoye, the intimate friend of Louis XIV. Had I not noticed the L's and O's beneath the torn bronze coronet over the gateway? Those had been his— made as much like the chiffre of Louis XIV as possible. Hugo de Groot and of course many important women had lived there—the Duchesse de Villars, the Marquise de Courcelles, the Princesse des Ursins. Once I knew the stories of all these people my interest in the house would be greater than ever, the French savant explained; and promised to bring me the books and memoirs from which he had gathered his information.

The first visit with the agent was a melancholy affair. Beautiful old rooms with exquisite boiseries, the grande salle des fêtes in ivory and gold, the gracefully curving stone staircase in the entrance hall, the fine old marqueterie floors, the tall spacious windows—everything had been given over to the tenants who seemed to think this was a place merely to afford shelter or to be used as shops. And as for the garden—an extensive plot of more than four hundred square feet which was reached by a broad terrace and steps—surely it had not had the care of a gardener for more than a century! Some fine old trees were still standing, reaching up beyond the roof of the house.

I came away from this second visit with the fixed determination to own the old house. I told my lawyer to treat with the tenants who were occupying the rooms and the shops. Long discussions ended with their being paid to leave—all but one family that persisted, and still do, in remaining in the apartment over the garage. They are still there. In a way I feel rather sympathetic towards them. I probably would be as immovable as they once I was installed in such rooms.

Finally my lawyer handed over my cheque for the purchase of the house and with the signatures the matter was closed. My bankers had purchased a cheque on the Bank of France, as this was the only one the owner would accept.

I drove straight to what I now called my house. It was twilight when I reached there. The narrow rue des Saints Pères was fading mystically into the shadows of the evening. I pushed the great door open, this time with the assurance of ownership. I hurried into the courtyard in spite of the still protesting concièrge, and stood gazing up at the old house. Mine!

In the ensuing months I had plenty to do in tracing the past history of my new home.

I discovered that it had been built in 1640 by Daniel Gittard for Paul Bailly. The following year it was rented to Hugo de Groot—the famous "Grotius," Ambassador of Marie-Christine, Queen of Sweden, who occupied it until he was recalled. From that time I found no record of its tenants until I came to the name of Louis d'Oger, Grand Maréchal des Logis de la Maison du Roi, in the reign of Louis XIV, personal friend of the Roi Soleil, and one of the most picturesque figures of his age, created Marquis de Cavoye by the King.

Louis de Cavoye's name appears in most of the memoirs of the period. Saint-Simon speaks of him as "sure, discreet, faithful; a good and honourable friend." Joseph de Maistre tells us that the "Marquis de Cavoye possesses in the highest degree the sentiment of dignity and personal respect which we call honour." D'Artagnan in his memoirs says: "Here is the rarest thing at Court. Behold Cavoye, a man who never told a lie." Dangeau, Boileau, Massillon, Madame de Sévigné, the Marquis de Souches, Bussy-Rabutin and many others have something to say about him, and of course Racine, his close friend; nearly all of them refer to his extraordinary resemblance to Louis XIV—who in his youth and prime was considered the handsomest man in France. His portrait which hung in the Château de Beaufort in Picardy depicts a handsome man in his late thirties—a grand seigneur wearing a reddish-brown perruque which seems to increase the effect of hauteur. Though darkened by age, it is easy still to discern in the background the arms and coronet of the Marquis; and the costume suggests a cuirasse over which is thrown a mantle of leopard skin.

He married Louise Philippe de Coëtlogon who came with her father the Marquis of that name to Versailles. She was just eighteen and destined to fill the place of "demoiselle d'honneur" to the Queen, left vacant by the death of Mademoiselle de Fontanges (who had just died in child-birth after her affair with the King). She came from a long line of distinguished ancestors, much more so even than the family of Cavoye. Louise was all virtuous, she was gentle and sweet, guileless and pious; she quickly won the love of Maria Theresa the Queen of France. Saint-Simon refers to her as "la laide de la Cour" for she was of a healthy, rosy type, while the ideal at Court was to be pale and thin, and hints that it was this deplorable lack of beauty that endeared her to her mistress. At any rate it must have been a great satisfaction to the Queen to have in her suite one demoiselle d'honneur who was not mixed up in love intrigues. Yet Louise in her simplicity lost no time in falling in love with the handsomest cavalier of the Court circle, Louis de Cavoye; and more than that in confessing it quite openly—a fact which interested the gay group immensely. When Cavoye was sentenced to the Bastille in punishment for fighting a duel she was not ashamed to beg permission of the King to visit him in prison and offer what solace she could to the gay courtier, and during the years of his incarceration she wore neither mouche (the black courtplaster patch) nor flowers, nor ribbons. She feared neither ridicule nor gossip. . . .

The marriage took place in the church of St. Paul in Paris on February 3rd, 1677. The "Mercure Galant" says of the wedding . . . "This union, of which everyone spoke for so long a time, took on the proportions of an event. All the Court manifested its joy."

"Le Beau Cavoye" was now thirty-seven years old, a high officer of the Crown, and full of the importance and dignity of his great position. He was admitted by everyone to be the most intimate friend of the King. Naturally one of so high a rank as Grand Maréchal des Logis de la Maison du Roi must own a hôtel in Paris that was worthy of his position. During the rare intervals in which he could leave the Court, his entertainments must be, if not so splendid as those at Versailles, at least not wanting in lavishness; his mode of life must reflect credit in every possible way upon the sovereign who had conferred so many honours upon him. And so the hôtel in the rue des Saints Pères was decided upon as being the most fitted for city life—and bought.

The close friendship between Louis XIV and Cavoye lasted throughout the great monarch's life. When Cavoye wanted to give up his bâton and sell his charge to the Marquis de Canay, the King said: "Cavoye, mourons ensemble" (Cavoye, let us die together)—and so he remained at Versailles until after the death of the monarch on September 1st, 1715.

After the death of Louis XIV, Cavoye returned to his house in the rue des Saints Pères and from then on rarely left it. He spent his last days peacefully with the ever faithful Louise de Coëtlogon. They had enjoyed splendours together, they had suffered over the death of their only only child, a son who was born and died in infancy in the "Chambre-à-Parade" (now my bedroom) and they were content to spend their last days in tranquillity. The house and garden now became their world, they received only a few friends, they devoted themselves wholly to good and pious works.

Exhorted by his devoted and saintly wife, "le beau Cavoye" died with the comfort of the Sacraments of the

Church on February 3rd, 1716—just five months after Louis XIV, his paragon and master for many years. He was the only man of his family on record who had died like a bourgeois, in bed, instead of on a field of battle. We must except his brother's tragic fate as the "Iron Mask." He was interred with great pomp and ceremony in his Parish church of St. Sulpice. Louise Philippe, his wife, survived him thirteen years.

And so ends the story of the two people whom I have grown to look upon as the real owners of my house. Often, during the restoration of their old home, I caught myself up with the question: Would Louis d'Oger have done this? Would he have liked this piece of furniture placed there? Would the Marquise have approved of the colour of the curtains in her bedroom—now mine? Such questions have brought them much closer to me. Even now, when I go down to the grande salle and wait there to welcome my guests, I almost feel their presence.

· · · · · · ·

And now I come to the end of my own story—which finishes fittingly with the realisation of a dream.

In this house which has known the happiness of others, I too have found happiness. It has been my privilege to restore it to its ancient glory, to revive its past splendours. In return it has given me peace. I have learnt to read its message, to know that beauty which is eternal is a consolation for many sorrows. At last I can look back on the past without bitterness.

Harry Lehr is dead, so are many who walked along

the road with me. Time heals all things. These walls within which I live have seen the end of many resentments; so let it be with mine.

I have my friends—the years have added to them. In the warmth of their affection I live some of my happiest hours.

I look to the future, not the past.

EXTRACTS FROM HARRY LEHR'S LOCKED DIARY

1916

January 2nd. As usual a miserable rainy damp day. We went to the twelve o'clock Mass at our parish church of Sainte Clotilde, where I saw no one we knew. We came home and lunched alone and then we went to the Opera which was mediocre—"Rigoletto." I was much exhausted from the hot air and the awful atmosphere. I came out and went home just leaving some notes in the motor. Then I went for a walk in the dark—which I hate doing, as I find it so depressing. I came home and we dined en famille, the cook is very bad—and she won't be sent away. The food is beyond any words of mine.

January 4th. I was up early and very busy. I find that after several holidays falling together there is always an awful lot to do. I drove out alone and came home to luncheon and after luncheon I went out to the American Ambulance and gave the tea to the doctors and nurses as is the custom. This time we had Laura Allien and Madame Gaston Legrand to help. I drove Madame Legrand home and went later and spent the evening and night at Neuilly with my old friend Paul Rodocanachi.

The rest did me good—and the change, to get away from the servants and the housekeeping.

January 6th. Another dark rainy day—we have always clear mild nights and the days are dark and overcast. I was out all morning hard at work and I lunched at the Hotel Ritz. In the morning, Mrs. Frank Lawrence (Ava Astor's sister) called me up on the telephone and told me she understood that the report she had been spreading about my father was untrue and that she would contradict it. I drove out with Bessie in the afternoon and I later tried on the telephone to get Mrs. Lawrence to tell me who had made the trouble. I dined with Mrs. Charles Carroll en garçon, plain but good food.

January 7th. The weather is still miserable and wet and our household in a most unsettled condition. I saw Mrs. Lawrence again today but she gave me no opportunity of asking who her informant was. I lunched at home with Bessie and afterwards I drove out alone to pay a visit to the Duchesse de Bassano and afterwards I dined with Madame de Sinçay—a most amusing dinner—the John Carters, Prince Ghika, etc. The food was not up to the usual mark.

January 8th. The weather is still very dull and damp and it seems impossible to get a clear decent day. I drove out in the morning and shopped. I stopped in at the Ritz where I saw Mrs. Lawrence and more talk ensued—it all seems so endless. My nephew has been terribly wounded, he fell from his aeroplane and has been badly burnt. I am in despair. I came home to luncheon. There

I found my stepson. I drove out with Bessie and had tea with the Baroness Teilleire and we dined with the Lawrence Benets to meet some English people. Eugene Higgins was also there.

January 9th. A fine clear day. I went to the half-past eleven o'clock Mass at St. Roch and took a nice walk in the Avenue du Bois with Randolph Wilson. He looks very smart in his uniform. I came home to lunch. After luncheon during my walk my little dog Hippodale was run over by a taxicab and almost crushed to death at Longchamps! We drove home as quickly as we could and he was put on my red sofa in my bedroom. Two doctors were summoned and we are fighting to save his dear life. We dined of course at home—alone, miserable. One of the vets remained to dinner.

January 17th. A mean changeable day. I was up very early and lunched at the Ritz with Anthony Drexel, who now has his divorce at last, but I am very much afraid his troubles are far from finished. He seems in good spirits and very well contented with everything, but it is an anxious moment. Louise arrived from New York today, looking pretty and was most entertaining at dinner as usual. She told us the story of her recent divorce. Her frankness was most amazing.

January 23rd. A better, brighter day. I was up early and wrote my letter to my mother and also one to Sydney Dyer and we went to the half-past eleven o'clock Mass at St. Roch. As we had many notes to leave I am afraid we were a little late for Mass. We lunched at home and drove out into the country to pay some visits. We found all the people out. The afternoon was fine and the drive lovely. We dined at home alone and I began my preparations for our trip South. We are off on February 3rd to stop with the James Gordon Bennetts at Beaulieu—if nothing prevents.

January 29th. A dark cloudy day but no rain. A busy morning—the baggage was prepared for the Beaulieu trip. I was out all morning and came home and got Bessie and the boy and we lunched with the Walter Greys and Bessie and Jack went to the Cinema. I could not stand the bad air so I did not try it but walked around Longchamps instead. I finished up some of our affairs and tried on some clothes and came home. We dined at the George Munroes'. At ten o'clock there was a Zeppelin alarm. It seemed so horrid and gloomy.

January 30th. A dull day, but no rain. In the morning I made my usual round. Twelve o'clock Mass at the Church of St. Pierre de Chaillot, first going to the Post Office and sending some registered letters, and then home to luncheon en famille. Those awful Germans sent a Zeppelin over Paris last night and succeeded in killing a number of women and children and some men. We dined with my Godmother the Duchesse de Bassano en famille. I found her looking very tired.

February 4th. Beaune, Côte d'Or. I did not sleep—a high wind sprang up during the night and the latticed window shades flapped and beat against the windows. We got off at half-past eight and began a most unpleasant experience. I never saw such a wind. We reached Macon at eleven-thirty, where we were obliged to leave the motor as it had become dangerous in the high wind—so we took an awful train to Lyons packed with soldiers and officers and their wives. The train was over an hour late and we arrived almost dead in Lyons. Nothing could have exceeded it all.

February 5th. Lyons. Thank heaven the wind has stopped, but a mean misty rain. We were off early and made Avignon for lunch at the Hotel d'Europe—we are now in Vaucluse. We got away early and made Marseilles at five-thirty. Here we found Mr. and Mrs. James Gordon Bennett, Mrs. Leeds, Miss Yznaga, Anthony Drexel and a small regiment of valets and maids and motors, etc., and from now on we move as a sort of caravan. Mr. and Mrs. Bennett had us all to dinner. There were a great many English officers and soldiers and much movement. I found everyone well and very good and kind—and they seemed glad to see us.

February 12th. Beaulieu-sur-Mer. Downcast and cloudy, but no rain. I am anxious about Hippodale, who is not very well. I went out in the morning in the motor and we had company for luncheon—Jennie Tiffany and M. and Mme. de Montgomérie and their daughter. After lunch we drove over to Nice and had tea with Mrs. Tiffany who was, I must say, pretty tactless and not very agreeable. We dined at Mrs. Leeds', a very pleasant and agreeable dinner; we remained until quite late. I find as always Bertie Paget charming.

February 21st. A fine clear day. I am glad of it as we are moving today and going for a fortnight to stop with Mrs. Leeds at Cap d'Ail, where she has taken the big Villa Primavera. We lunched with the Bennetts, alone, and I am very sorry to leave them, they have been more than kind. After luncheon came the moving. We came over in the car with Zelia, my wife's maid, and Hippodale. We had tea at home and Emily Yznaga came. After tea she and I walked and we dined and went to bed early. I felt very tired from the moving.

February 22nd. A dull dark cold day but no rain. I am sure it is getting ready to rain. In Paris it does nothing else and the Seine is rising rapidly. My room here is very large with a fine bath adjoining. We lunched with the James Gordon Bennetts, a large luncheon, Mrs. Leeds, Countess Tyshkiévitch, Miss Yznaga, Mr. Pratt, Mr. Drexel, etc. I had a nice talk with Emily Yznaga and we all dined informally at home. Nancy Leeds has a fine cook and we are very comfortably lodged.

February 26th. A mean cold rainy day, like winter. We went out to luncheon with the James Gordon Bennetts at Beaulieu and had a very pleasant time. Nancy lent us her motor as it was a closed one and we came home in it. I then walked to and from Monte Carlo. It began to rain again just as I entered the house. I gave a dinner of ten people for the Grand Duchess Anastasia of Russia who afterwards took us all in her loge to the Opera. It was the opening night—"The Demon," which I saw for the first time. I found the music spirited and fine. They say there is no gasoline in Paris, so we shall have to return by train.

March 18th. A bright but cloudy day. We had a busy morning and finally got off for Paris on the one-thirty-five train. It was just nerve-racking about getting off and we were not really sure we would until we were on the train. The Station Master said any of the trains might be mobilised at a moment's notice. We said good-bye to Harry and Emily with a heavy heart, they are always so nice and kind. I did not sleep much on the train; this did not surprise me, as I never can manage it, in consequence I was worn out.

March 25th. Paris. A fine bright sunny day which was most welcome I can assure you. I found a most annoying mix-up first thing in the morning for Bessie had asked young Baron de Reuter to dine with my stepson Jack and Jack had accepted an invitation to dine at our Embassy! I finally arranged matters so that he and young Sharp came here to dine as did also Harry Leeds. In the meantime we lunched at home, Bessie, Jack and I. I would not lunch at the Ritz with them as Jack's uniform was so abominably shabby. I ordered a new one for him at Hill's today which I hope will prove a success.

March 31st. A magnificent clear mild day, divine. I drove out alone in the morning and came home to lunch alone with Bessie. I am progressing well with my work, and much is in order that was not so before I came home. In the afternoon Bessie and I drove out together and I went afterwards to see Ingram Carroll and had a nice talk. I came home to a dinner en famille. After dinner I worked until late at night on my petit-point chair and did not get to bed until long after twelve o'clock and slept soundly which, alas, I don't always manage.

April 23rd. A fine bright Easter morning. I was up early and went to Mass at seven o'clock in our parish church of Sainte Clotilde, where I went to Holy Communion. There were masses of communicants; I was most edified. I came home and went back to Mass with Bessie and Jack, who is home for a two days' rest. We then lunched with Anthony Drexel; Mrs. Leeds and Miss Harry were there. Then Bessie and I went to see my Godmother de Bassano. Then we came home and Bessie went to bed with a bad cold and I dined alone with Jack.

April 25th. A fine clear mild spring day. It cheered the heart to see the sun once more after all these months of rain. It is our day at the American Ambulance. We lunched at home en famille. We went out to the Ambulance in the afternoon and I thought the tea went off very well. There seemed a big crowd and I am sorry to say not an attractive one. We dined at home alone.

April 30th. Another brilliant beautiful day. In the morning I went to our parish church for the eleven o'clock Mass. I came home and drove out to luncheon with Helen Gwinne. We had a very pleasant day and I remained there all afternoon until tea. Two young men from the American Ambulance came to tea; one was young Hamilton, Edith Gould's cousin. He is very handsome, the most beautiful creature I have even seen. He likes everyone to think that he is very rich, which is unfortunately not the case, for he is one of those souls not suited for poverty. I went to dine with Emily Yznaga at her apartment. I had a very satisfactory long talk with her and never got home till eleven.

May 13th. A mean dark rainy day. I was late getting out and very busy. The boy came home from the Ambulance and we went to the Hotel Ritz for our luncheon. There did not seem to be the usual crowd. After luncheon Bessie and the boy went shopping and I came home. Then I went out in good and earnest. I went to Tardiffs' about some framing, to Cartier's and paid him five thousand dollars on the tiara, to the electrician's, etc., and then went to an amusing tea at Howard Sturgis' and came home to dinner. Bessie and Jack went out.

June 4th. A dark, threatening day and some rain in the afternoon. I went to the twelve o'clock Mass in my parish church with Bessie and came home and we lunched alone. Then at half-past two I took the big motor and filled it with all the old linen in the house and called for my Godmother de Bassano and she and Mrs. Blount and I drove out and spent the afternoon with the Belgian refugees. I gave them the linen and then we came home. The roads were in a fearful state. In the evening I dined with Charly Carroll of Carrollton en garçon and was home early. I have just heard that there has been a frightful scandal at the American Ambulance. It seems that one of the drivers (a young man related to the best families in New York) took out his ambulance as usual to meet the Red Cross train, but when he failed to appear with his load of wounded at the hospital everyone grew very alarmed and imagined that there had been an accident on the way. All sorts of inquiries were made, but there was no trace of either the ambulance or its driver. Now days afterwards the news has leaked out. Feeling bored with the monotony of his daily round he decided to have a little sport as a diversion. So he invited several of his friends to go on a shooting trip with him, using the ambulance as a private car. They all drove off to the country together with their guns packed in beside them and put in some good days shooting. They actually had the impudence to drive back to Paris with the Ambulance filled not with wounded but with dead game. Of course the matter was reported to Headquarters and there has been a nice row, I can tell you. I hear that the young man has been put under arrest.

June 13th. Another mean damp day and some rain. My cold is even worse. I did not go out but remained in all day. Paul Rodocanachi came to lunch and Bertie Landsberg and Madame Massolis Séchiari and a Mlle. Vassiliadis, who is staying with them. They and Bessie all went afterwards to the American Ambulance to pour the tea and I remained at home alone. Later I joined them to see about giving an Ambulance to the field service and they attended to the interesting function of pouring tea. We dined at home alone and I went to bed still very miserable indeed.

June 20th. A vile cold mean dark rainy day. In the morning I was out early in the motor and left some notes and bought some cakes for the Ambulance and then I came home and went to the Ritz where Emily Yznaga and Bertie Paget and Mme. de St. Aldegaude lunched with me. Then came the tea at the Ambulance—Mrs. Moore poured and Emily Yznaga—and I must say they did very well and we came home late. Jack has now joined the field service; he went on his first call this evening. We dined at home by ourselves—and he did not get in until after eleven o'clock.

July 10th. A changeable day, and little or no rain. I was out in the morning paying bills as usual. I came home to luncheon and we lunched alone en tête à tête. In the afternoon I had a nap and then drove out in the motor and did some few commissions and came home to tea—we had some people in to tea, Marie Kemp and Mrs. Cotton and so on. I enjoyed myself very much. I dined at home and drove out in the evening. The weather was mild and fine. The news is bad from Mexico and I am sure we will have war. The German gold backs them.

July 16th. A mild clear morning. Lunched at home and then went out with Bessie to Versailles to Miss de Wolfe and there we saw Maurice and his wife dance. It was very well done. The entire affair was very well organised and most amusing. We came into town quite early and remained in for dinner. I wrote some letters and I played cards until quite late, and did not get to bed until after twelve. F. D. and his wife have arrived from New York. They have only just been married. He is to drive an ambulance over here and she would not be left behind. She is awfully pretty and amusing. They seem very much in love.

July 18th. An uncertain mild day. I was out very early and got the doughnuts and sandwiches for our tea at the Neuilly Ambulance. Then came luncheon and then I called for Mrs. and Miss Sherman and took them to the Ambulance, left a note at Neuilly and came to the Ritz. There I helped with the entertainment given there for the American Ambulance. There has been quite a great deal of feeling against this entertainment by the French, God only knows why, and the Marquise de Ganay has given it a snub, but it went off very well and many French people were there. I dined at home and drove out to Neuilly afterwards.

July 31st. Another awful scorching day, dry as dust and no comfort to be found anywhere. Bessie leaves to-day and of course we are very long making our arrangements. I went out in the motor for a few minutes, the heat was intense, and came into lunch en famille. After lunch I went out alone. F. D. and his wife dined with us. Miss X—— was there too and at once struck up a great friendship with Mrs. D. She wants her to join her at her hospital. X—— says that she can very well live at her house at —— so she will be well looked after. F. D. seemed rather reluctant at first, but I think he will be talked over.

August 12th. (Brides-les-Bains) A fine clear day. I saw

the doctor, he says my heart and liver are fat, I must re-
duce. So at eleven I took my first glass of water. I was immediately ill and had to stop my cure. We lunched at the
hotel; the food is awful. In the afternoon I rested and
walked again and went to see the doctor who gave me
some drops to stop this awful indigestion I have. Then
I sat about with Mrs. Whitney Warren and Emily Yznaga
until we went to dine with Mme. de Croisset, where we
had an excellent simple good dinner, which I can tell
you I enjoyed.

August 23rd. A cloudy clear day with no rain. I was up
early in the morning as usual and took my water and had
my breakfast with Emily Yznaga and came home. I feel
much better this morning and have not got these pains
in the abdomen. I lunched with Miss Yznaga as usual and
took a long rest and did not go out until five o'clock
when I went for my water. I feel very much better this
afternoon and the time commences to pass. I have some
hopes of standing it. In the evening Miss Yznaga felt ill
and did not come to dinner. I dined alone with Mrs.
Whitney Warren and came home.

September 1st. My cure being finished this morning, I
left Brides-les-Bains at ten o'clock for Paris alone in the
big motor. The weather was very fine and we made good
time, blowing one tyre which lost us about an hour and
a half. I lunched at Aix-les-Bains and then we went on
until we came to Bourg-en-Bresse where we almost had a
bad accident. But all went well and we arrived in Beaune
where I spent the night. I feel very much tired out, but

I am very glad to have gotten away from that awful nest.
    September 2nd. I was up early, it was a fine morning
and we started about half-past eight. I was a little nervous
about the motor as the opening valve of the radiator
came off yesterday and we have a cork in it, but things
went along all right and we lunched at Saumur, after
losing our way and getting into the Army zone and
almost being arrested. I arrived in Paris in time for
dinner and went to bed quite early, being very tired and
slept soundly.

    September 4th. Bad weather seems to be setting in and
it has turned cold and damp. I was up and out early. I
paid some bills and tried to engage a footman and telephone Stanley Mortimer to invite him to luncheon tomorrow and I came home and we lunched alone. In the
afternoon I worked hard and arranged the household and
went out as usual. Later Mr. Burden-Muller came to tea
and also Harcourt Johnstone, the son of Lady Johnstone,
a splendid-looking young Englishman with a marvellous
skin. I went to bed at a very early hour.

    September 5th. Uncertain autumn weather but very
fine in spots. We lunched at home and then I had my
rest. Then there was a dreadful row, really it was too
awful for words. Just before tea F. D. burst into the salon
in a rage and began to abuse me and call me every name
he could think of. It seems that his wife joined Miss
X——'s hospital and went to stay with her at her quarters.
Then when F. D. got leave and went to see her she told
him some story that made him furiously jealous of her

friendship with Miss X——. So now he is wild with me for having introduced them. He says Miss X—— is a disgrace to the Red Cross and that he will not permit his wife to stay one day longer. I tried to pacify him but he says he means to have it out with Miss X——. I never felt more nervous or uncomfortable in my life, I can tell you. In the evening we dined at the de Waedel Jarlsburgs'. There was Emily, Nancy Leeds, Anthony Drexel, Antoine Sala, Howard Sturgis, Kingsland, Frankie Otis and me.

September 8th. The weather dark and changeable but no rain. In the morning came the manicure and then I got Emily and we went out and then I called for Laura Allien and we did some shopping. Then I met Bessie at the Hotel Ritz and we lunched at Nancy Leeds' table. After lunch we went up to see Junior. I saw the Duchesse de Noailles, Countess de Bourg, etc. We went home to tea. I hear that Miss X—— and F. D. have had another frightful row. Miss X—— says it is all a misunderstanding, but he won't accept her explanation. He goes round telling everybody that she has tried to ruin his marriage.

October 13th. Very dark and threatening but no rain. In the morning I did nothing much as the date is such an unlucky one (Friday the 13th). We lunched at the Ritz; we saw quite a number of people there. After lunch I came home to tackle the situation about Jack. I hope now that I won't have to go to Switzerland, the place seems to be filled with these awful Germans. We dined at home alone.

October 30th. Much clearer and better. I was out late and lunched alone at the Marlborough Tea Rooms, an excellent but badly served meal. I walked home and had my rest and then drove out to find more things for the table which I required tonight. Then I came back and Bessie went out to buy the flowers and I remained in all afternoon and occupied myself about the house. In the evening we gave a dinner of twenty, for Lady Sarah Wilson. The dinner was not up to the mark in my opinion as regards service and food—we had cold plates! I sat between the Marquise de Castega and the Countess de Chevigné.

November 16th. A fine clear cold winter day, I drove out in the morning with Emily Yznaga with my usual list of shopping and note-leaving and finally came back home to luncheon after having left her at the Hotel Ritz. We drove out to tea with Miss X—— who is back. I was simply astonished to see F. D. and his wife there—all perfectly amicable. They are both staying with Miss X——. Afterwards when we were alone I said I supposed he had made up his quarrel with Miss X——. He just stared at me . . . "What are you talking about? We never had any quarrel." I reminded him of how he had come to see me about it some months ago. He laughed and replied . . . "My dear man you must have imagined it. I was only joking of course. I think Miss X—— is a charming little woman! . . ." I do not understand the whole thing. We got back to Paris and dined at home alone.

November 19th. Dreary and dark but no rain. We went to the eleven o'clock Mass in our parish church and then afterwards I went to see Mattie de La Rochefoucauld and took her a small bunch of violets. I saw her and she looked very badly and she took me in to see her mother (Mrs. Mitchell, just dead). She looked very peaceful, but very, very old. I then went back and got Bessie and we lunched with Nancy Leeds at the Ritz. There was an immense crowd of uninteresting people. I then went home and had my rest and then we went to the Madeleine for a fine big religious concert—beautiful music. Boldini came to dinner. He made himself quite agreeable and admired the house very much but he was just as malicious as usual, and attacked people right and left.

December 4th. Cold and dreary and dark but some sunshine in the morning about ten o'clock. I drove out about eleven. I did many small and uninteresting things and came home to luncheon en famille, and not very good at that. The war news is very bad, and I am sure it will make an awful effect when the Germans take Bucarest, for take it they certainly will. I had my rest after luncheon and drove out with Bessie after. I am very busy at home as we have been promised all kinds of horrors— such as no coal, no electric light and so on. We dined en famille and spent an interminable evening quarrelling and disputing all the time.

December 7th. Dark and cold—but no rain. It has become very cold indeed. There were workmen in the house this morning who were putting in a Salamandra for the servants in the top floor and in the cellar seeing about the hot water machine. Moncure Robinson came to see me and I lunched with him at the Ritz. Anthony Drexel came to dinner. He seemed very much depressed. I think that the general behaviour of the John Fells in London has been a great shock to him. I believe it is the story of the Duke of —— that upsets him most.

December 13th. A very dark day but no rain. I drove out alone, I did some small errands and I came home as soon as I could. I went to my tailor's to see about some of my winter things. Marie Kemp came to luncheon. I was so very glad to see her again. In the afternoon we drove out together and I took a long walk. We dined with Mrs. Hollox, Frankie Otis and Emily Yznaga. Emily was taken ill almost immediately after dinner and at one time I was afraid we could not get her home, but about eleven o'clock she was able to pull herself together and we came home leaving her en route.

December 17th. Cold and dark but no rain. It is now so difficult to obtain anthracite coal that we are obliged to suppress the big furnace. The discomfort is very great. We went to twelve o'clock Mass at our parish church and then came home to luncheon after leaving some notes. I rested after lunch and then we went out and went to the cinema at the Colisée with Mrs. Moore; there we found quite a lot of people we knew; Emily Yznaga, Alexandre de Gabrillac, etc. In the evening

Laura Allien came down to see us and remained to dinner. We spent a pleasant evening.

Christmas Day. A wonderful clear fine day—we went to the eleven o'clock Mass in our parish church and then we left some Christmas presents and came home. Bessie lunched at the Hotel Ritz with Emily Yznaga and the two young Yznaga children. I lunched at home with a dear young Roumanian friend of mine. We had a wonderful time together. Then I had my rest and went to a children's party at Marthe Hyde's which was very gay and pleasant and then we came home. We had some friends to dine in the evening—Mrs. Moore, Emily Yznaga, Countess Tyshkièvitch, Jean Bérand, Frankie Otis and so on.

December 28th. A mild wet rainy day—the Seine is rising and the coal famine continues. I am most anxious to obtain some coal. Jacques Seligmann came to see us and I drove out with Emily Yznaga. We lunched with Bertha and Larry Ronalds, who is still boasting of being natural son of Napoleon III, and met the James Hydes and Louisa Clews. After luncheon I came home and went on a coal hunt, without much effect, I am afraid. However, I did manage to get some kindling wood. I bought candles today and some petroleum. We dined at home en tête à tête. I wrote to Alice and went to bed very early.

December 31st. Mild and rainy. I drove to the Hotel Ritz where I got Helen Gwinne and Bertie Paget, who came home to luncheon, after which I drove Helen home to Sèvres. Then I returned home and Emily Yznaga and

Laura Allien and Francis Potter and Pierre de Polignac came to dinner. Then we went to supper at Laura Allien's, where we saw the Old Year out and the New Year in—we were joined there by Jack Dahlgren and Mr. Wilcox.

INDEX

323

Printed in the United States
55448LVS00003B/1-90